Coaching Students with Executive Skills Deficits

The Guilford Practical Intervention in the Schools Series

Kenneth W. Merrell, Founding Editor
T. Chris Riley-Tillman, Series Editor

www.guilford.com/practical

This series presents the most reader-friendly resources available in key areas of evidence-based practice in school settings. Practitioners will find trustworthy guides on effective behavioral, mental health, and academic interventions, and assessment and measurement approaches. Covering all aspects of planning, implementing, and evaluating high-quality services for students, books in the series are carefully crafted for everyday utility. Features include ready-to-use reproducibles, lay-flat binding to facilitate photocopying, appealing visual elements, and an oversized format. Recent titles have companion Web pages where purchasers can download and print the reproducible materials.

Coaching Students
with Executive Skills Deficits

PEG DAWSON
RICHARD GUARE

THE GUILFORD PRESS
New York   London

© 2012 The Guilford Press
A Division of Guilford Publications, Inc.
72 Spring Street, New York, NY 10012
www.guilford.com

Printed in the United States of America

This book is printed on acid-free paper.

Last digit is print number: 9   8   7   6   5   4   3   2

The authors have checked with sources believed to be reliable in their efforts to provide information that is complete and generally in accord with the standards of practice that are accepted at the time of publication. However, in view of the possibility of human error or changes in behavioral, mental health, or medical sciences, neither the authors, nor the editor and publisher, nor any other party who has been involved in the preparation or publication of this work warrants that the information contained herein is in every respect accurate or complete, and they are not responsible for any errors or omissions or the results obtained from the use of such information. Readers are encouraged to confirm the information contained in this book with other sources.

Library of Congress Cataloging-in-Publication Data

Dawson, Peg.
  Coaching students with executive skills deficits / Peg Dawson, Richard Guare.
    p. cm.—(The Guilford practical intervention in the schools series)
  Includes bibliographical references and index.
  ISBN 978-1-4625-0375-9 (lay-flat binding)
  1. Executive ability in children.   2. Executive ability in adolescence.   3. Children—Life skills guides.   4. Child development.   I. Guare, Richard.   II. Title.
  BF723.E93D388 2012
  158.3—dc23
                                                                                        2011037133

About the Authors

Peg Dawson, EdD, is a staff psychologist at the Center for Learning and Attention Disorders at Seacoast Mental Health Center in Portsmouth, New Hampshire, where she specializes in the assessment of children and adults with learning and attention disorders. She is a past president of the New Hampshire Association of School Psychologists, the National Association of School Psychologists, and the International School Psychology Association. Dr. Dawson is a recipient of the National Association of School Psychologists' Lifetime Achievement Award.

Richard Guare, PhD, a neuropsychologist and board-certified behavior analyst, is Director of the Center for Learning and Attention Disorders at Seacoast Mental Health Center. He serves as a consultant to schools and agencies in programs for autism, learning and behavior disorders, and acquired brain injuries. Dr. Guare has presented and published research and clinical work involving attention, executive skills, and neurological disorders.

Drs. Dawson and Guare's website is *www.smartbutscatteredkids.com*.

Preface

In their book *Driven to Distraction*, Hallowell and Ratey (1994) devote a single paragraph to the concept of *coaching* individuals with attention-deficit/hyperactivity disorder (ADHD). From this brief description, a virtual industry has emerged, with a focus on helping students with attention disorders achieve success in school. At a recent annual conference of Children and Adults with Attention Deficit/Hyperactivity Disorder, a full 10% of the breakout sessions were devoted to the topic of coaching, with titles such as Motivational Interviewing: A Powerful Coaching Tool; Co-Active Coaching: A Tool to Promote Successful Transition to College; and How ADHD Coaches Can Expand Their Toolbox and Help Their Client Get Organized. Another 15% of the breakout sessions focused on helping students with ADHD develop executive skills. Interestingly enough, with only one exception, the abstracts describing the coaching sessions failed to mention executive skills, nor did the abstracts for the executive skills sessions refer to coaching.

In 1998, we published a manual called *Coaching the ADHD Student* (Dawson & Guare, 1998). Since then, we have written several books on executive skills, with different target audiences in mind—school psychologists and other educators (Dawson & Guare, 2004, 2010), parents (Dawson & Guare, 2009), and adults working in a corporate environment (Martin, Dawson, & Guare, 2007; Martin, Guare, & Dawson, 2010). Although our coaching manual preceded our work with executive skills, we soon realized that coaching is an ideal intervention strategy to help students of all ages improve executive functioning. This book is designed to marry those two concepts in a practitioner-friendly way.

The strength of our coaching model lies in the fact that it is built on a theoretical foundation well grounded in the behavioral literature. Since its development, it has been the basis for a number of research studies (e.g., Plumer & Stoner, 2005; Merriman & Codding, 2008) that have applied the model to varied student populations, with diverse outcome measures targeting different behavioral goals. On the basis of such studies, we are confident that coaching, as we have defined it, is evidence based and, therefore, a worthy addition to the repertoire of interventions for underperforming students.

Furthermore, coaching is a versatile intervention that lends itself to modification to suit the needs of a variety of student populations, thus making it an ideal tool for schools that employ a three-tiered response-to-intervention (RTI) model. At Tier 1, it can be used as a whole-class intervention by classroom teachers to help students acquire the skills necessary to organize tasks and remember homework assignments. At Tier 2, it can serve as a small-group intervention for at-risk students who may be struggling socially because of weaknesses in executive skills such as response inhibition and emotional control, or academically because of weaknesses in time management, planning/prioritization, or organization. And at Tier 3, it can form the basis of an individual support plan for students who may be failing because of more severe executive skills weaknesses.

While *Coaching the ADHD Student* provided a good beginning, we have now had many more years' experience with the model, and we believe we can now provide a more comprehensive description of coaching. In the text, we offer enough detail to provide schools with the tools they need to institute coaching programs or to provide individuals who work with students with executive skills weaknesses a structure around which to build their work.

One of our favorite cartoons, from the syndicated comic *F Minus*, depicts an interview between a prospective employer and a job applicant. The the employer is saying, "The job you are applying for will require you to know state capitals, cursive writing, and long division" and the caption reads "Dale's 4th grade education pays off." This illustrates in fewer words why schools have to teach more than content area subjects. Whereas some students acquire executive skills fairly easily because of innate strengths or good parenting, many others fail to acquire these skills, which are critical to life success, without external support and direct instruction. Coaching provides a vehicle for this support and instruction.

OVERVIEW OF THE BOOK'S CONTENTS

This manual is divided into three units. In Unit I, we present the theoretical and research background that supports our coaching model. Chapter 1 provides a brief overview of executive skills, placing them within a developmental context, with a particular emphasis on how they emerge throughout childhood and adolescence. Because coaching as we envision it is an intervention strategy for students with weak executive skills, any discussion of coaching must be preceded by a solid understanding of executive skills development.

In Chapter 2, we turn to the theoretical and research base on which our coaching model was developed and that demonstrates its efficacy. This includes a description of correspondence training as well as research in the areas of self-regulation and self-management that shows that students can be taught how to manage behaviors that are relevant to social and academic success, including goal setting, self-monitoring, and self-evaluation. We also summarize studies that provide support for the efficacy of this model as a behavioral intervention.

In Unit II, we present our original coaching model, which was designed as a secondary school intervention to help underachieving students achieve academic success. We now conceptualize coaching as a two-level process: basic and advanced. Chapter 3 describes basic coaching by laying out the fundamentals of the coaching model, including how to assess whether or not a student is a good candidate for coaching, how to conduct the goal-setting interview, how to conduct daily coaching sessions, and how to fade the process so that the student achieves independence with respect to the skills being taught or supported. In addition, it includes suggestions for how to teach executive skills, how to use reinforcers and motivational strategies, and how to collect objective data in order to monitor progress and determine success. This chapter also discusses how the standard coaching model, which is intended for use with high school students, can be modified to meet the developmental needs of both younger students and older, college-age students. Interview outlines, checklists, and forms for use with both the goal-setting interview and the daily coaching sessions accompany this chapter.

Chapter 4 is a primer on advanced coaching techniques. It includes skills modules that provide coaches training in (1) effective communication skills; (2) techniques to improve the executive skills of students being coached; (3) measurement procedures to document coaching effectiveness; (4) problem-solving procedures coaches can use with students to help them solve academic or social problems; and (5) the special education and Section 504 process and procedures as well as a description of RTI so that coaches understand how coaching can fit into any of these service options.

Chapter 5 describes the steps involved in setting up a school-based coaching program, including identifying and selecting a coaching pool (either adult or peer coaches), identifying students who may benefit from coaching, soliciting students' willingness to participate, obtaining parental permission, supervising the coaching process, and evaluating coaching outcomes, including methods for collecting pre- and postintervention data.

Unit III is devoted to special applications of coaching. Chapter 6 outlines how to set up a classwide peer coaching program. This chapter includes the sequence of steps required for developing a peer coaching program, a description of how to train peer coaches, and sample permission forms, goal-setting forms, and record-keeping forms for progress monitoring.

Chapter 7 presents a model for coaching that is designed to help students improve social skills. The chapter is written by Pamela Plumer, the primary author of a study that compared classwide peer tutoring with peer coaching to help students with ADHD develop positive social behaviors.

The book concludes with Chapter 8, in which we frame the coaching method in terms of its ultimate goal: to help students develop *self-determination*. In this chapter we summarize a recent qualitative study conducted with college students who describe how coaching helped them become more effective students and how it differed from other intervention strategies commonly available for students in need of support services.

Several years ago, Stanley Pogrow (1996) wrote an article titled, "Reforming the Wannabe Reformers: Why Education Reforms Almost Always End Up Making Things Worse." In this article, he referenced Peter Drucker's understanding of successful innovations. Drucker said, "Historically, the vast majority of innovative ideas and changes throughout human history have failed to take root. Most remain just interesting ideas." Drucker proposed the following three characteristics of "innovations that stick":

1. Innovations that become successful innovations represent a solution that is clearly definable, is simple, and includes a complete system for implementation and dissemination.
2. Successful innovations start small and try to do one specific thing.
3. Knowledge-based innovations are least likely to succeed and can succeed only if *all* the needed knowledge is available.

In writing *Coaching Students with Executive Skills Deficits* it is our intention to provide a solution that is clearly definable and includes a complete system for implementation and dissemination. Although we present a number of variations on coaching that have proven effective, we encourage the reader to start small, select one target population with one set of needs, and try it out in a small-scale way. When we first started working with our coaching model, we used it on each other, a method we eventually termed *reciprocal coaching*. This enabled us to understand how coaching worked firsthand and to identify the elements of the model that were critical to its success. Since there is no substitute for firsthand experience, we encourage readers to consider reciprocal coaching as a way to get their feet wet. We are excited about coaching and its promise as a way to meet the needs of struggling students. We hope our readers will be too.

Contents

UNIT I

THEORETICAL AND RESEARCH BACKGROUND

CHAPTER 1

Executive Skills
and Brain Development

Consider the following scenarios:

Sean is a bright 15-year-old who wants to be an engineer when he finishes his schooling. He has great ideas for things he wants to invent, and he often daydreams about them when he's sitting in class or when he should be doing his homework. He knows that to achieve his goals he has to do well in school in order to get into a college that will give him the training he's looking for. The problem is, much of school bores him. He has trouble paying attention in classes that don't relate to his interests, and he finds most of his homework assignments so tedious he can barely get himself to do them. And with his lack of interest and his daydreaming, he often misses important instructions, like what exactly he's supposed to include in his U.S. history project or when his next Spanish exam is. His parents give him a hard time and do the best they can to keep him on track, but they feel like they're chasing a moving target. They can't go to school with him and listen to his teachers for themselves, so how can they help him?

Ellen is a 14-year-old social butterfly. Her life revolves around her friends and what's happening with them at the moment. She is empathic and insightful, and her many girlfriends always look to her for advice, for a shoulder to cry on, and even to mediate disputes among her fellow cheerleaders. She's flattered by this and thinks that maybe she would like a career in psychology. Ellen is a bright eighth grader, and her teachers tell her that the quality of her work is good when she makes the effort. Unfortunately, her extracurricular activities make it very difficult for her to get her schoolwork done. She has the best of intentions to begin long-term assignments well before the due date, but then a friend texts her or she gets pulled into a conflict playing out on Facebook, and she completely loses track of the plan she's made. Too many deadlines are missed, and Ellen's midterm progress report shows that she's failing a couple of subjects and earning C–'s in others. Never mind that her parents are furious at her—Ellen is mad at herself!

Anton wants to make friends, but his temper and impulsivity keep getting in the way. In school, he lives for recess but more often than not it goes badly for him. Anton gets into altercations

3

that put him "on the wall" for much of the period, or he says something stupid and the kids he wants to play with walk away from him. He thinks if he tells them what a great soccer player he is, he'll get chosen to play on a team, but this just seems to annoy his classmates. When recess is over, he gets a tight knot in his stomach, and then he just feels like kicking his desk or throwing something through the window. And try to focus on math in the afternoon when you feel that way!

These youngsters contend with different challenges and different developmental tasks, but they all have one thing in common—they struggle with some executive skills weaknesses that interfere with their ability to get along with others, their ability to perform in school, or both. *Executive function* is a neuropsychological concept referring to the cognitive processes required to plan and direct activities, including task initiation and follow-through, working memory, sustained attention, performance monitoring, inhibition of impulses, and goal-directed persistence. Although the groundwork for development of these skills occurs before birth, they develop gradually and in a clear progression through the first two decades of life. But from the moment that children begin to interact with their environment, adults have expectations for how they will use executive skills to negotiate many of the demands of childhood, from the self-regulation of behavior required to act responsibly to the planning and initiation skills required to complete chores and homework. Parents and teachers expect children to use executive skills even though the children may not quite understand what these skills are and how they impact behavior and school performance.

Youngsters with poor executive skills are disorganized or forgetful, have trouble getting started on tasks, get distracted easily, lose papers or assignments, forget to bring home the materials to complete homework, or forget to hand homework in. They may rush through work or dawdle; they make careless mistakes that they fail to catch. They don't know where to begin on long-term assignments, and they put the assignment off until the last minute, in part because they have trouble judging the magnitude of the task and how long it will take to complete it. Their work spaces are disorganized, and teachers may refer to their desks, backpacks, and notebooks as "black holes." Some youngsters with weak executive skills are like Anton—their problems with self-regulation have to do more with controlling behavioral excesses, like managing impulses or emotions, than with behavioral deficits, such as problems with planning, organizing, initiating, or completing tasks such as schoolwork.

Luckily, there is an intervention available to help youngsters develop more effective executive skills. It is called "coaching," and it differs from other interventions to address academic or behavioral problems in some critical ways. First, it focuses on self-management or self-regulation, in that its goal is to give youngsters tools they will be able to use eventually on their own to function more effectively in a variety of problem situations. Second, it generally targets only one or two behaviors at a time through the use of goal setting. Targeted behaviors are specific and measurable, so that there is no question about whether the plan has been followed or the goal achieved. Third, it is a *daily* intervention, at least in the early stages. The goal of coaching is habit formation, and we know that habits are formed through daily practice. If they are challenging habits to acquire, we cannot expect youngsters to practice them independently without daily check-ins and monitoring to assess how the practice is going.

Before we introduce coaching in greater detail, the reader needs a firm grounding in executive skills, what they are and how they develop throughout childhood and young adulthood, as well as the research base that supports the coaching process.

BRAIN DEVELOPMENT

At birth, infants are by and large "stimulus bound"—they are drawn to whatever stimulus in their environment is the most salient. Being stimulus bound also sparks impulsivity because infants have little capacity to control what they are responding to. Gradually over the course of the first year of life, they develop the capacity to direct their attention and inhibit some responses. With a growing ability to retain past experiences, they can adjust responses depending on what they learned the last time they were in a similar situation. They also find that if they behave in a certain way, a predictable response will come from others around them. If they cry, for instance, they will get fed or have their diaper changed. If they smile or laugh, others will smile or laugh too, and so they will get a pleasing, reinforcing reaction from others. These are the early signs of emerging executive skills. These skills will become more sophisticated as childhood progresses, but they serve the ultimate purpose of allowing children increasing control over their environment—and their own actions within that environment.

Neuroscientists have learned a number of critical facts about executive skills development. First, although multiple brain systems may be involved, executive function resides primarily in the prefrontal cortex—that part of the brain located just behind the forehead. Second, the brain develops from back to front; thus, the prefrontal cortex is the last part of the brain to mature. Furthermore, neuroscientists generally agree that the frontal lobes are not fully mature until around age 25—and that's in *typically* developing individuals (DeLuca & Leventer, 2008; Steinberg, 2008). Experts on attention-deficit/hyperactivity disorder (ADHD) have found that these skills develop more slowly in individuals with this diagnosis, with a developmental lag of about 5 years in adults with ADHD.

Skills develop through repetition and practice, and this accentuates the importance of a third fact about brain development. The brain is composed of two kinds of cells: neurons and glial cells. Neurons consist of a cell body; an axon, which transmits information to other neurons; and dendrites, hairlike branches that extend from the cell body and receive information from other neurons. Neurons communicate with each other at junctions that connect axons and dendrites, called synapses. The development of skills—or sequences of behaviors—involves information being passed quickly from one neuron to the next. Synaptic connections grow and strengthen depending on use.

Early on—from birth to age 3—the brain produces significantly more dendrites and synapses than it needs. Beginning at age 3, it begins to slough off the nerve cells it doesn't need based on neuronal activity. Those not used regularly by the toddler are eliminated in a process called "pruning." However, even in adolescence, this process of overproduction and concomitant pruning of excess nerve cells continues. Those that are used by the developing brain are retained, and those that are left unused are eliminated. This process has led to the expression "use it or lose it" to describe brain development during adolescence. Thus, childhood and adolescence are key stages for habit formation. Those behaviors and habits that are practiced—sports, video games, learning to drive a car—are retained and strengthened. If students are not practicing important habits, they are losing a tremendous opportunity to build skills at a time when the brain is programmed to do just that. This is why coaching has such potential to help students develop habits that will serve them throughout their schooling—and, indeed, throughout life.

One other brain process is worthy of mention in our discussion of habit building. As the axon transmits information to other nerve cells, a fatty substance called myelin (composed of glial cells) wraps itself around the axon and acts as insulation. Just as insulation wrapped around an electric cord speeds the transmission of electrical impulses, so myelin enables nerve cells to communicate more quickly and efficiently. The more the nerve cell is used, the more myelin builds up. The thicker the myelin, the faster the impulse is transmitted. Fast transmission translates into better developed, more efficient skills. At a cellular level, then, coaching enhances myelin production.

Myelin is released to neurons in stages depending on the developmental level of the individual and other factors such as environment and heredity. As noted previously, however, the part of the brain where executive skills reside, the prefrontal cortex, is the last to develop. This means that adults—parents, teachers, coaches—have a comparatively long period of time to influence the growth of executive skills.

A TAXONOMY OF EXECUTIVE SKILLS

A survey of the literature on executive skills shows that early efforts to understand and catalogue these skills were done so in the context of traumatic brain injury (Lezak, 1983). Individuals with injuries to the prefrontal cortex have predictable executive functioning weaknesses, and one of the best descriptions of the kinds of skills governed by this part of the brain comes from a 1993 article by Hart and Jacobs published in the *Journal of Head Trauma Rehabilitation*. The authors summarized the critical functions of the frontal lobes in the management of information and behavior:

1. The frontal lobes decide what is worth attending to and what is worth doing.
2. The frontal lobes provide continuity and coherence to behavior across time.
3. The frontal lobes modulate affective and interpersonal behaviors so that drives are satisfied within the constraints of the internal and external environments.
4. The frontal lobes monitor, evaluate, and adjust. (pp. 2–3)

Since then, a number of different researchers have developed different schemes for organizing executive skills. Russell Barkley (1997) has proposed a developmental model in which he describes the emergence of key executive functions in the first year of life. He has suggested that response inhibition is the first executive skill to develop shortly after birth, followed by nonverbal working memory, self-regulation of affect, internalization of speech (or verbal working memory), and finally "reconstitution" (a problem-solving capacity that combines cognitive and behavioral flexibility, fluency, and creativity).

Tom Brown, developer of the Brown ADD Scales (1996), organizes executive functions somewhat differently (1996). He describes six clusters of executive skills: activation (including organization, prioritizing, and activating for work), focus (focusing, sustaining, and shifting attention), effort (which includes alertness, processing speed, and sustaining effort), emotion (managing frustration and controlling emotions), memory (i.e., working memory), and action (monitoring and self-regulating action).

The developers of the Behavior Rating Inventory of Executive Function—the BRIEF (Gioia, Isquith, Guy, & Kenworthy, 2000)—have divided executive skills into two broad categories: skills associated with behavior regulation, such as controlling emotions, managing impulses, and dealing with situations requiring cognitive flexibility; and skills involving *meta-cognition*, or thinking, such as initiating tasks, sustaining attention, keeping track of what needs to be done, planning and organizing tasks, and monitoring behavior based on feedback from the environment or the reactions of others.

Typically, researchers identify five to eight executive skills, although the terms and descriptors vary. In our work with children and teenagers, we have chosen to identify a larger number of more discrete skills. Our rationale for doing so is this: The more precise we can be in our description of specific executive skills, the better able we are to design interventions to address critical weaknesses. It is not uncommon, for instance, for researchers to combine planning and organization into a single skill. Our experience is that these are two related but discrete skills, and we often see youngsters with strengths in planning and weaknesses in organization or vice versa. Because our goal is to design interventions to address specific behavioral weaknesses, we prefer to be as precise as possible in our description of each executive skill. The 11 executive skills that we feel are most likely to have an impact on academic performance and social adjustment are presented in Table 1.1, along with definitions and examples of how the skill manifests in younger and older children.

In other publications (*Executive Skills in Children and Adolescents: A Practical Guide to Assessment and Intervention* [Dawson & Guare, 2010] and *Smart but Scattered* [Dawson & Guare, 2009]), we have detailed a variety of methods and strategies for helping young people acquire these executive skills at a level of proficiency to support academic success. In this manual, we choose to focus on one intervention in depth: coaching. We initially developed this approach with a target population of students with ADHD in mind; however, our and others' evolving experience with the model has demonstrated that it is ideally suited for youngsters who are underperforming in school as a result of weak executive skills, whether or not they have an identifiable disability. Thus, it is a flexible strategy that is effective for a wide variety of students—and probably for a wide variety of reasons. Chapter 3 addresses in greater detail the student populations we think are most likely to benefit from coaching.

Chapter 3 also describes in considerable detail the coaching process. As a lead-in to this discussion, Chapter 2 focuses on the theoretical underpinnings that guided our development of coaching and that underlie its success. In brief, coaching involves an initial session at which a written plan, including goals and objectives, is jointly developed by the coach and the student, followed by regular brief "coaching" sessions to evaluate progress and develop new goals and plans. At each daily session, the coach and student review the plan made at the previous coaching session, evaluate how well the plan was followed and whether the goals were met, identify what the student wants to work on next, and create a new plan.

TABLE 1.1. Definitions of Executive Skills

Executive skill	Definition	Examples
Response inhibition	The capacity to think before you act; this ability to resist the urge to say or do something allows your child the time to evaluate a situation and how his or her behavior might impact it.	A young child can wait for a short period without being disruptive. An adolescent can accept a referee's call without an argument.
Working memory	The ability to hold information in memory while performing complex tasks. It incorporates the ability to draw on past learning or experience to apply to the situation at hand or to project into the future.	A young child can hold in mind and follow 1- or 2-step directions. The middle school child can remember the expectations of multiple teachers.
Emotional control	The ability to manage emotions to achieve goals, complete tasks, or control and direct behavior.	A young child with this skill can recover from a disappointment in a short time. A teenager can manage the anxiety of a game or test and still perform.
Sustained attention	The capacity to keep paying attention to a situation or task in spite of distractibility, fatigue, or boredom.	Completing a 5-minute chore with occasional supervision is an example of sustained attention in the younger child. A teenager can pay attention to homework, with short breaks, for one to two hours.
Task initiation	The ability to begin projects without undue procrastination, in an efficient or timely fashion.	A young child is able to start a chore or assignment right after instructions are given. A teenager does not wait until the last minute to begin a project.
Planning/ prioritization	The ability to create a roadmap to reach a goal or to complete a task. It also involves being able to make decisions about what's important to focus on and what's not important.	A young child, with coaching, can think of options to settle a peer conflict. A teenager can formulate a plan to get a job.
Organization	The ability to create and maintain systems to keep track of information or materials.	A young child can, with a reminder, put toys in a designated place. A teenager can organize and locate sports equipment.
Time management	The capacity to estimate how much time one has, how to allocate it, and how to stay within time limits and deadlines. It also involves a sense that time is important.	A young child can complete a short job within a time limit set by an adult. A teenager can establish a schedule to meet task deadlines.

(cont.)

TABLE 1.1. *(cont.)*

Executive skill	Definition	Examples
Goal-directed persistence	The capacity to have a goal, follow through to the completion of the goal, and not be put off by or distracted by competing interests.	A first grader can complete a job to get to recess. A teenager can earn and save money over time to buy something of importance.
Flexibility	The ability to revise plans in the face of obstacles, setbacks, new information, or mistakes. It relates to an adaptability to changing conditions.	A young child can adjust to a change in plans without major distress. A teenager can accept an alternative such as a different job when the first choice is not available.
Metacognition	The ability to stand back and take a bird's-eye view of yourself in a situation, to observe how you problem-solve. It also includes self-monitoring and self-evaluative skills (e.g., asking yourself, "How am I doing?" or "How did I do?").	A young child can change behavior in response to feedback from an adult. A teenager can monitor and critique her performance and improve it by observing others who are more skilled.

Note. From Dawson and Guare (2009). Copyright 2009 by The Guilford Press. Reprinted by permission.

CHAPTER 2

Theoretical Underpinnings for Coaching

In their book *Driven to Distraction*, Hallowell and Ratey (1994) include a one-paragraph description of an intervention for adults with attention disorders, which they refer to as "coaching." At the time we read that description, we were operating off a "case manager" model for helping students with ADHD navigate the complex channels of middle school and high school. We immediately recognized that the concept of a coach, using the same sports analogy as Hallowell and Ratey, better fit the needs of ADHD students. They didn't need someone to *manage* them as much as they needed someone to *coach* them, especially as Hallowell and Ratey described:

> an individual standing on the sidelines with a whistle around his or neck barking out encouragement, directions and reminders to the player in the game. The coach can be a pain in the neck sometimes, dogging the player to stay alert, in the game, and the coach can be a source of solace when the player feels ready to give up. Mainly the coach keeps the player focused on the task at hand and offers encouragement along the way. (p. 226)

Once we recognized this as the metaphor we wanted to work from, we surveyed the literature to find empirical evidence both to help us design our coaching model and to support its efficacy. In the years since we wrote our first coaching manual, we have come to recognize that the process is suited not only for students with ADHD but for any student who is struggling in school as a result of executive skills weaknesses. We have also looked to evidence-based practices in both the behavioral and the cognitive-behavioral fields for strategies that can be incorporated into the coaching process. In the following sections, we present several strands of research that we believe contribute to our understanding of coaching and why it is an effective intervention.

GOAL-DIRECTED PERSISTENCE
VERSUS CONTEXT-DEPENDENT SUSTAINED ATTENTION

As noted previously, executive skills take a full two decades or longer to mature, and one of the last skills to develop fully is *goal-directed persistence*. This executive skill actually incorporates other executive skills, including the ability to set a goal, to develop a plan to achieve the goal, to keep the goal in mind over the length of time required to fully implement the plan, and to sustain attention long enough to achieve the goal.

We've recognized for some time that in younger children and those with developmental delays in the acquisition of executive skills (such as those with ADHD), goal-directed persistence is a long time in coming. More recently, research studies (e.g., Reyna & Farley, 2006; Steinberg et al., 2009) have demonstrated that a key characteristic differentiating adolescents from adults is a lack of *future orientation*. Because of both a lack of experience as well as immature brain development, teenagers tend to make poor decisions under some circumstances despite well-developed reasoning skills. This is because the part of the brain that controls logical reasoning, which consists of the outer regions of the brain that include the lateral prefrontal and parietal cortices and the parts of the anterior cingulate cortex to which they are connected, develops more quickly than the socioemotional network, which includes the paralimbic areas of the brain, an interior region that includes the amygdala, ventral striatum, orbitofrontal cortex, medial prefrontal cortex, and superior temporal sulcus (Steinberg, 2007). As a result, these two brain regions compete for dominance in decision-making situations. When the individual is not emotionally excited, he or she is able to make logical decisions. However, as noted by Reyna and Farley (2006), "In the heat of passion, in the presence of peers, on the spur of the moment, in unfamiliar situations, when trading off risks and benefits favors bad long-term outcomes, and when behavioral inhibition is required for good outcomes, adolescents are likely to reason more poorly than adults do" (p. 1).

With diminished future orientation or in the absence of goal-directed persistence, as Barkley (1997) has articulated so well, individuals are under the control of the immediate environment. This means that they have little difficulty sustaining attention to tasks that are novel and intrinsically interesting and for which extrinsic consequences (rewards and penalties) are imposed. Youngsters with ADHD, for instance, attend well when playing video games, watching favorite television shows, or engaging in other preferred activities. They also tend to be successful in classrooms where the subject matter is of particular interest to them or the teacher's instructional style is engaging or entertaining. Unfortunately, it is very difficult for these individuals to sacrifice an immediate reward either to gain some longer term reward or to avoid some later harm. They are under the control of what is happening *right here and right now*, which Barkley labeled context-dependent sustained attention. When there is a conflict between immediate activities (e.g., playing World of Warcraft) and long-term goals (getting a good grade in chemistry), youngsters who lack, using Barkley's term, *goal-directed persistence* have little incentive to set aside the immediate fun activity in favor of the effortful work required to achieve a long-term goal.

We believe that interventions need to be keyed to behaviors that will facilitate achievement of longer term goals—or goal-directed persistence. The model of coaching we have developed seeks to do just this, particularly in Phase 1, in which students are asked to identify long-term goals and begin to design action plans to achieve those goals.

CORRESPONDENCE TRAINING

The daily coaching sessions that take place following the long-range goal-setting session draw on correspondence training research to support the process. Correspondence training has a long history in the behavioral literature, dating back to Risley and Hart (1968) and more recently applied by Paniagua (1992) to a population with attention-deficit disorder. As defined by Paniagua, *correspondence training* refers to a chain of behaviors that "include a verbalization or report about either past or future behavior and the corresponding nonverbal behavior" (p. 226). In other words, when individuals make a verbal commitment to engage in a behavior at some later point, this increases the likelihood that they will actually carry out the behavior. In our model, for instance, we ask students to report what tasks they intend to accomplish before the next coaching session and to specify when they intend to accomplish them.

Correspondence training is a well-established intervention that has proven effective with a variety of populations. In their 2004 review of the literature, Bevill-Davis, Clees, and Gast found 33 empirical studies that employed the technique, primarily with young children but also with older children with disabilities. They concluded that the approach held some promise but recommended further research. Some of the recommended practices gleaned from this review of the literature are summarized in Table 2.1.

Correspondence training is an important part of the coaching process and is integral to the daily check-ins that coaches conduct with students. However, we have found that, in addition, it is critically important to build in a mechanism to verify student reports. Without this, coaches may be inadvertently reinforcing students for making promises rather than for keeping them.

GOAL SETTING

Another critical component of the coaching process is goal setting. Extensive empirical research (see Locke & Latham, 2002, for an excellent overview) has documented the value of goal setting in promoting high levels of performance. Although much of this research has been done with adults in a work environment (Locke & Latham, 2002), there is ample evidence that the same rules apply to children and youth in the school environment (see a review by Schunk, 2003).

According to Locke and Latham (2002), goals serve four primary functions. First, they *direct* behavior—toward goal-relevant activities and away from goal-irrelevant activities. Second, they *energize*—high goals lead to greater effort than low goals. Third, they encourage *persistence*. Finally, they motivate individuals to discover or use task-relevant knowledge or strategies.

Coaching, in all its forms, is built around goal setting. Whether we're working with a second grader on task completion, a fifth grader on social skills, or a high school student on passing classes, the process begins by having students set goals.

Table 2.2 summarizes key findings about the most effective ways to use goal setting to improve performance.

Locke and Latham (2002) affirm that the efficacy of goal setting is well documented and that the process plays a significant role in producing high performance. They also suc-

TABLE 2.1. Keys to Success with Correspondence Training

What the research says	Guidelines for practice
"Say–do" is more effective than "do–say"	Have the student state in advance the behavior that he or she intends to do (e.g., "I will raise my hand during circle time"; "I will spend 1 hour studying for my social studies test tonight").
Reinforcing students for performing the behavior they've promised to do works better than reinforcing them for making the promise.	Praise students *after* they have performed the target behavior ("I saw that you raised your hand four times during circle time—you did what you said you would do!").
For students who lack verbal skills, verbalization of intent can be replaced by rehearsal or demonstration of the desired behavior.	This approach could be used with students with autism—for example, having them point to a picture of a student sitting with another student in the cafeteria to show that they will initiate social contact.
Correspondence training may be particularly effective when the youngster is allowed to choose the behavior he/she intends to engage in.	Although correspondence training can be effective when the target behavior is prescribed by an adult, whenever possible, involve the youngster in selecting the target behavior, either using free choice or providing options to choose from.
There is some evidence suggesting that in some cases correspondence training can include both positive and negative consequences (e.g., the use of a short time-out from reinforcement for failing to perform the promised behavior).	This should be attempted only after a positive-reinforcement-only condition fails to produce the desired result.
Several studies have been able to facilitate generalization of behaviors to different settings (e.g., in a small room next to a classroom, students were taught to recruit praise from teachers in two classes, one in the class period immediately following the training and the second later in the school day).	Generalization may be more likely to occur if specific feedback and error correction are incorporated into the correspondence training.

cinctly summarize the conditions that impede the effectiveness of goal setting. These include "not matching the goal to the performance measure, not providing feedback, not getting goal commitment, not conveying task knowledge, setting a performance goal when a specific high-learning goal is required, not setting proximal goals when the environment is characterized by uncertainty, or not including a sufficient range of goal difficulty levels" (p. 714). This summary should serve as a guideline for coaches in their evaluations of the effectiveness of the coaching process.

TABLE 2.2. Keys to Success with Goal Setting

What the research says	Guidelines for practice
Specific goals are more effective than urging people to "do their best."	Help students make goals that are measurable (e.g., spend 45 minutes studying for a chemistry test; complete math homework during sixth-period study hall).
There is an exception to the above: When a task is complex, urging people to do their best may produce better results than setting specific goals because it reduces evaluative pressure and performance anxiety.	Help students determine whether the goal they want to set is "simple" or "complex." Encourage them to make some of their goals complex but allow for a looser evaluation of results (let them use a "pass/fail" grading system for these goals).
Complex tasks are more likely to be achieved if accompanied by short-term interim goals (also called *proximal goals*) that specify steps to be followed to achieve the complex task.	For complex tasks, always incorporate a planning component that specifies steps to be followed and establishes interim goals for each step. Proximal goals act as an "early warning system" to let the student know whether the long-term goal is feasible.
When people are trained in proper strategies, they will use those strategies for high-performance goals. If they lack those strategies, however, they will perform better with easier goals.	Make sure that students have the strategies they need to carry out goals. If necessary, teach them the steps they will need to follow to achieve goals.
When individuals can control how much time they spend on a task, hard goals prolong effort, but there is often a trade-off between time and intensity of effort.	Give students a choice of working faster and more intensely for shorter periods of time or more slowly and less intensely for longer periods of time; help them identify which pace works best for them.
Goals can either be assigned or determined jointly by coach and student. Assigned goals may be effective, but only when the individual understands the purpose or rationale behind them. In general, when allowed to set their own goals, people tend to set higher goals and to have a higher level of performance in achieving them.	Since the goal of coaching is self-determination, it is better, whenever possible, to have students set their own goals. They may need help with this in the beginning, in which case suggesting a goal, along with the rationale for it, may be helpful.
People with high self-efficacy (confidence in their abilities) set higher goals than those with low self-efficacy; they are also more committed to achieving those goals and are more likely to identify effective goal attainment strategies.	With students who have experienced a lot of failure and who lack confidence in their ability to achieve goals, encourage them to set easier goals in the beginning and to gradually increase their reach.
Self-efficacy can be increased by (1) ensuring adequate strategy training; (2) role-modeling; and (3) using persuasive communication that expresses confidence in the individual's ability to achieve a stated goal.	Coaches assume all of these roles in the course of the coaching process.

(cont.)

TABLE 2.2. *(cont.)*

What the research says	Guidelines for practice
Learning goals (the skills or knowledge one hopes to acquire) produce different results than performance goals (the tasks one wants to complete). When a student sets difficult learning goals, goal specificity is critical.	There is a place for both learning and performance goals, particularly with the student who is failing in school because of failure to complete assigned tasks. Coaching often focuses on performance goals, but good coaches look for ways to incorporate learning goals as well because these are often accompanied by a higher level of motivation and intrinsic interest.
Performance feedback informs individuals about progress toward goals. Goals plus feedback is more effective than goals alone.	This is another reason for helping students create measurable goals. Daily coaching sessions should incorporate performance feedback (e.g., "How many of the goals you set yesterday were you able to achieve?" "You said you wanted to earn a grade of 85 or better on your math test. Were you able to?")
Performance feedback is enhanced when accompanied by attributional training (i.e., training students to attribute success to effort or strategy use and failure to lack of effort or strategy use rather than to lack of ability).	Coaches should ask students, "To what do you attribute your success (or failure)?" and should steer them toward explanations that involve behavior they have control over (e.g., "I tried hard"; I studied for a long time") versus other explanations (e.g., "I got lucky"; "It was an easy test").

SELF-REGULATION/SELF-MANAGEMENT

The ultimate goal of coaching is to enhance the self-regulatory capacities of youngsters, so that they are no longer reliant on others to cue them, coach them, or reinforce them for using their executive skills to achieve personal goals. Self-regulation has been defined as "the internally-directed capacity to regulate affect, attention, and behavior to respond effectively to both internal and external environmental demands" (Raffaelli, Crocket, & Shen, 2005, pp. 54–55).

Self-regulation applies to a broad array of behaviors designed to facilitate the acquisition of self-control and self-direction in a variety of contexts. *Self-regulated learning*, a related concept, is also relevant to this discussion because coaching is frequently designed to promote this skill more specifically. This has been defined as "the self-directive *processes* through which learners transform their mental abilities into task-related academic skills" (Zimmerman, 2001, p. 1). In other words, "students are self-regulated to the degree that they are metacognitively, motivationally, and behaviorally active participants in their own learning process" (Zimmerman, 2001, p. 5).

Self-regulated learners are able to use an array of cognitive strategies to accomplish academic tasks. They also have the metacognitive skills to understand what any given learning task requires, so that they can select the most appropriate strategies to accomplish the task. They are also able to monitor their performance and make adjustments based on shifting situational demands.

An important component of self-regulation and self-regulated learning that is sometimes overlooked in the literature is the regulation of motivation. Wolters (2003) noted that students use metacognition to process, construct, or understand academic content. Regulating motivation, however, involves students' "willingness to process information, construct meaning, or to continue working" (p. 192). Metacognitive strategies involve *how* one performs a task, according to Wolters, whereas motivational strategies relate to *why* and *how long* one engages in a task. For many students with executive skills weaknesses, lack of motivation has as much to do with their inability to apply themselves to academic tasks than lack of cognitive or metacognitive skills. Thus, coaching is as much about helping students activate motivational strategies as cognitive or metacognitive strategies. Table 2.3 summarizes research on strategies to enhance motivation regulation (see Wolters, 2003, for a more complete discussion of these strategies).

Self-management refers to a set of strategies students use to alter their behavior in order to achieve behavioral or academic goals. These strategies include self-monitoring, self-evaluation, self-instruction, and self-reinforcement. Table 2.4 provides descriptors and examples for each of these strategies.

Self-management of behavior in classroom settings has been the focus of research since the late 1960s (Fantuzzo & Polite, 1990; Fantuzzo, Rohrbeck, & Azar, 1987), with some impressive results supporting this approach to changing student behavior. Fantuzzo and colleagues identified 11 different elements of self-management interventions where students can be responsible for the management of the intervention: (1) selecting the target behavior; (2) creating an operational definition of the target behavior; (3) selecting primary reinforcers; (4) setting the performance goal; (5) administering the prompt to engage in the target behavior; (6) observing the target behavior; (7) recording the occurrence of the target behavior; (8) evaluating whether the performance goal was met; (9) administering secondary reinforcers when the goal is met[1]; (10) administering primary reinforcers when the goal is met; and (11) monitoring the occurrence of the behavior over time using charts or graphs. Ways to incorporate these elements of self-management in the coaching intervention are presented in Table 2.5.

Chapter 3 describes in more detail how correspondence training, goal setting, and self-management strategies can be incorporated into the coaching process. We conclude the current chapter with a brief look at studies that document the efficacy of coaching.

STUDIES INVESTIGATING THE EFFICACY OF COACHING

When we first developed coaching as an intervention strategy, we were fairly confident that it would work because of the research supporting its key components. We conducted a pilot study at a high school in Portsmouth, New Hampshire, in which we trained school personnel, including guidance counselors and special education aides, to act as coaches for five students (10th and 11th graders) with ADHD who volunteered to participate in the study. After completing a

---

[1] The authors' definitions of primary and secondary reinforcers appear to deviate from the more commonly accepted definitions of these terms. Technically, a primary reinforcer is biologically predetermined to act as a reinforcer, such as food or water. A secondary reinforcer, also called a conditioned reinforcer, is anything that acquires reinforcing properties by being paired with a primary reinforcer, such as token, points, or money.

TABLE 2.3. Keys to Success for Enhancing Motivation

What the research says	Guidelines for practice
Students who reward themselves for achieving goals or accomplishing tasks are more productive than those who punish themselves or do not self-consequate.	Encourage students to identify a way to reward themselves when they achieve a goal or accomplish individual steps toward achieving a goal. This might include something they can look forward to doing when the task or subtask is completed.
The use of self-talk has been associated with higher levels of task engagement and performance outcomes. Mastery self-talk is associated with greater use of planning and self-monitoring strategies and with self-reported effort. Performance self-talk is associated with rehearsal and regulation strategies and with classroom performance.	Teach students how to use both mastery self-talk (e.g., "I'm going to work at this algebra problem until I understand how it works!") and performance self-talk (e.g., "Great job. I stuck with my math homework and didn't quit until I finished it!").
Individuals can improve task performance through the use of interest-enhancement strategies to make tasks more enjoyable, interesting, or challenging.	Help students identify ways they may turn tasks into games, challenge themselves to complete tasks within self-selected time limits, or find a purpose for doing the task (e.g., by creating a question they want to answer in a reading assignment or forming an opinion regarding key points covered in a reading assignment and looking for evidence to support or refute their position). For some students, social engagement enhances interest in any learning task; encourage them to study with a friend or partner.
Some students engage in "self-handicapping" strategies (such as leaving assignments until the last minute or pulling "all-nighters"). Although these students report that this motivates them, research is equivocal, and the practice may be associated with creating a cycle of low effort and low task performance because students may use procrastination as an excuse for poor-quality work.	If students say they work best under the pressure of immediate deadlines, coaches may want to challenge this belief. Explain that a large body of research supports the superiority of distributed practice (spreading the work out over time) versus massed practice (doing all the work at one time, such as cramming for exams).
Proximal goals and self-set goals increase student motivation for task completion and performance.	See Table 2.2 for practice suggestions.
Motivation can be enhanced through emotion regulation techniques.	Teach students ways to decrease negative emotions (e.g., through relaxation techniques or thought stopping) and increase positive emotions to support the task at hand (e.g., by focusing on the pride they will feel in their efforts or their sense of accomplishment at completing a challenging task).

TABLE 2.4. Types of Self-Management Strategies

Type	Description	Example
Self-monitoring	Student recognizes occurrence of target behavior and records some aspect of the behavior.	Student checks off whether paying attention at the sound of electronic tone occurring at random intervals.
Self-evaluation	Student compares his or her behavior to previously established criterion set by self or adult (e.g., teacher or coach).	Student compares neatness of homework to example representing criterion performance.
Self-instruction	Student uses self-talk to direct behavior.	Student generates list of motivating or problem-solving statements to get through homework ("You can't walk away from this" or "If I can't figure it out, I'll ask my dad for help").
Goal setting	Student selects behavioral targets to work for.	1. Finish homework by 9:00 P.M. 2. Study 30 minutes per night for four nights for biology test. 3. Ask two teachers to write college recommendations by end of school day on Friday.

TABLE 2.5. Elements of Self-Management

Element	What does student participation look like?
Selection of target behavior	Student helps identify what behavior problem needs to be addressed.
Definition	Student is involved in developing operational definition of the target behavior (e.g., "Keep hands to self during circle time").
Selection of primary reinforcers	Student is asked to identify possible reinforcers; helps create a reinforcement menu.
Performance goal	Student helps set a reasonable goal for the target behavior (e.g., "Remember to raise my hand x percent of the time").
Instructional prompt	Student helps decide the best way to remember to prompt for the behavior (e.g., use of kitchen timer or random self-cuing for on-task behavior).
Observation	Student is responsible for monitoring the target behavior.
Recording	Student is asked the best way to record the presence or absence of the target behavior.
Evaluation	Student is at least partially responsible for determining when the goal was met (may include a system for verifying accuracy).
Administration of secondary reinforcers	Student gives him- or herself points or tokens for exhibiting target behavior.
Administration of primary reinforcers	Student chooses reward from reinforcement menu when he or she has accumulated enough points or tokens.
Monitoring	Student is responsible for charting or graphing performance over time.

long-term goal-planning session, the students met with their coaches daily to make study plans consistent with their long-term goals. Although the study included no control group, we were able to compare the grades these students had earned the year before coaching began with the grades they earned during the two marking periods in which coaching took place. Table 2.6 depicts the results. As can be seen, whereas before coaching the majority of the grades students earned were C's, during coaching, the majority were B's or better.

A study examining the impact of our coaching model on math homework completion and accuracy among high school students with ADHD (Merriman & Codding, 2008) also produced promising results. Using a multiple baseline approach, the sample of three 9th and 10th graders established both long- and short-term goals related to homework completion and accuracy rates and participated in daily coaching sessions, in which students met individually with their coach for 10–15 minutes to perform the following tasks: (1) score and graph on an Excel spreadsheet the percentage of math problems attempted and completed accurately for the prior day's homework assignment; (2) review and evaluate their success following the previous day's plan and meeting the goal; (3) establish a new plan for the day; and (4) determine a new short-term goal if the previous goal had been met. Systematic fading was incorporated into the process by reducing the frequency of sessions to every other day once long-term goals were reached and to once a week when homework completion and accuracy rates stabilized across four coaching sessions. Coaching was discontinued when rates remained at high levels for four additional sessions.

Study findings showed that prior to coaching the students were submitting an average of 29% or fewer homework assignments, with average accuracy ratings of 29% or lower. Compared with baseline performance, the percentage of problems completed and accuracy increased for all three students, and two met their long-term goals and were able to fade and then discontinue coaching with continued success. The third student showed improvement over baseline but did not improve enough to meet her long-term goals.

A second study applied our coaching model to the development of social skills in children with ADHD (Plumer & Stoner, 2005). This is described more extensively in Chapter 5, but is noteworthy here because it applied coaching to a younger population (late elementary school age) and used peers as coaches. Plumer and Stoner found that not only did coaching significantly increase positive social behaviors among the three student participants, but the gains appeared to generalize to other settings as well and positively impacted interactions with children other than the peer coaches.

More recently, Vilardo and DuPaul (2010) implemented coaching using cross-age tutors to improve peer interactions among first-grade students exhibiting symptoms of ADHD. In this study, four focus children, two girls and two boys ages 6–7, were matched with four older children, ages 8–9, to work on prosocial skills. The focus children set long-term goals and then met with their coaches, who were trained by graduate students in school psychology and special

TABLE 2.6. Effect of Coaching on Report Card Grades

Percent grades earned	B or better	C	D
Before coaching	19	61	19
During coaching	63	32	5

education, every day to select a daily goal and practice the goal through modeling and role play-ing. Rewards were administered for successful demonstration of daily goal behaviors. Outcomes were assessed using a standardized social skills improvement measure and an intervention rat-ing profile. In this study, boys exhibited improvement on the outcome measures but girls did not.

These three studies were all based on our coaching model. In addition, studies that use coaching without following our model explicitly or that include all the elements of our model without calling it coaching have also supported the efficacy of the process. For example, Ander-son, Munk, Young, Conley, and Caldarella (2008) described a process for teaching organiza-tional skills to junior high school students that used most of the elements of coaching, including direct instruction of organizational skills, data collection, individualized adult support, positive reinforcement, goal setting, and behavioral contracting. Students in a life skills class were shown how to organize their notebooks and were taught to use a daily checklist to help them come to class prepared, write down assignments, complete and turn in assignments, and track their performance on assignments. As the year progressed, they added two other features: goal set-ting and behavioral contracting. Three of the four students in the study significantly improved report card grades in the subjects in which they applied the process, one student improving the science grade from a D– to a B– and two others improving grades from C and C– to A's.

Coaching has also been employed effectively at the college level. Swartz, Prevatt, and Proc-tor (2005) described a coaching intervention for students with ADHD that included an initial goal meeting at which the coaching process was explained and long-term goals were established. Decisions were also made regarding rewards and consequences for meeting or failing to meet goals as well as the frequency and nature of the ongoing coaching contacts, with participants choosing weekly or biweekly face-to-face contact at the campus assessment center, phone calls, and/or e-mails. Weekly objectives (interim steps to be followed to achieve the long-term goals) were also developed at the initial session and reviewed and revised at each subsequent coaching session. The authors provide a single-case study of a fourth-year nursing student who partici-pated in the coaching process in order to address problems with procrastination, concentration in class, and time management. A comparison of pre- and posttest data showed that the student improved on a majority of the goals she selected to work on, showed improvement in her study time, and achieved her goal of earning a B in the course.

Although coaching has not been extensively studied, the research to date is encourag-ing in that it has shown that coaching can be an effective intervention with students ranging from elementary to college age and can be used to address both academic and social goals. In the chapters that follow, we present a how-to guide for establishing coaching interventions to address the needs of individual students and, more programmatically, of groups of underper-forming students at all grade levels.

UNIT II

OUR COACHING MODEL

CHAPTER 3

Basic Coaching for Academic Success

The coaching process described in *Coaching the ADHD Student* (Dawson & Guare, 1998) was designed primarily for use with adolescents. It is a versatile strategy that, as we noted in the previous chapter and expand on later here, has been employed successfully with both younger students and college students. In this chapter, we first outline the coaching process as it works with teenagers.

Coaching is fundamentally a process that helps students establish a link between long-term goals, which may also be described as hopes and dreams, and the daily behavior they need to perform in order to achieve those long-term goals. Many underachieving teenagers have experienced years of failure prior to coming to coaching. This has eroded their self-confidence and made them wary of investing in anything that has the potential to produce another failure experience. Thus, it is all the more critical that the coaching process be well thought out and presented in a way that offers hope to students without overpromising the results.

WHO BENEFITS FROM COACHING?

As we have documented, coaching can be implemented for students at all levels of education—from elementary school to college—to address both academic and social skills deficits. In addition, we see coaching as working most effectively for students of average to near-average capabilities. Furthermore, although it can be effective with students whose school performance problems fall under a variety of disability categories, coaching is likely to be more effective with those whose problems do not fall at the extreme end of any of those disorders. Thus, students with behavior disorders profound enough to make it unlikely that they can get through a typical school day without having meltdowns or multiple discipline infractions would not be likely candidates for coaching. Nor would students with ADHD whose impulsivity or distractibility is extreme and not controlled with medication. However, for students whose attention problems are mild to moderate, it is an ideal intervention because it allows them to practice the skills they need to manage, overcome, or work around their attention problems. Youngsters with Asperger syndrome are also likely to benefit from coaching because they tend to be rule governed, do well with procedures that can be spelled out in a step-by-step fashion, and are able to focus and keep tasks and goals in working memory. Students with learning disabilities may respond well to a coaching intervention as long as their working memory deficits are not so profound that they have trouble holding in mind the plans or commitments they have made.

Coaching is also an ideal intervention for students who are underachievers by virtue of the fact that they have weak executive skills apart from a diagnosed disability. We have found over the years that students may struggle with individual executive skills weaknesses, such as poor organization or weak time management skills, and it is these skills deficits that prevent them from working at their potential or achieving their goals. By pinpointing executive skills strengths and weaknesses, coaches can help students strengthen weaknesses or maximize strengths to compensate so they are able to achieve more consistently the high-quality work they are capable of.

BEFORE COACHING BEGINS

We view coaching as a process in which a student voluntarily agrees to participate. The voluntary nature of this relationship is essential for two reasons. First, the rapport established between the coach and the student is critical to success: Coaching is not only a *process*, it is a *relationship*. Coercing a student to work with a coach places the process in jeopardy and should be avoided whenever possible.

Second, an important goal of the coaching process is to assist students in becoming independent learners who can make the daily and long-term decisions necessary to achieve important self-selected life goals. We believe that a desire to set long-term goals as well as a willingness to work toward them is a prerequisite that students must bring to the coaching process. Students who are unwilling to set and work toward long-term goals are unlikely to reap the benefits this process offers.

This is not to say we discourage parents and teachers from trying to persuade the reluctant participant to buy into coaching. Certainly, this student can be walked through the long-range goal-setting session prior to determining whether the process will be an effective intervention. A student who approaches this session with a negative or apathetic attitude may find the process of setting long-term goals satisfying, possibly sparking an interest in school that up until now lay dormant. However, if at the end of the long-range goal-setting session the student still feels the process is not worthwhile, we recommend it stop there. The coach can leave the student with an open invitation to reconsider this intervention should he or she be interested in trying again at some later point. The option of choosing someone else to act as the student's coach should also be offered.

SELECTING A COACH

Once a student had decided to try coaching, selecting the coach may be the most critical element in the success of the process. Many students for whom coaching has been suggested have had chronic problems throughout school. Some students with whom we have worked do not balk at the coaching model itself but at the necessity of working with school personnel with whom they have a negative history. Because of the nature of their problem behaviors, these students—and particularly those at the junior high and high school levels—are often judged by teachers to be "lazy," "irresponsible," "indifferent," and so on. Some students have heard these labels applied to them for so long that they are reluctant to put themselves in a situation where more of the same may be forthcoming.

This concern is legitimate because coaching will subject these students to a high degree of monitoring in areas where they have been most vulnerable in the past. At the same time, however, we have found that, except for those who are new to a school (such as freshmen beginning a new year), most students are able to identify at least one adult, usually a member of the school staff, with whom they feel comfortable and are willing to at least start the process.

Our coaching process is designed specifically to be implemented by someone outside the student's family, most commonly in a school setting, although coaching can also be conducted successfully outside of school hours by someone not connected to or employed by the school.

A coach need not be someone with an advanced degree in mental health. At the high school level, it could be a guidance counselor or also a caring teacher, a resource room teacher, a gym teacher or sports coach, or an assistant principal. One should not rule out custodians, school secretaries, teacher aides, or school nurses as possible coaches, particularly when the primary purpose of coaching is to provide students with a caring adult who is committed to checking in daily to make sure the students are staying on track with their goals. Possible coach candidates are listed in Figure 3.1. It could even be another student, with an adult "coaching supervisor" acting as a backup. In later chapters, we discuss peer coaching and the training considerations for this style of coaching. In this chapter, we focus on training adults to act as coaches.

What personal qualities define a good coach? Figure 3.2 summarizes the primary attributes. A good coach is reliable, able to make plans and keep schedules. Clear thinking helps: When a student describes a goal that is vague or grandiose, a coach needs to be able to help translate it into something practical. A good coach is not only a skilled problem solver but, more importantly, knows how to empower students to solve their own problems. A good coach doesn't lecture or instruct; rather, using a Socratic method, he or she primarily asks questions that lead students to identify solutions for themselves. A coach also needs to be enthusiastic and

> - A school psychologist
> - A special education teacher
> - A favorite teacher
> - A guidance counselor
> - An intern
> - A paraprofessional (classroom or personal aide)
> - A trained volunteer
> - Another school employee (e.g., secretary, custodian, nurse, assistant principal, sports coach) to whom the student feels well connected

FIGURE 3.1. Possible coaching candidates.

- They like kids and relate to them in a natural way.
- They are empathic and good listeners.
- They're reliable, organized, and have good planning skills.
- They teach more through questions than lectures.
- They have training in coaching.

FIGURE 3.2. Characteristics of good coaches.

supportive—someone who can find the silver lining in the cloud. When plans don't work, the coach is able to highlight the positive, bring students back to the long-term plan, and remind them how far they've come. Finally, a good coach is invested in the students without taking setbacks or disappointments personally.

To select a coach, the student must first understand the role of the coach. Although a coach offers significant support, he or she also helps to problem solve and troubleshoot day-to-day plans and sometimes must push the student or hold the student accountable for poor follow-through. The student must recognize these duties of the coach and select someone with whom he or she can tolerate such interaction.

This is particularly important in the early stages of the relationship, when the entire process is susceptible to breakdown. In some cases, we have asked the students themselves to approach their prospective coaches to invite them to participate, and this has worked well. Willingness on the part of the student to make the initial contact indicates a fair degree of trust and confidence in the person selected. Additionally, it conveys to the coach the student's motivation and commitment to participate in the process. If the selected individual agrees to become a coach, the student should inform him or her that additional details will be provided by the coaching supervisor (often a school psychologist, counselor, or special education teacher).

The coaching process may work in one of two ways: either individually, on a case-by-case basis, or as a systemwide intervention in which a cadre of coaches are trained and made available to students. On an individual basis, coaching may be activated following a psychological evaluation or a referral to a school psychologist or guidance counselor. We activate the coaching process in our clinic when we see students for consultation or for an attention disorder evaluation. When it seems appropriate, we discuss with students and their parents the coaching process and ask students to consider whether they would find it helpful to work with a coach. We talk further with interested students and ask them to identify someone they would like to have coach them, and we may then meet with that person to review the coaching process. Occasionally, we have coached high school students ourselves, via direct meetings and telephone contact, although logistically this is more difficult to arrange.

Coaching can also be introduced as a more broad-based intervention service. Here, someone in the school setting takes responsibility for overseeing the coaching process and serves as a coach coordinator/supervisor. For instance, a school psychologist assigned to a high school might begin by making a presentation to faculty describing the process, then recruit volunteer coaches from those attending the presentation, and train volunteers in after-school sessions. The coach coordinator can then inform the student body that the service is available to interested students and provide enrollment instructions. As part of the enrollment process, students are given a list of volunteers from which to select their coach. They might also be invited to ask someone not on the list to serve as their coach, an approach that is described in more detail in Chapter 5.

THE COACHING PROCESS

Step 1: Identifying the Need for a Coach

This often comes as a result of an evaluation in which the student's academic problems are identified. In a school that makes coaching available as a publicized service, the need for a coach may be identified through either self-referral or referral from a teacher, guidance counselor, private therapist, or parent.

Step 2: Obtaining the Student's Commitment to Coaching

The coaching process is described to the student and his or her agreement to participate is solicited. A script for explaining coaching to students may look like this:

"Chris, your guidance counselor contacted me because he was concerned that the grades you're getting may not be good enough to get you into the kind of college you've talked about wanting to go to. I'm wondering if you'd be interested in working with an academic coach to help you bring your grades up. Academic coaches work sort of like sports coaches: They help you decide what you want to achieve and then meet with you on a regular basis to make sure you're on track to reach your goals. At first, it'll be a daily check-in with your coach, who'll help you get organized, make sure you've written down all your homework assignments, and help you plan your time so you can get everything done you need to do.

"Coaches aren't there to tell you what to do; they're less of a 'boss' and more of a partner. Mostly they ask questions to make sure you remember everything you have to do and have a game plan for getting it done. If you seem stuck on something, they can help you figure it out—like how to plan a project or to track down things you need to complete assignments or how to get extra help from your teachers if you need it. If you want, you can work with a coach for something small, like getting all your homework done in one class. Or you may want to use a coach to help you work on bigger goals, like how to pass all your classes or bring your grades up so you make the honor roll. It's up to you how high you set your sights. Some kids we work with start small so they can achieve some success and then reach for something bigger after that.

"Coaching doesn't take a lot of time—kids usually find 10 minutes either during the school day (like just before lunch or in the first part of study hall) or just before or after school. It's not a big time commitment, but especially in the beginning we ask that students commit to meeting with their coach every day. As times goes on and it gets easier to make plans and meet goals, we drop back the coaching sessions to a less frequent schedule—like every other day, then twice a week, then once a week, and so on.

"Coaching isn't mandatory. In fact, we've found it doesn't work if kids feel they *have* to do it. And if they agree to try it and it doesn't work out, no one will make them continue (although we may try to figure out what went wrong and try to fix it).

"So what do you think? Is this something you might be interested in trying?"

Step 3: Matching the Student with the Coach

As already stated, coaching works best when students are able to select someone they already know and feel comfortable with. If the school has a coaching program in place, students should be provided with a list of possible coaches and asked to select one they think they can work well with. If the intervention is being offered on an individual basis, brainstorm with the student to identify a compatible coach from among the school staff. This might be a favorite teacher, a sports coach, an administrator with whom they feel comfortable, or a guidance counselor, classroom aide, or special education staff person. We generally recommend that the coach be someone who works at the student's school because this makes it easier for the coach to meet with the student and to contact teachers to verify student follow-through on goals. However, a student may choose an individual who is not affiliated with the school, and steps for setting up this type of coaching intervention are discussed later in the chapter.

Step 4: Setting Up the First Meeting with the Coach

This is the point where the specifics of the relationship are agreed upon and long-term goals established. If a coach coordinator is involved (such as a school psychologist), it may be helpful for that person to sit in on this meeting to assist with the long-term goal-setting process, a more detailed description of which is provided shortly. Also at this meeting, the coach and student determine the time and location of daily coaching sessions.

Step 5: Beginning Daily Coaching Sessions

As noted previously, we strongly recommend that coaching sessions occur daily at first, with the goal of reducing their frequency as success is achieved. The coach and student should identify a procedure for notifying each other if either is unable to attend an agreed-upon session. Details regarding how daily coaching sessions are to be conducted are presented shortly.

LONG-TERM GOAL SETTING

This process involves identifying the student's long-term goals, determining what criteria must be met in order to meet those goals, and delineating the barriers that stand in the way of meeting those goals. This process takes place before coaching begins and then as a periodic check to determine whether the long-term goals are still applicable and whether adequate progress is being made toward achieving those goals.

Many high school students fail to recognize that demands and expectations shift when they reach this level. Unlike in elementary or middle school, in high school students have more latitude in course selection. At the same time, high school students have distribution requirements—in order to graduate from high school, they must earn sufficient credits in specific subject areas (e.g., math, history, English, science, physical education). If high school students plan to go to college, other requirements must be met, in terms of courses selected, of arranging to take the SATs, and performing the tasks that are necessary prerequisites for college acceptance.

Students with executive skills weaknesses are particularly prone to "living for the moment." However, when taken through a goal-setting process that includes having them describe what they want to accomplish through and beyond high school, they are often able to set realistic goals and begin to make the connection between their daily performance and the achievement of cherished goals.

Long-term goal setting with secondary-level students includes setting goals with respect to both high school graduation and post–high school plans. If these plans include college, it also makes sense to identify what kind of college the student hopes to attend (e.g., 2-year or 4-year school, state university, liberal arts college). If the student has a particular college in mind, this can be included as part of the goal.

With middle school youngsters, setting goals beyond high school or even middle school may not be possible. However, we encourage coaches to begin this goal-setting process with a discussion about longer term goals, if only to help students recognize that these decisions will need to be made eventually. Nonetheless, they may ultimately settle on shorter term goals (e.g., passing enough classes so the student is eligible to play sports) at this stage in the coaching process.

We see the goal-setting phase as lying at the heart of the coaching process. For most under-achieving students, the ability to set and keep long-term commitments is a fundamental weakness that has resulted in recurrent failure. Coaching them to set and achieve goals will help them establish a track record of success and motivation toward self-management. In addition, long-term goals provide a conceptual and motivational link to the demands of day-to-day performance. Without this link (which the coach repeatedly reminds students of), the effort of day-to-day tasks can leave students opting for more immediately enjoyable or rewarding activities. Finally, for some students, this may be their first opportunity to engage in setting specific goals that they believe are truly attainable. Although it is important not to overemphasize this in the beginning stages, the possibility of reaching goals builds confidence and motivation. We have found it particularly helpful to have these goals to return to when students encounter the obstacles that are a normal part of the process of changing long-standing and entrenched behaviors.

There may be times when the initial goal-setting session is conducted by both the coach and the coaching supervisor (e.g., a school psychologist or counselor). In many cases, it is the coaching supervisor who already knows the student who has recommended coaching, and he or she can help set the process in motion by conducting the goal-setting session. At times, as we have found, it may be helpful for parents to sit in on this session in order to help further clarify the student's long-term goals.

Step 1: Gathering Background Information

If the coach and student are new to each other, it may be helpful for the coach to gather some background information on the student to inform the coaching process. This can be done through a combination of student questionnaires and structured interviews. Two forms that can be used for this purpose are included in the appendices.

The first form (Appendix 1, Getting to Know You, p. 165) asks students to identify how they prefer to spend their leisure time and what they see as areas of talent and personal strength. It also asks them to identify areas in which they would like to become "expert." This question can serve multiple purposes by bringing to light what the students feel passionate about that the coach can use to relate to the learning process. First, it can serve as a conversation starter between student and coach. Asking students about their interests creates positive energy, which gets the process off to a good start. It also gives students the opportunity to share their knowledge and expertise, which communicates to them that the coaching experience will be different from prior relationships with teachers or other educators that may have caused them to feel inferior. Finally, some students have trouble identifying their post–high school goals. By asking them to share their passions, they may be helped to translate those passions into meaningful goals.

The second form is a semistructured interview (Appendix 2, p. 167) designed to identify executive skills strengths and weaknesses. The more a coach knows about trouble spots and competencies before coaching begins, the better able he or she will be to steer the long-term goal-setting interview in a useful direction and to draw on this knowledge once the daily sessions begin. For example, if a student acknowledges in this structured interview that she is really lousy at figuring out how long it takes to complete homework assignments and as a result consistently runs into time crunches as due dates arise, the coach can use this information to help the student make plans, particularly where long-term assignments are involved.

Step 2: Defining the Long-Term Goals

Once the background information is collected, the coach then asks the student to describe long-term goals, using the Long-Term Goal-Setting Form (Appendix 5, p. 178). These goals may be vague at first and need to be refined through clarifying questions from the coach:

"Do you plan to graduate from high school?"
"Are you taking college, general, or vocational track classes?"
"What do you hope to do after you finish high school?"—for example, continue with further schooling or job training; get a job (what kind?); the coach should help the student be as specific as possible.

Some students, even those in high school, are not ready to think much about life after high school. Although we always recommend beginning with that question, if it becomes apparent in the course of the interview that students' ideas about postgraduate plans are vague and likely to remain so, it makes sense for the coach to focus on a more immediate goal by asking, "What is *one thing* you would like to get out of school?" For students who are disaffected or discouraged about school and their likelihood of success, moving to this question quickly in the interview process may be advised.

Step 3: Determining the Steps to Achieve Long-Term Goals

Working with one goal at a time, the coach and the student determine what steps the student needs to take in order to achieve that goal. This may be as simple as getting passing grades in all classes, or it may be more complicated. If a student is applying to a competitive college, for instance, the steps may include making the honor roll, enrolling in honors-level classes, participating in extracurricular activities and signing up for the kinds of classes the college requires. Figures 3.3 and 3.4 are examples of student responses to the first two questions on the Long-Term Goal-Setting Form (Appendix 5).

LONG-TERM GOAL: LIFE AFTER HIGH SCHOOL. What do you see yourself doing after you finish high school? Do you plan to go to college? What kind of college? Do you plan to get a job? What kind of job? Create a picture of what you see your life like after high school. If this question is too difficult to contemplate, then think about this: What is *one thing* you would like to get out of school?

> I would like to go to college and train to be a marine biologist. I would like to study sharks in particular because I'm very interested in protecting our beaches without having to kill these fish. My plan is to get a bachelor's degree at a 4-year college and then work as a lab assistant for awhile before possibly returning to school to get a graduate degree. I see myself working at a university or in a research institution.

Identify a single goal to focus on now—highlight it in the list above. Now list the things you need to do in order to meet your goal.

> Do well enough in high school to be able to go to college. To meet my goal I need to:
> - Get A's and B's in most of my classes.
> - Volunteer at the Seacoast Science Center.
> - Identify which colleges have good biology departments.
> - Visit potential colleges to decide which ones I like.

FIGURE 3.3. Long-term goal-setting example 1.

LONG-TERM GOAL: LIFE AFTER HIGH SCHOOL. What do you see yourself doing after you finish high school? Do you plan to go to college? What kind of college? Do you plan to get a job? What kind of job? Create a picture of what you see your life like after high school. If this question is too difficult to contemplate, then think about this: What is *one thing* you would like to get out of school?

> I would like a job that involves computers or video games, but I'm not sure what that might be. Video game design would be awesome, but I don't know if that's realistic. I've already done some web page design, so maybe I could get more training for that. I'd also like to learn computer programming because I've heard programmers make a lot of money. But I've also heard that computer programming is pretty boring, so that may not be the best choice for me.

Identify a single goal to focus on now—highlight it in the list above. Now list the things you need to do in order to meet your goal.

> Take whatever computer classes are available to me now so that I can learn more about possible job options. To do this, I should:
> - Apply to Seacoast School of Technology (SST; a high school vocational program).
> - Find out what kinds of grades I need to earn to get into that school.
> - Find out what kinds of classes I should be taking next year to prepare me for this school.
> - Put in the work to earn the grades I need to get into SST.
> - Once I have a clearer idea of what aspect of computers I want to focus on, I should look to see what kind of postgraduate training I might need (community college, technical college, or 4-year college).

FIGURE 3.4. Long-term goal-setting example 2.

The coach may feel that some students, especially those in middle school and early high school, would be better served by focusing on *marking period goals* rather than long-term goals. A Marking Period Goal-Setting Form is included in Appendix 6 (p. 182) for this purpose. The process involves having students identify either a grade they want to earn or a specific set of tasks they want to accomplish for each class (e.g., hand in 80% of math homework on time; maintain a B– average or better on history exams). If students choose to set a goal of earning a specific grade in each class, the coach should help them identify exactly what they have to do in order to earn that grade. When working with students who have set the goal of earning higher grades, we ask them what they will have to do differently in order to make this happen.

Step 4: Discussing Obstacles to Achieving Long-Term Goals

The coach discusses with the student what obstacles will need to be overcome to achieve the goals set. Many of these obstacles will be behavioral: for example, choosing to do more interesting things than homework; leaving assignments to the last minute, leading to poor-quality work; skipping classes; forgetting to hand in homework; getting suspended because of fights; or being placed in detention because of skipping or disrupting classes. Having conducted the executive skills interview, the coach may be able to suggest possible obstacles if the student seems at a loss as to how to answer this question.

Step 5: Developing Ways to Overcome the Obstacles

The coach and student next discuss how the student can work to overcome the identified obstacles. For instance, if procrastination or time mismanagement is an obstacle, the student might decide that making and following a timeline for long-term projects could help. If forgetting homework is a problem, the coach and student might develop a homework-recall cuing system. We recommend that the coach and student work together to identify one or two strategies to address each obstacle. Figure 3.5 provides examples of obstacles and student response.

Step 6: Developing Interim Goals

For most teenagers, especially those with a history of underachievement, setting a goal they want to achieve by the time they graduate from high school, no matter how well thought out, is still too distant to act as a motivator on a daily basis. For this reason, we ask students to set interim goals that are closer at hand. In addition, because interim goals are more specific and measurable, they lend themselves well to progress monitoring, so students can see they are moving toward their long-term goal.

Students choose to receive academic coaching because they want to improve school performance. This usually involves working on one of the following interim goals:

- Improving class attendance.
- Improving homework completion.
- Handing in more homework on time.
- Improving grades on homework assignments.
- Improving test or quiz grades.

What are some of the potential obstacles that might prevent you from reaching your goal? How can those obstacles be overcome or avoided?	
Potential obstacle	**Ways to overcome the obstacle**
1. Spending too much time on Facebook	• Don't let myself go on Facebook until my homework is done. • Find a block that will keep me from going to Facebook for 3 hours every evening.
2. Watching ESPN when I should be doing HW	• Allow myself 1 hour for watching ESPN every day. • Ask my mom to monitor this to make sure I don't break my rule.
3. Talking with friends during study hall instead of doing HW	• Don't sit near my friends in study hall. • Study with my friends (e.g., preparing for tests together or doing math homework together and comparing answers). • Explain to friends that I've decided to use study hall time better and ask them to remind me to study.
4. Getting kicked out of U.S. history class for talking back to teacher.	• Tell myself at the beginning of class, "I'm not going to let Mr. C. get on my nerves today." • Sit in the front of the class so I don't get drawn in by friends sitting in the back of the class.

FIGURE 3.5. Examples of obstacles and how to overcome them.

- Improving class participation.
- Decreasing discipline referrals.

For interim goal setting, therefore, we ask students to select among the choices just listed or others that they and their coach may identify. Table 3.1 contains a list of sample interim goals and how they might be measured. As with the long-term goals, this process should be accompanied by a discussion of potential obstacles to achieving this goal and how those obstacles can be addressed.

Chapter 2 (Table 2.2) contains additional suggestions for how to set goals that have the greatest likelihood of being met with success.

Step 7: Completing the "Interim Goals" Section of the Long-Term Goal-Setting Form

Here, the coach and student take the list of interim goals they have selected and refine it further still by:

1. Estimating current performance. If the goal is to improve performance, it helps to know what level the student is starting at. This can be a rough estimate if there are no specific data to refer to (e.g., the student might say, "I'd guess that I show up late for math class at least a couple of times a week"), but the more precise the current performance level estimate, the more likely it is that the interim goal will be realistic.

2. Writing down the interim goal. This can be selected from among the goals listed previously (and in Appendix 5, Long-Term Goal-Setting Form).

TABLE 3.1. Examples of Interim Goals

Goal	How will it be measured?
Complete 80% of homework assignments 4 days out of 5.	Graph percentage of homework completed daily.
Complete math homework with 80% accuracy 4 days out of 5.	Graph percentage of accuracy daily.
Study at least 30 minutes for all Spanish quizzes.	Graph number of minutes spent studying for each quiz.
Earn grades of 80 or better on all science quizzes and tests.	Graph test and quiz grades.
Attend math class 9 days out of 10.	Graph number of math classes attended weekly.
Hand in all English homework on time.	Graph percentage of English assignments handed in on time per week.
Participate in French class.	Keep tally sheet during class; graph number of times hand raised per class.
Keep biology notebook organized and up to date.	Create a scoring rubric with a 1–5 scale; along with coach, rate the notebook at each coaching session; graph daily score.
Bring P.E. clothes to every gym class.	Graph number of days per week student brings clothes to class.
Arrive to first-period class on time.	Graph percentage of days per week on-time arrival.
Attend after-school math help sessions at least twice a week.	Graph number of math help sessions attended per week.
Break down long-term projects into subtasks, with timelines.	Complete long-term project planning form; graph percentage of steps completed on time.

3. Specifying the classes to which the goal will apply.
4. Identifying one to two strategies the student will use in order to achieve the goal.
5. Specifying the success criterion, preferably in terms of a percentage or an average (e.g., hand in 85% of math homework on time; earn an average of 80 or better on 90% of chemistry tests/quizzes).
6. Determining the length of time the student will meet his or her success criterion before setting a new goal or fading coaching. You may want to delay making a decision about this until the coaching process is in place for a few weeks because it may be difficult to make this determination without weekly performance data. For instance, it may take the student awhile to develop some consistency in terms of meeting daily or weekly

goals, and you may want to take this into account before deciding on an end point. We discuss fading in more detail later in this chapter.

Table 3.2 provides additional examples of interim goals.

Step 8: Identifying Ways to Enhance the Likelihood of Success

This step in the process focuses on how students can motivate themselves on a daily basis to stick with their plan to achieve their goals. There are a number of ways to do this, including the following:

- Create an objective way to track progress or to quantify success. The Daily Coaching Form (Appendix 7, p. 184; discussed shortly) enables students to quantify how many of their daily goals they met; these can be turned into a percentage and placed on a graph (a spreadsheet program can facilitate this process). Data sheets can be created for some goals. For example, if attending class is a goal, a sheet like the following can be used:

TABLE 3.2. More Examples of Interim Goals

Current performance	Interim goal	In what classes?	Strategies to achieve goal	Success criterion	Length of time at criterion before beginning new goal or fading coaching
Math homework—completed 50% of the time; English homework—completed 75% of the time	Improve homework completion rates	Math; English	• The student will write down assignment in assignment book • The student will plan with coach for when homework will get done • The student will do homework before playing video games or going on computer	Math: 80%; English: 95%	6 weeks for each subject
Approximately three of six assignments handed in late every week	Hand in homework on time	All classes	• The student will use a checklist to remind him- or herself to place homework in homework folder and place homework folder in backpack • The student will ask his or her mother to check in before bedtime to make sure the student has put his or her homework in the proper location	Hand in 95% of homework assignments on time	6 weeks

Date	Class attendance	
	Yes	No

• Ask students to think of things they can say to themselves to stay focused on their goal or to resist temptations that might interfere. This could be, for example, a mantra (e.g., *You can't walk away from this* or *Remember what you're working on*) that could be written down and posted prominently (e.g., on a bulletin board at home where the student studies, as a screensaver on the student's laptop, or as "wallpaper" on his or her cell phone).

• Role-play with students how they can stay focused or resist temptation. For example, the coach could play the role of a friend calling the student with an invitation to a social event on a night when he or she planned to study for an exam.

• Ask students to identify ways they can structure the environment to support their plan. For instance, discuss and identify the best place and time to study, ask about typical distractions when studying and how these could be reduced or eliminated, find out if the student would find cues or reminders helpful and how these can best be delivered (e.g., by a friend or a parent or through technology using programmed alarms on a cell phone or computer calendar programs). Table 3.3 lists other environmental supports and modifications that students should consider when making decisions about studying.

• Have students identify a reward to work for. This can be as simple as students planning something they can look forward to after they complete their daily plan (e.g., watching a favorite TV program), or the reward may be a larger one that they will work for over time. This may require cooperation from parents if an expense is involved. We have worked with students who have arranged with their parents to earn new video games, a laptop computer, or a new pair of skis in exchange for following a plan to improve school performance. Typically, this is done using a points system: establish how many points can be earned for specific behaviors (e.g., completing daily goals) and how many points are needed to earn the reward. Depending on the size of the reward, points are adjusted so that the reward can be earned in a specific period of time (1–2 weeks or over the course of a marking period). Points are recorded on a graph (we favor something like the thermometer often used by United Way and other community fund-raisers) and prominently displayed so students keep the goal in mind and see their progress. If students are working toward a tangible reward, we also recommend posting a picture of the reward to help them keep their "eyes on the prize."

Step 9: Reviewing the Plan

The last step in this session involves the coach checking with the student one last time to ensure that the plan being developed is realistic and within his or her capabilities. Although plans can be revised as necessary as the coaching continues, every effort should be made to develop a plan at the outset that has a reasonable chance of success.

TABLE 3.3. Suggestions for Environmental Modifications to Promote Good Study Habits

- *Choose study times based on energy patterns.* People in general tend to have specific times in the day when they have more energy than others. Encourage students to track their energy patterns to discover their peak energy times.

- *Identify optimal study environments.* This includes the best place to study (e.g., bedroom, dining room table, library) as well as other study conditions (e.g., alone or with a friend, in a completely quiet environment or with background music).

- *Create a study schedule that works.*
  What to start with: Some students do best when they get the "hard stuff" out of the way first. Others have to ease into a homework session by beginning with something easy or enjoyable. Some students need to finish one assignment before starting the next one. Others can't tolerate more than 15 minutes on a task at any one time, so they switch back and forth between tasks until all are done.
  Breaks: Some students do best with breaks every half-hour or so; others find that completing a task before breaking is a good motivator. Schedules might include sandwiching a favorite TV show in the middle of a study period or completing all one's homework before turning on the TV.

- *Identify the right organizational system.* Some students prefer to have a separate notebook for each subject, while others find that too overwhelming and want to keep all their work in one large notebook. Color coding work sometimes helps (e.g., unfinished assignments go in a red folder, completed assignments that are ready to hand in go in a green folder). Organizational systems also may include "tickler" systems to remind students what has to be done when. Having Post-its handy to write down reminders and posting them prominently where they will be seen may be useful. Post-it digital notes on the computer screen can be used in the same way.

- *Find effective study strategies.* Active strategies are more effective than passive ones (e.g., "rereading the chapter" or "looking over notes"). Active strategies include making flash cards, creating "practice tests," studying with a friend by asking questions back and forth, writing out a set of questions to consider before reading a chapter (ideas for questions can be generated from headings and subheadings, pictures, graphs, words printed in bold, or review questions at the end of the chapter). Learning how to use highlighting in a thoughtful way may also help.

Given the importance of this stage of the coaching process, it may be advisable to break this session into two shorter sessions. A logical sequence would be to use the first session as a "get acquainted" time to gather background information. The session could end with a preliminary discussion of long-term goals and, between the first and second sessions, having students think about what those long-term goals might look like.

DAILY COACHING SESSIONS

The purpose of the daily coaching session is primarily to help the student plan what tasks he or she has to accomplish before the next coaching session and to identify when the task will be completed. With the exception of the first session, each session follows the same format based on the acronym REAP (**R**eview, **E**valuate, **A**nticipate, **P**lan).

First Session

We recommend that the first session begin with a review of the outcome of the long-range goal-setting session. The coach should prompt with an open-ended question such as "What was it we talked about when we met before?" or "Tell me what you remember about the goals you set at our last meeting." The Long-Term Goal-Planning Sheet should be available to refer to, but the student should begin by answering this question based on his or her own recollection of that meeting. The parts omitted can then be filled in by looking at the sheet. It may be helpful to have the student again consider those goals and recommit to working toward them.

After this, the coach should bring out the Daily Coaching Form (Appendix 7). The long-term goals should be written briefly in the appropriate place at the top of the form. The next section, labeled "The Big Picture," involves identifying any longer term obligations the student may have. This includes upcoming tests and quizzes, long-term assignments, and other responsibilities (e.g., sports activities, clubs, jobs).

Then the coach asks the student to identify what he or she hopes to accomplish before the next coaching session ("Today's Plans"). This should include all academic tasks, including homework due the next day as well as beginning long-term projects or spending time studying for upcoming tests or quizzes. Here, the student may need help developing timelines or setting reasonable study goals for tests. The student may also want to work on behavioral goals (e.g., "answer more questions in Spanish class" or "stay after school for extra help in biology"). Once the student has identified these specific tasks, the coach should have him or her describe when he or she plans to do each task. The student should be as specific as possible with respect to *when* the task will be accomplished (e.g., "during eighth-period study hall" or "between 7:00 and 8:00 P.M. this evening").

The meeting concludes with a brief assessment of how the session went and words of encouragement. Both the student and the coach should have a copy of the Daily Coaching Form to take away from the session. We have found it useful to keep the sheets in a three-ring binder with the most recent sheet on top.

To give the reader a sense of how the process works, let's create a dialogue that might take place between a high school student and his coach. Let's assume the following conversation takes place in the first daily coaching session.

> COACH: Joe, you've set as a goal for the marking period to bring your English grade up to a B. This will take some work on your part, since at the last marking period you got a C. Do you remember what you said you were going to try to do differently to improve your grade?
>
> JOE: Yes, I'm going to study for my weekly vocabulary tests, I'm going to stay on top of my reading assignments, and I'm not going to leave papers until the night before they're due so I'll have time to edit and revise.
>
> COACH: Excellent. All good ideas. If you can follow through on them, I'm sure your grade will improve. The coaching we're going to do should help you with this. What we will do when we get together every day is to make a plan for the day that will help you reach your goal. So why don't we begin by taking a look at what's coming up in English. Do you have anything due for that class tomorrow?

JOE: Yes, I'm supposed to read the first chapter of *Lord of the Flies*.

COACH: Anything else—any study questions to answer or reader response you have to write?

JOE: No, except we're supposed to keep an eye out for something that might *foreshadow* later events in the book.

COACH: How are you planning on doing that?

JOE: Well, Mrs. Henderson told us we should look for tensions between characters that might be likely to get worse as the book goes along. Or maybe look for things that are important to characters or maybe personality traits or character flaws that might get them in trouble . . . things like that.

COACH: Sounds good. How are you going to keep track of your ideas?

JOE: I have my own paperback copy of the book, so I thought I would put the letter F in the margin by each detail that might be foreshadowing.

COACH: Sounds like a good plan. When do you think you'll be able to do this assignment?

JOE: I was planning on doing it in my seventh-period study hall.

COACH: Do you think that will give you enough time?

JOE: I think so, but if not, I can finish it after basketball practice and just before dinner.

COACH: OK. Let's talk about upcoming English assignments. What's on the horizon?

JOE: (*consulting his agenda book*) I have a vocabulary test on Thursday, and by next Monday I have to read the first three chapters of *Lord of the Flies* and write a reader response.

COACH: So you have three nights before the vocab test. Have you thought about how you might use the time to study?

JOE: (*a little sheepishly*) I wasn't even going to think about this until Wednesday night. That's a big improvement over last marking period, when I didn't study at all!

COACH: There's actually some good research to show that spreading out studying into several short sessions is a more effective way to learn material than cramming the night before. But tell you what, let's use this week as a baseline. Why don't you plan to study the night before and we'll look at your quiz grade. Then we can decide if you might want to try a different approach next week . . . So, what's your plan with reading the rest of *Lord of the Flies* and writing the response?

JOE: I thought I'd read the other two chapters on Saturday and write the response on Sunday night.

COACH: Let me make a suggestion. You may want to look at how many pages you'll have to read for the second and third chapters and divide the total by the number of days you have left until Sunday. If you can read a little each day, it'll be easier to stay on top of the reading. Maybe you can take advantage of little pieces of time, like in study hall or while you're waiting for dinner.

JOE: I like that idea. I'm a slow reader, so what's gotten me in trouble before is not allowing enough time to do all the reading *and* write the response.

COACH: You've left the paper until the night before it's due. One of your strategies was not to do that.

JOE: Oh, I meant leaving *big* papers until the last minute. This is just a little thing I should be able to whip off in less than an hour.

COACH: Do you need help thinking about how to write your paper?

JOE: Nah, I'm good at that. I did lousy before because I'd only do half the reading and then I'd try to fake it. If I can get the reading done, the paper should be a piece of cake.

COACH: All right. I think we have a plan for today. With the work you have set for English, do you think you'll be able to fit in your other homework too?

JOE: I think so. English has always been bad because I don't like it and I kept putting it off. If this'll help me stay on top of the work, I should be fine.

COACH: Great! I think this process will work well for you. I've written down on this sheet what you committed to do. Take a look at it and see if it captures what we talked about. [See Figure 3.6.]

JOE: (*Looks over the plan.*) Yeah, this looks good—can I keep this sheet as a reminder?

COACH: Sure, but let me make a photocopy for me to keep in my coaching notebook.

COACH: You're off to a good start. You did a nice job writing down your assignments and keeping track of what's due when. That's an important part of the process, and it seems like you do that well.

JOE: Yeah, well, having enough teachers drum into me the importance of writing things down finally got through to me. See you tomorrow, "Coach!"

Later Coaching Sessions

The second session and all coaching sessions thereafter begin with a *review* of the tasks the student had planned to do at the previous coaching session to determine whether they were carried out as intended. Referring to the Daily Coaching Form filled out at the previous session, the coach should read each item on the list and ask whether the student did the task. The student should then be asked to rate (*evaluate*) how well he or she accomplished the task, using the 5-point rating scale detailed on the Daily Coaching Form. A brief discussion about the goals set and the student's performance should follow. For instance, if the student failed to carry out a task, it may be helpful to identify what prevented the task from being done. The positives as well as the negatives should be touched on, however. If the student committed to studying for a test for an hour and followed through, it may be helpful to ask, "What was it that helped you carry out this task as you said you would?" The coach may want to make some notes at the bottom of the sheet to highlight this discussion.

The next step is to have the student *anticipate* work that he or she has to do in the near future. Using a new monitoring sheet, together the coach and the student fill out "The Big Picture" section. This will mean transferring relevant information from the previous coaching session and adding any new assignments, tests, or responsibilities that may have come up since then. The final step, as in the first session, is to have the student *plan* what will be done before the next coaching session. Again, the session should end with words of encouragement from the

Name: _Joe_   Date: _Monday_

LONG-TERM GOAL(S): _Earn a B in English by (1) studying for weekly vocab tests; (2) staying current with reading assignments; and (3) starting writing assignments before the night before due date._

THE BIG PICTURE:

Upcoming tests/quizzes:	Long-term assignments:			Other responsibilities:	
Subject:	**Date:**	**Assignment:**	**Date due:**	**Task:**	**Date:**
Vocab test	_Thursday_	_3 chapters L of F_ _Write reader_ _response_	_Monday_		

TODAY'S PLANS:

What are you going to do?	When will you do it?	**LOOKING BACK:** Did you do it?		How did you do?*
Academic tasks:				
1. _Read ch. 1 L of F (F = foreshadow)_	1. _7th-period study hall_	Yes	No	1 2 3 4 5
2.	2.	Yes	No	1 2 3 4 5
3.	3.	Yes	No	1 2 3 4 5

*Use this scale to evaluate: **1—Not well at all; 2—So-so; 3—Average; 4—Very well; 5—Excellent**

OTHER NOTES/REMINDERS: _Talked about dividing the reading assignment by the number of days and reading a little each day; will study for vocab test on Wednesday, look at test score, and consider spreading out study time over several days if grade is low._

GENERAL OBSERVATIONS REGARDING GOALS/PERFORMANCE:

FIGURE 3.6. Example of a completed Daily Coaching Form.

coach. This could include praise for meeting the previous session's goals and positive feedback regarding the student's attitude and effort in the coaching session. Asking the student to assess his or her own performance may help the student develop self-appraisal skills and give the coach the opportunity to provide further encouragement.

As an example, let's follow Joe as he meets with his coach for his second session.

COACH: Hey, Joe. Welcome back. How's it going?

JOE: Not bad—are you impressed that I remembered to come?

COACH: I was pretty sure you would—did you surprise yourself?

JOE: No—I programmed it into my cell phone. [*Note:* Many schools do not allow students to use their cell phones during school hours; for students with executive skills weaknesses, it may be possible to obtain permission to use them to schedule alarms as reminders for things they need to do or to remember.]

COACH: Clever idea . . . so let's start by looking at the plan we drew up yesterday. As you can see, at the top of the plan is a reminder of what your goal is—earning a B in English—and the three things you said you wanted to do to accomplish the goal. I've photocopied new coaching forms with the goal written down, so we don't have to write it repeatedly—but I suggest that for the next few sessions, we take a look at it just to refresh our memories. Are you still on board with the goal—and do you still think the steps you've written down will get you to that goal?

JOE: I'm all set—reading the chapter on time sure made it easier to stay awake in class—I was even able to participate in the discussion! Mrs. Henderson almost fell on the floor when she saw I raised my hand to answer a question!

COACH: I guess that answers my next question—did you follow your plan? Sounds like you did.

JOE: Yep. My friend Chad tried to distract me, but I just told him I had to get some work done, and he left me alone.

COACH: Were you tempted to set aside your plan? We haven't talked yet about how to handle things that get in the way of following the plan, but it sounds like you passed the first test on your own.

JOE: He did look at me kind of funny—like, *Who are you and what did you do with my friend Joe?* but I told him I was trying to turn over a new leaf. He said, "We'll see how long *that* lasts," but I just smiled and opened my book.

COACH: Nice job. I'm impressed. OK, so you read the chapter—did you make notations for foreshadowing?

JOE: Yeah, that was easy—and it actually made it more interesting to read the book—gave me something to think about while I read. Those notations helped with the class discussion too. That was the question I raised my hand to answer that surprised my teacher.

COACH: So, if you were going to rate how well you followed your plan, sounds like you'd give yourself a 5—for excellent?

JOE: I think so.

COACH: OK, so now we make a plan for today. Let's go back to "The Big Picture" and see if there's anything we need to add—the vocab test is still on Thursday, right? And you have to read two more chapters and write the reader response for Monday, is that correct?

JOE: Yes, nothing's changed.

COACH: Has Mrs. Henderson mentioned any other upcoming tests or long-term assignments we should add to the list?

JOE: She said something about a paper we have to write when we've finished the book, but she hasn't given us a due date yet.

COACH: OK, let's add that to the list just so we don't forget it. We'll put a question mark down for the due date. Has she talked about what the paper is supposed to be about?

JOE: Not yet. She said she'll talk more about it on Monday after we've done our first reader response.

COACH: OK, so what do you have to do for English for tomorrow?

JOE: Nothing—we have an assembly during that period tomorrow.

COACH: Remember what we talked about yesterday—doing a little of the reading assignment every day so you don't get backed up on Sunday? This might be a good chance to start doing that.

JOE: I'm willing to try that. I've got a couple of assignments due for other classes early next week, so it might be good to get ahead of the game. (*Pulls out his copy of* Lord of the Flies *and together he and his coach count out the number of pages in the two chapters and divide it by 5, so that he finishes the reading by Saturday.*)

COACH: OK, so that means you have about five pages per night to read—do you think you can manage that?

JOE: Piece of cake.

COACH: So when will you do today's reading?

JOE: Today Chad and I are actually working on a biology lab during study hall so that won't work. I'll have to do it tonight.

COACH: It would be a good idea if we could write down a time—either an actual time or a marker, like "right after dinner."

JOE: Maybe right *before* dinner actually.

COACH: What time do you usually eat dinner?

JOE: My mom's like clockwork—5:30 on the dot every weeknight.

COACH: So, 5:00 might work?

JOE: Yeah, that's reasonable.

COACH: And how will you remember?

JOE: Just for you, Coach, I'll set an alarm on my phone.

COACH: Well done, Joe. Now, you don't want to get a head start studying for your vocab test?

JOE: Don't push your luck. Besides, we were doing an experiment, right? Comparing how I do when I only study the night before and when I space it out?

COACH: OK, we'll make a study plan tomorrow for that then. Hey, Joe. This has gone really well so far. I'm impressed with your willingness to try to make this work.

JOE: I'm trying—see you tomorrow, same time same place.

The coaching session can also be used as a place to talk about and solve problems the student encounters. While the coach can lend a sympathetic ear, he or she needs to remember that coaches are not counselors. If the student brings up personal problems that are interfering with the ability to follow plans and meet obligations, the coach should refer the student to an appropriate counselor. When the problems raised relate directly to obstacles that are interfering with the ability to meet the goals established at the beginning of the coaching process, however, the coach can help the student brainstorm ways to overcome them. For instance, if a student feels a teacher has misunderstood him or her, the coach can help the student figure out ways to talk to the teacher to clear up the misunderstanding. If the student doesn't know how to approach the teacher or is unsure what to say, the coach may help the student role-play the situation until he or she feels more comfortable. Again, the coach should not impose solutions on the student, but by asking questions, helping the student brainstorm alternatives, or suggesting role plays, the coach can assist the student in identifying the best course of action.

Coaching sessions usually last no more than 10 or 15 minutes and occur daily at first. As the student becomes adept at setting realistic goals and accomplishing tasks reliably, the coaching sessions can gradually be reduced. The student should be involved in deciding when the time is right to cut back on coaching sessions. A logical sequence would be to reduce the sessions from daily to every other day, to twice a week, and then once a week. If slippage occurs, more frequent sessions can be reintroduced. If the student reaches a point where he or she feels coaching sessions are no longer necessary, we would still recommend that the coach contact the student every other week for 4–6 weeks and then once a month. During this fading process, it may be necessary to monitor the student's performance independently, such as through weekly contact with teachers, to make sure the student is on track.

We recognize that during the daily coaching phase there may be times when a session needs to be missed. When this happens, it is vitally important that the coach contact the student via a phone call, note, or e-mail to ensure some continuity. Likewise, if the student is unable to keep a coaching appointment, efforts to communicate with the coach should be made.

Verifying Students' Reports

The correspondence training research discussed in Chapter 2 shows that making a public commitment to performing a task is an effective way to increase the likelihood that the task will be done. In our years of working with the coaching process, we have learned through hard experience that public commitments alone do not guarantee that students with executive skills weaknesses will actually do what they say they are going to do. For this reason, whenever possible, we recommend building into the coaching process a way to verify that students actually follow the plans they make.

With younger students, such as those in middle school, this verification process is presented as a "given" (i.e., part of the coaching process). Most frequently, the goals students set at that age revolve around completing homework and handing it in on time. Goals of earning passing grades on tests and quizzes are also common. Schools that use an Internet-based tracking system (such as PowerSchool) make verification of these kinds of goals relatively easy. The coach and the student may want to use the coaching session on Friday to check the Internet to make sure the student has made an honest report.

When schools do not use a Web-based tracking system, or when teachers are not reliable in keeping it up to date, the coach will need to arrange another tracking system with teachers. The system that we've found works most effectively is for the coach to e-mail teachers once a week and ask them to report back before the Friday coaching session so that their report can be incorporated into the last coaching session of the week. It helps to have a backup plan in place at the start of the process for teachers who are not reliable in responding to this request. In one case we were involved with, a non-school-site coach contacted teachers weekly. If a teacher failed to respond to e-mails a couple of weeks in a row, the coach contacted the parent (who had hired the coach), and the parent then contacted the school's vice principal, with whom she had a good working relationship. The vice principal then met with the teacher to emphasize the need for consistent communication.

Sometimes schools want to place the responsibility for obtaining feedback from teachers on the shoulders of the student being coached. We generally do not favor this approach, at least in the beginning, for a couple of reasons. First, kids with executive skills weaknesses have trouble remembering to do things like this. These are kids who routinely forget homework assignments, forget to bring home the materials they need to do their homework, forget to place their homework in their backpack so that it comes back to school, or forget to hand in the homework. Do we really want to give them the opportunity to forget one more thing?

Second, kids with executive skills weaknesses often already feel badly about their performance in school. They are more likely to be reprimanded by teachers for some slipup or other on their part, and are likely to feel self-conscious about these reprimands and mistakes, especially if they occur in front of their friends and classmates. To ask them to do anything that makes them stand out in front of their peers in yet another negative way not only is insensitive but reduces the likelihood that the student will persist with coaching. Coaching is designed to solve problems, not create new ones, and if the student feels stigmatized, this will hurt, not help, the process.

For this reason, the issue of verification needs to be handled delicately with older teenagers who are participating in the process voluntarily. In some cases, depending on the goals, verification is built into daily coaching sessions. Let's say a student sets the goal of keeping his science notebook organized. He and his coach may develop a checklist of all the things that need to be done to maintain that organization. The student brings his science notebook to each coaching session, and he and his coach go through the checklist together to make sure he's following the steps.

In other cases, however, there will be no way for the coach to verify student reports in the actual coaching session. We recommend that coaches obtain permission from their students to either check in with teachers or go on the school website periodically to track progress. In Joe's case, for instance, it may be difficult to verify that he is following his daily plans (although his coach might ask him to write down start and stop times for when he is working on his plan). However, because his goal is to earn a B in English, Joe and his coach can monitor his grades to make sure he is on track to meet his goal. In general, we recommend that this tracking be done once a week. For students with executive skills weaknesses, if things start to fall apart, they tend to do so very quickly—and then it becomes extremely difficult to repair the damage. The goal is for the coach to catch problems quickly so that the damage can be repaired in time to avert all-out failure.

When Plans Aren't Followed and When Goals Aren't Met

Sometimes students have difficulty following their daily plans despite the best of intentions. Unless coaches have built-in verification mechanisms, it may take them awhile to realize that their students are not following through. This is because, in our experience, students don't want to let their coaches down and try to cover up the fact that they are falling short. Some students will be honest about small shortcomings ("I know I said I was going to do all my math homework last night, but I only did about two-thirds of it") but cover up the larger ones. Others gloss over the small failings too, hoping their coach won't catch them in their cover-up.

It may be helpful for the coach to have a discussion with the students early in the process to let them know that the process is unlikely to go smoothly 100% of the time. A script for this might read like this:

"Here's what I've learned about coaching from doing it for awhile [or from the reading I've done about it]. Kids begin the process with a lot of enthusiasm. Because of this, they usually meet with success initially. This can be reinforcing and when they see things turning around, it motivates them to continue with the process.

"Sometimes, though, as time goes on they lose sight of the fact that the process is not magic but takes hard work and consistency for it to succeed. When this happens, kids may begin to fudge a little. They tell their coaches that they followed their plan when they didn't. Or they say they studied an hour for a test like they promised they would when, in fact, they spent less than half an hour. They do this not because they're liars or because they don't want to get yelled at by their coaches (good coaches don't do that), but because they don't want to let their coaches down.

"This process doesn't work well, though, if there is a loss of trust between us. If you find it hard to stick to your plan, that means either the plan is too ambitious and needs to be scaled back or we have to find other tactics or strategies to make it easier for you to follow the plan. The coaching process is sort of like losing weight. If you're overweight, it's relatively easy to lose the first few pounds, but as time goes on it takes longer and more effort to shed more weight. In the beginning, you may be excited by how well coaching is working and think, 'Wow! This is easy.' But as the weeks go by and school demands pile up, you may get too tired or too busy to be quite so conscientious. When you feel this happening, let me know and we'll make adjustments. I have a lot of tricks in my bag, but I can only pull them out when I know they're needed. My job is not to blame you when we run into trouble but to work with you to get back on track, even if that means changing the track if necessary."

As implied in this script, when students begin to fall short of the mark on a more consistent basis, then it may be time to revisit their interim goals to see if they are realistic. Maybe Joe runs into a major science project that eats up so much time that his English grades start slipping. At this point, the coach may want to discuss with him whether earning a B in English is still a realistic goal. If Joe says it is, then his coach can have a discussion with him about time management. Is Joe trying to do too much? Is he spending a bit too much time playing video games on weekends? Is there an extra half-hour several days a week he can eke out to devote to English? Is there something more he could do to motivate himself? Are there other resources he could tap into? Maybe he has a friend he could study his vocab with or pair up to read with? If he could download his reading assignments to his iPod and listen while he's working out at the gym, would that help? The point of this discussion is to get Joe to look at his slipping grades as a problem to be solved, with multiple possible solutions.

If Joe and/or his coach decide it's unlikely that he can reach his interim goal this marking period, rather than abandoning the goal—or coaching—altogether, they should revise the goal and figure out what needs to be done to make it work. This may mean doing some math. Maybe Joe's average with 3 weeks to go in the marking period is a C+. Joe and his coach could look at the remaining assignments and make a realistic estimate about what grades he is likely to be able to earn on them. They could plug different numbers into the formula and compute his class average based on those. If Joe still wants to reach a little higher, the coach might advise him to talk with his English teacher about possible extra-credit activities he could do to bring his grade up. This is where a coach may act as a go-between or mediator, helping Joe set up a meeting with his English teacher to negotiate a deal. The coach may attend such a meeting to help with the negotiations or, if Joe prefers to go it alone, may get permission from Joe to talk with the English teacher before the meeting to share his observations and discuss what might have affected Joe's performance. The coach could also role-play with Joe how he will handle the meeting to increase the likelihood that his English teacher will be sympathetic to his request.

In situations like this, it is not the job of the coach to get a student off the hook. However, teachers who don't understand executive skills don't always appreciate how hard kids with executive skills weaknesses have to work just to get by in some cases. If Joe's coach feels Joe worked hard but misjudged the effort needed, then intervening to help his English teacher understand may be advised.

Scaling back goals is an art in itself. If students repeatedly fail to follow their daily plans and begin to get discouraged, the coach can have them set a very small goal that can be easily attained. When they meet with success, they can set a similar goal for the next day. Then the coach can very gradually increase the goal. This is most easily done when the goal involves time or quantity. If a student promises to spend an hour working on her biology project for several days in a row and fails to follow through, the coach can ask her to cut the goal back to 10 minutes. Or if a student has five overdue lab reports and promises to do one each night but then can't get started, the coach can ask him to commit to writing the first section of the first lab report.

We sometimes ask students to rate how effortful they find a task using a 1 to 10 scale, with 1 being a task that's so easy they could sleepwalk through it and 10 being so effortful that it feels like climbing Mt. Everest. When they rate a given task as an 8, 9, or 10, we ask what could be done to turn that task into a 3 or 4. If they can do that, then they are more likely to follow through than if the task remains an 8, 9, or 10.

Fading Coaching with Success

As students internalize the skills that are the focus of coaching, their need for coaching diminishes. Coaching lends itself to a fading process that can be well defined and that ensures continued student success.

Fading a support of any kind usually involves either time or distance, or both (see Appendix 8, Plan for Fading Coaching, p. 185). A fading schedule for coaching that involves time might look like this:

- *Step 1:* Daily coach sessions.
- *Step 2:* Sessions held every other day.
- *Step 3:* Sessions held twice a week.
- *Step 4:* Sessions held once a week.
- *Step 5:* Sessions held every 2 weeks.
- *Step 6:* Sessions held once a month.

Fading coaching in terms of distance might look like this:

- *Step 1:* Face-to-face coaching.
- *Step 2:* Telephone coaching.
- *Step 3:* Electronic coaching (e-mail, texting, Facebook).

Deciding when to begin the fading phase depends on how successful the student is in meeting goals. In most cases, interim goal attainment can be used as the basis for this decision. As each goal is met according to the criteria specified, the coach and the student decide whether to take on a new interim goal or to fade coaching. Table 3.4 gives some examples of interim goals and how the fading process might be defined.

COACHING FOR DEVELOPMENT OF EXECUTIVE SKILLS

One of the activities we recommend coaches do before beginning the coaching process is to gather background information by using a structured interview to assess students' executive

TABLE 3.4. Making Fading Decisions

Interim goal	Success criterion	Length of time at criterion before beginning new goal or fading coaching
Attend math class.	4 days out of 5	6 consecutive weeks
Complete science homework.	80% of the time	4 consecutive weeks
Complete math homework with accuracy.	90% accuracy 4 days out of 5	4 consecutive weeks

skills strengths and weaknesses. The way the coaching process is structured, it helps students improve executive functioning. Table 3.5 shows how each executive skill is addressed through coaching.

As coaches work with students, they may find that extra attention needs to be paid to particular executive skills weaknesses that are obstructing progress in students' efforts to meet their goals. At this point, coaches may want to share their observations with the students to see whether they are willing to address the area of concern. For instance, with students who routinely forget things coaches may want to brainstorm ways to help them remember. If lack of organization is contributing to poor performance, coaches may want to see whether the students are willing to create an organizational checklist to help them address the problem. Further suggestions for helping students identify either environmental modifications or strategies to tackle executive skills weaknesses can be found in our book *Executive Skills in Children and Adolescents: A Practical Guide to Assessment and Intervention, Second Edition* (Dawson & Guare, 2010). This book also contains a number of teaching routines (e.g., how to study for a test, how to plan a long-term assignment) that may facilitate the coaching process by providing a set of "mini-lessons" addressing specific skills deficits. A number of these are also included in the Appendices to the present volume.

COACHING DOS AND DON'TS

We have outlined in some detail the coaching process, but our list of the "dos and don'ts" of coaching presented in Table 3.6 may serve as a handy, quick reference guide to help prospective coaches understand how the process works best and pitfalls to avoid.

COACHING MODIFICATIONS

This chapter presents academic coaching in its most comprehensive form. Not all students who may benefit from this intervention require "the full dose." Modifications that we have seen used include:

• *Omitting or reducing in scope the long-term goal-setting process*. Most middle school students and even some 9th and 10th graders are not at a stage where they can think about what they want to do after they finish high school. Rather than incorporating this portion of the coaching process if they are not yet developmentally ready, coaches should focus on having them set interim goals. For some middle school students the time horizon may need to be quite short (goals to accomplish "this week" or "by the time progress reports are issued"), whereas for others, and for high school students, setting marking period goals as the time horizon is reasonable.

• *Making the daily sessions more general*. Some students need more specificity with the daily check-ins than others. In the examples we provided, we have recommended that the coach help students create goals that are specific and measurable and daily plans that are precise in terms of the tasks to be accomplished and the timelines for doing so. We have seen a subgroup of students, though, for whom the coach acts more as a mentor than as a planning partner. The

TABLE 3.5. How Coaching Facilitates Development of Executive Skills

Executive skill	How coaching addresses this skill
Goal-directed persistence	This is the overarching purpose of coaching: by engaging in the process students learn how to make and achieve long-term goals.
Planning/ prioritization	• In goal-setting session, student is asked to develop a plan to achieve desired goals. • In daily coaching session, student makes daily homework plan.
Metacognition	• In goal-setting session, student is asked to consider potential obstacles to achieving goals and to think of ways to overcome obstacles. • In daily coaching session, student is asked to assess how well the previous day's plan went and how to improve likelihood of success in the future if problems arose.
Time management	This skill is developed through making daily plans; coach has student estimate how long each task will take and to think about how to fit in non-school-related activities, such as job, sports, and so on, along with homework, including studying for tests and working on long-term assignments.
Organization	Coach can use homework such as writing assignments or notebook checks to help student develop organizational schemes.
Emotional control	Student learns to manage frustration associated with obstacles to goal attainment or to successful completion of daily plans.
Flexibility	Students with weaknesses in this skill practice it not only by managing obstacles and changes in plans as they arise, but also, if necessary, by working with the coach to handle assignments such as open-ended tasks, which are often difficult for inflexible students.
Task initiation	By asking student to specify when a given task will be started, the coach helps the student follow through on plans and begin tasks in a timely fashion.
Sustained attention	By asking student to commit to a daily plan, student learns that tasks need to be seen through to completion.
Working memory	Asking students to make a daily plan prompts them to remember all the work they have to do, including daily homework and long-term assignments. The daily plan itself serves to jog students' memory to ensure all work is completed as scheduled.
Response inhibition	By making a plan and learning to set and meet daily goals, students are also learning to avoid the temptation of setting aside work to engage impulsively in whatever fun activities arise to compete with work.

TABLE 3.6. Coaching Dos and Don'ts

Good coaches do . . .	Good coaches don't . . .
Ask questions.	Lecture.
Sympathize/empathize.	Bail out students.
Act nonjudgmentally.	Take it personally when students fall short of their goals.
Help students problem solve.	Offer their own solutions (unless asked, and even then do it carefully).
Explicitly relate daily performance to long-term goals.	Assume students see this relationship.
Praise specific behaviors (e.g., "I like the way you avoided being tempted by your friends in study hall").	Either praise or criticize in a global fashion (e.g., "What a smart kid you are! You're just being lazy").
Provide honest, fact-based feedback on performance.	Exaggerate how well students are doing.
Communicate their faith in their students' ability to achieve personal goals.	Raise doubts without offering options or alternatives.
Know students well enough to personalize the process.	Rigidly follow the same procedure with all students they are coaching.
Maintain confidentiality if that is the agreement.	Share personal information about students with others.
Make appropriate referrals to therapists or other relevant professionals.	Provide counseling or therapy.
Ask for help when they've reached the limits of their expertise.	Go beyond their training when a "sticky" situation arises.

research on dropout prevention shows that some students at risk for school failure achieve success simply by finding a caring adult in the school setting. In this case, coaches may help students set long-term goals and then act as a cheerleader as students strike out on a path to achieve those goals—helping them through the rough patches, celebrating their victories along the way, and simply communicating that there is another person in their world who cares whether they make it or not. These are students who probably have fairly intact executive skills to start with and who just need to be encouraged to use them consistently.

• *Using coaching as a brief intervention.* For students with significant executive skills weaknesses, coaching is a long-term intervention. At a minimum it lasts a marking period, and at a maximum it may be used, in one form or another, throughout high school. There may be times, however, when a brief coaching intervention can be used to get students over a particular obstacle, and teachers may incorporate it into a particular class assignment. For instance, if a student has a difficult time managing long-term projects, the teacher could arrange for a coach to help the student plan and carry out a single assignment. For students who need more intensive coaching but are reluctant to commit themselves, this may be a way to persuade them to give the process a shot, with the understanding that if they find it helpful they may be willing to sign up for a longer tour of duty. If a high school has a pool of coaches available, this brief coaching approach could be easily facilitated.

• *Using coaching as a group intervention.* We have worked with schools that arrange for students to make daily homework plans as a group. In this case, either regular classroom teachers or resource room teachers set aside time at the end of the day for students to create a homework plan (the Daily Coaching Form can be used for this purpose, but an alternative Daily Homework Planning Form is also included in Appendix 9 on p. 186). Students may work in pairs to fill out their homework plan or they may work individually, with supervision from the teacher.

• *Coaching via e-mail or telephone.* Although we believe that coaching is most likely to be successful when the coach is available in the school setting, this is not always possible. In cases where a private coach is used, the daily coaching sessions can be conducted by telephone or e-mail. The same general process is followed as outlined previously, but verification or accountability is both critically important and more difficult. Off-site coaching works best when check-ins with teachers via e-mail on a weekly basis are built into the process to verify that students are completing the tasks they have committed to doing or are earning the grades they say they are earning. When the school uses a Web-based tracking system such as PowerSchool, coaches should arrange to have access to students' accounts so they can check on upcoming homework assignments (when posted by teachers) and verify completed assignments as well as grades on tests, quizzes, and homework. Off-site coaches also need to establish a procedure to follow if teachers are not reliable in their e-mail communications, an example of which was given earlier: The coach contacted the parent, who contacted the school's vice principal, who then communicated with the teacher in question.

COACHING DISAFFECTED OR DISENGAGED STUDENTS

We have stated that coaching with teenagers works best when it is a voluntary process and when the students are motivated to improve school performance in order to achieve some self-selected long-term goal. Obviously, every high school has students in danger of failing who do not satisfy these selection criteria. For these students, it may be possible to modify the coaching process as a strategy to help them become more engaged in school. This is understandably a more complicated process with a greater risk of ultimate failure attached to it. For skilled coaches who like taking on this kind of challenge, we suggest a different tack.

Rather than asking disengaged students to select a school-related goal, expand goal setting to include anything they might want to achieve or acquire. The Getting to Know You form (Appendix 1) may offer some clues as to what this might be. We have also achieved good results through the use of material reinforcers that may have nothing directly to do with school but that reward students for engaging in behaviors that have the effect of improving academic performance. With younger children (elementary and even a surprising number of middle school students), rewarding them with school "dollars," which can be used to purchase small items at the school store, when they work on goals designed to improve school performance can be remarkably effective. The key here is to hold out the reward but ask the students to set a specific goal that they would like to work on in order to earn it. Offering students a menu of goals to choose from may be the easiest way to do this, but coaches should not select the goals for the students because the point of this approach is to help students learn the power of goal setting and goal attainment.

With older students (middle school and high school), it is more likely that parents are the key to reinforcers powerful enough to persuade their children to participate in coaching. These may include (1) access to privileges (such as computer and video game time or use of the family car), (2) special outings (e.g., a trip to the mall or tickets to a movie), or (3) the opportunity to earn a tangible reward, such as a new cell phone or video game. When tangible rewards are involved, students generally earn points for daily or weekly behaviors (such as handing in all homework on time), with the understanding that once they have earned an agreed-upon number of points, they will earn the reward.

In our work, we have sat down with parents and teenagers and asked them explicitly what they want to get from the other. We ask parents to identify what behaviors they want from their child that he or she is not currently doing. We then ask the child, "What will it take?" Using a method similar to labor or contract negotiations, we then bring both sides together and hammer out an agreement.

Coaches can facilitate this process by acting as a mediator. Parents may resist this approach because it seems so far removed from their real goal (i.e., for their children to be self-directed and successful students), but if they can be persuaded that this approach may be the only way to connect their children to even a modicum of school success, they may be willing to underwrite the rewards and participate in the negotiation process.

We must reiterate that this is not a role for novice coaches to take on and is likely to be tackled most successfully by coaches with a background in mental health counseling.

COACHING ELEMENTARY SCHOOL STUDENTS

In educational settings, coaching is most easily conceptualized as a process for high school and college students. However, we believe it has applications at the middle school and even upper elementary levels. Use of the coaching procedure at these age levels requires an adjustment in the goal-setting process and in the management of day-to-day objectives. At the younger age levels, students are not as likely to be focused on or perhaps even aware of longer term goals. *Whereas goals with teenagers extend to months or marking periods, with younger students, it is more useful to think in terms of minutes and hours.*

Those who use this model with younger children should keep in mind Barkley's (1997) notion of "context dependent sustained attention." Young children in particular are governed by immediate stimuli in their environment. They are easily drawn off task when something more interesting than their work is happening around them, and their behavior is shaped by immediate consequences (both positive and negative) that occur in response to their actions.

Young children have difficulty delaying gratification, and they are less likely to have a goal in mind toward which they are working to counteract the immediate force and attraction of things happening around them. To give a concrete example, a child who has been instructed to finish a piece of seatwork has a hard time persuading himself to get back to work when the two children seated behind him (who may have already finished their work) pull out a toy to play with or carry on a lively conversation about what they plan to do at recess.

Coaching with a younger child might encompass the following steps:

- *Step 1:* The coach (who may well be the child's teacher) arranges a conference with the child to discuss the kinds of problems he or she is having in the classroom. Common academic problems include difficulty completing work (both classwork and homework), producing sloppy work, disrupting the class by talking out or interrupting, and failing to remember homework assignments or to bring home everything needed to complete homework.
- *Step 2:* Identify a behavior or two that the child might like to work on. Allow the child some control over the choice of behavior. If the child fails to choose something the coach feels is important, a second behavior could be added at the suggestion of the coach, or the coach might decide to defer addressing the behavior of concern to the teacher.
- *Step 3:* Brainstorm ways the child can improve with respect to the target behavior. This might mean asking him or her what could be done to make the target behavior easier to do or how the teacher might help the child use the target behavior (e.g., to raise his or her hand before speaking out).
- *Step 4:* Write down the goal behavior and the strategies the child might try to use. Appendix 10 (Coaching for Kids Form, p. 187) can be used for this purpose.
- *Step 5:* Check in with the child early each day to remind him or her of the goal being worked on and the strategies being tried.
- *Step 6:* Check back with the child at the end of the day to review how the day went with respect to the goal. A rating scale might be used to evaluate this (as shown in Appendix 10). Having the child and the teacher do independent ratings (where possible) would serve as a reality check and help the child learn to monitor his or her own behavior more accurately.

We now identify some elements of the coaching process with younger children that we believe contribute to its success:

- Many children respond positively to the novelty of being approached by an adult who will work with the child *as a partner* rather than as an authority figure. This communicates a sense of respect and equality, which can have a very powerful effect on a child's willingness to engage in the process.
- Building choice into the coaching process can also produce significant effects. Having children brainstorm possible solutions, and then allowing them the freedom to choose which solution they want to try, increases their investment in the process. For many young children, school problems often revolve around work completion. In these cases, choice can be incorporated into the coaching process by giving them a choice of tasks to perform, the opportunity to negotiate alternative assignments at times, or some freedom in choosing the order in which the tasks will be completed.

- As with older students, the verbal commitment to a plan helps make coaching successful.

- By identifying one problem behavior at a time, children gain a sense of efficacy as success is achieved, and new goals can be established.

- This process can also be combined with the use of an incentive system for those students who do not respond to coaching alone. For instance, the rating scale on the Coaching for Kids Form can be converted into points that the child can earn, which can be traded in for rewards either at school (most frequently, activity rewards) or at home. Although this can be very effective, we believe that coaching by itself can be a very powerful process and can be attempted without using a reinforcement system first because this will move the child toward self-regulation faster than if extrinsic reinforcers are required.

COACHING COLLEGE STUDENTS

The coaching process we have outlined for high school students can also work effectively with college students. Unfortunately, although colleges provide services to students with disabilities that include tutoring, scheduling help (e.g., finding the best classes for students with disabilities), and classroom accommodations (such as note takers and testing modifications), most colleges do not recognize that executive skills weaknesses often account for class failure and dropout. Nor do they understand that an intervention such as coaching is ideally suited to address this cause of college dropout.

Coaching for college students follows the same basic outline as coaching for high school students: (1) Collect background information regarding executive skills strengths and weaknesses; (2) establish long-term goals (in this case, what the students hope to achieve by the time they graduate and what they hope to do following graduation); and (3) arrange for regular coaching sessions (in the case of college students, coaching sessions may not occur daily nor may they be face to face).

In our experience with coaching college students, the issue of verification is as important at this level as it is with high school students. We once set up a coaching program for a college student in which he met daily with someone from the school's center for students with disabilities for the purpose of drawing up a study plan. The plan was quite precise, and the student assured his coach every day that he was following the plan as drawn up. It wasn't until the student walked out of his first midterm exam without completing it that it came to light that, instead of studying in the library every night for several hours as reported, the student was, in fact, spending most of that time surfing the Internet.

College coaches are generally unable to check in with professors to make sure students are staying on top of their work. However, they can obtain from students a commitment to demonstrate that they are doing what they say they are doing. For instance, they can be asked to bring their laptops to the coaching session to demonstrate that they have begun to write a term paper, or they can be asked to bring reading assignments to show that they have used a highlighter when reading. This has to be done carefully and should be arranged as one of the ground rules for coaching. The coach may want to introduce this by saying something like:

"I've found that when working with college students, time sometimes gets away from them and they do not always follow the plans they make. And then they feel bad and want to cover up the fact that they've not followed their plans. What I'd like to do in the beginning is to have you bring to our coaching session the stuff you've been working on. This will let me know that the plans we're making are realistic. I'm not here to critique your work (unless you want me to), but it will help you avoid the temptation of telling me that you're following your plan when something got in the way. If it turns out you're having trouble carrying out your plans, then we can troubleshoot and figure out what needs to change—the plans or the strategies for following them."

For additional information about how to coach college students, with many suggestions for handling the kinds of pressures that college students typically face, we recommend *Coaching College Students with AD/HD* (Quinn, Ratey, & Maitland, 2000).

CHAPTER 4

Advanced Coaching Techniques

Many people who want to be coaches come to the role with years of background knowledge and experiences that are sufficiently aligned with the coaching process that they can easily implement the new role without additional training. Special education teachers, guidance counselors, school psychologists, intervention specialists, and behavioral consultants are likely to have the prerequisite skills and knowledge needed to be able to jump into the coaching process once they understand how it works. Others, particularly classroom aides or paraprofessionals, may never have received formal training in communication skills or executive skills. Those coming to coaching from outside school systems (e.g., from a counseling or clinical psychology background) may not have the detailed knowledge of how schools operate or the specifics of education law (special education/Section 504) to be effective coaches.

As we stated in Chapter 3, we believe that the process of basic coaching is sufficiently straightforward that it can be done by people with relatively little training, such as high school students, paraprofessionals, and school psychology practicum students or interns. There is room, however, for coaching to go well beyond a basic level and, in so doing, increase the likelihood that the students being coached will not only meet academic goals, such as earning desired report card grades, but also be able to significantly improve their executive skills to the point where they can begin to generalize what they have learned to new settings and higher aspirations.

For this to happen, coaches should have a skill base that includes communication techniques, specialized knowledge in executive skills as well as proficient executive skills of their own, skill in the problem-solving process, and an understanding of how schools are organized and how coaching might be included either as part of an individualized education program (IEP) through special education or as part of a 504 plan.

Appendix 20 (p. 209) lists both the skills and knowledge that coaches at the "advanced" level need to have as well as a job description outlining the kinds of tasks that they typically perform.

In the remainder of this chapter, we present a series of five training modules designed to give coaches an introduction to the skills we believe are critical for advanced-level coaching:

communication skills, executive skills, documenting coaching effectiveness, problem solving, and knowledge of Section 504 plans, special education, and RTI.

We do not mean to imply that basic coaching is not effective by itself—in fact, research to date has studied models that are best categorized as fitting our basic coaching model. Nonetheless, we believe that coaching can be taken to a higher level, helping students not only to improve their academic success (as measured by test scores and report card grades) but also to enhance their executive skills so that they can independently apply what they have learned to tackle new challenges and achieve higher goals.

HOW TO USE THESE TRAINING MODULES

Coaches can be trained either individually or in groups. For the skills coaches need, training is best conducted by an expert in a group setting, following steps such as:

1. Define the skill to be learned.
2. Provide examples and nonexamples of the skill through modeling, followed by a discussion highlighting the key elements of the skill.
3. Have participants practice the skill through role playing and other exercises or activities.
4. Provide corrective feedback to participants to improve their skill level.

Requiring this level of training can, unfortunately, actually be a barrier to coaching because schools often lack the personnel or resources necessary to support it. To overcome this barrier, and help bridge the training gap, in the remainder of this chapter, we focus on the skills and knowledge base that are essential to advanced-level coaching, presenting descriptions and examples of each skill. At the end of the book (pp. 135–149) are supplemental practice exercises, along with answers to selected exercises (pp. 150–158), that prospective coaches can complete to sharpen their skills. These exercises can be done individually, but they can also form the basis for group activities and discussion. Both the examples and the exercises are specific to coaching. For instance, in discussing communication skills, we focus on those that are most relevant to coaching rather than a broader array of communication skills. (We thus spend more time discussing active listening, paraphrasing, and asking open-ended questions versus "I"-messages or how to communicate in emotionally charged situations.) We conceptualize coaching as a partnership in which the coach's role is to support students' ability to set goals and manage tasks, not a therapeutic relationship with a goal of helping students understand and resolve trauma or interpersonal conflict.

MODULE I: COMMUNICATION SKILLS

The communication skills that are most in demand in the coaching process include paraphrasing, active listening, asking open-ended questions, scaffolding, delivering instructions clearly, and providing effective praise. Each of these are defined next, with examples as well as scenarios the coach in training can use to practice the skills.

Paraphrasing

Paraphrasing means capturing the essence of what someone has just said and stating it back to him or her succinctly. Paraphrasing serves several purposes: (1) It shows you've listened carefully; (2) it allows you to check the accuracy of what you heard; and (3) it allows the speaker to hear what he or she said so that the statement can be revised if it was not what he or she intended to convey.

Example 1

STUDENT: I've got to start my English paper this weekend, which means I have to finish reading the book and then figure out what aspect of the book I want to write about. And somehow I have to squeeze that in with the math test I need to study for and the chemistry lab report I have to finish. Oh, and I've got 2 hours of community service I need to do on Saturday morning!

COACH: Let me get this straight. You've got a math test to study for, a chemistry lab report to finish, 2 hours of community service, and an English paper to start—which means finishing the book and figuring out what to write about.

Example 2

STUDENT: Mrs. Dobson didn't like the essay I wrote on the New Deal. She said I didn't spend enough time talking about how the country reacted to it and the resistance raised by Republicans. She also said I needed to go into more detail about what was actually in the legislation. And then she said I made a lot of spelling and punctuation errors.

COACH: It sounds like she was looking for more information both about the content of New Deal legislation and how it was received by the country and the opposing party. And it sounds like she's asking you to proofread the paper before you hand it in.

STUDENT: Actually, I did proofread it—I'm just not very good at catching my mistakes.

In this second example, the coach made an understandable assumption that because the student made a lot of spelling and punctuation errors, he had not proofread the paper. By stating this as part of the paraphrase, it gave the student a chance to clarify. Now the coach has additional information to work with: This student may need to ask someone to proofread his work for him if it turns out he routinely has trouble catching his own mistakes.

Reflective Listening

This skill involves two components: listening carefully and responding reflectively. Reflective listeners work to understand in an empathic way whatever the person is saying from the speaker's viewpoint or internal frame of reference. Beyond empathy, however, the listener *accepts* what the speaker is saying without agreeing or disagreeing. Responding reflectively means picking up on the *feelings* contained in what the speaker is saying and not just facts or ideas. It means zeroing in on the personal elements of the speaker's statements, not the impersonal, and responding with acceptance and empathy rather than indifference or judgment.

Example 1

STUDENT: I left my math homework at home, and Mr. Hodgkins told me that the rule is that homework turned in late only earns half credit. I've got a C– in that class, and I can't afford another low grade! He knows I have ADD—you'd think he'd cut me some slack!

COACH: It sounds like you're nervous about your grade in that class, and maybe a little irritated that your math teacher doesn't understand the impact of your attention disorder.

Example 2

STUDENT: OK, so my plan was to spend my sixth-period study hall studying for my world history exam. But then Jenny and Caitlin were working on their humanities project, and since I had that class last marking period they kept asking me questions and wanting my help with it. I didn't want them to be mad at me, so I spent half the study period working with them. When I looked at the clock and saw I only had 15 minutes to study, I completely freaked. When I got the test, I just froze and couldn't answer half the questions—even the ones I studied for!

COACH: Wow! It sounds like you're a little mad at yourself for not being able to tell your friends you really needed to study. And then not having enough time to study made you so anxious it blocked your thinking once you got to the exam.

Open-Ended Questions versus Closed-Ended Questions

Open-ended questions are designed to gather more information about something a student is talking about. They help students use their executive skills: for example, working memory ("Tell me everything you have to do for homework tonight") or other skills such as planning ("What steps are you going to follow to complete your earth science project?") and metacognition ("How are you going to study for your sociology midterm?" or "How did your session with your study group go?"). Open-ended questions force students to think more deeply about how they approach learning and academic tasks.

Closed-ended questions are yes–no questions or any other question designed to elicit a precise answer. Coaches use both kinds of questions and need to know when to use which.

It should be noted that there are some populations with whom coaches may be working who have a great deal of trouble with open-ended questions. Students who are cognitively inflexible, such as those with Asperger syndrome or nonverbal learning disabilities, may find these questions very difficult to answer. When working with these students, coaches may need to alter the way they ask questions to suit their students' style. This usually means asking more closed-ended questions and giving students choices (e.g., "Let me describe a couple of different ways you might do this assignment and you tell me which one might work best"). Coaching may work best when the focus is narrower—for example, helping students make plans or helping them create checklists for things they have to do or remember.

With more typical underachievers, coaching employs a mix of open-ended and closed-ended questions. Some examples of how each kind of question is used in the coaching process follow.

Examples of Open-Ended Questions

- "What is your study plan for the weekend?"
- "How are you going to study for your Spanish quiz?"
- "How are you going to work around your school play practice given the homework load you have?"
- "What's your thought about keeping your science notebook organized?"
- "I've noticed you have a hard time estimating how long it takes you to write a paper. What do you think you could do to fix that?"
- "What will you say to your science teacher when he gets on your case about forgetting your homework?"
- "It seems like studying in your bedroom doesn't work for you because there are too many distractions. Do you have ideas for other places you could study?"

The purpose of all these questions is to encourage students to come up with strategies on their own or to generate their own solutions to problems. Very often, these kinds of open-ended questions are lead-ins that enable the coach to offer suggestions. For example, consider the following dialogue:

COACH: How are you going to study for your Spanish quiz?

STUDENT: I hadn't really thought about it. I guess I was just planning on reading down the list of vocabulary words in the chapter and cover up the Spanish term and keep doing it until I've got them all memorized.

COACH: What if your teacher gives you the Spanish term and asks you to produce the English translation?

STUDENT: Good point! I guess I should go back and forth between covering up the Spanish term and then covering up the English term.

COACH: How about making flash cards?

STUDENT: I hate that! It's way too much work.

COACH: Did you know there are computer flash card programs? For instance, iFlash for Macs.

STUDENT: No kidding? I didn't realize that. I use a PowerBook—I'll look into that. That might make studying a little more fun.

Notice the progression. The coach starts with a very open-ended question: "How are you going to study for your Spanish quiz?" When the student shares her strategy, the coach doesn't tell her it's probably not good enough, but asks another, somewhat less open-ended question designed to give the student additional information that she can then use to refine her studying process. It's only at this point that the coach asks a closed-ended question: "How about making flash cards?" Note that the coach does *not* say, "I think you should make flash cards" or "Try this—make some flash cards." By making it a question, the coach leaves it to the student to decide if that method will work for her. When the student rejects it, the coach finally offers a variation on flash cards that might appeal to her.

Examples of Closed-Ended Questions

- "What time do you plan to do your math homework today?"
- "What's the first step you have to do for your social studies project?"
- "How much time do you plan on studying for your French exam?"
- "Do you think you'll be able to resist goofing off with your friends during study hall?"
- "Did you hand in your English paper like you said you were going to?"

Because part of coaching involves having students make a commitment to carrying out a plan or working on a goal, closed-ended questions enable them to develop the plan with adequate specificity. Sometimes a single closed-ended question is not sufficient, however. Consider the following:

COACH: So what time do you plan to do your math homework today?

STUDENT: I think I'll do that first after I get home from school.

COACH: Do you usually start your homework right away when you get home from school?

STUDENT: I wish! No, I usually get a snack, then go on Facebook to check up on my friends.

COACH: How long does that usually take?

STUDENT: Oh, about an hour.

COACH: So if you get home from school at 3:00, then if I put down 4:00 on the planning sheet, do you think that's reasonable?

STUDENT: Yeah, that should be fine.

COACH: And how will you remember to start your homework?

That idiom *the devil is in the details* should be a framed display on the office wall of every coach. The coach in the prior example used closed-ended questions to help the student refine his study plan. The last question, though, is another open-ended question. Students with executive skills deficits can be walked through a planning process so that when they leave the coach's office they have a detailed schedule for what they plan on accomplishing that day. But if they don't remember to follow their plan, the planning is for naught. "How will you remember to . . . ?" should be asked at least once in almost every coaching session, particularly in the early stages of coaching.

Scaffolding

Scaffolding is a technique that often incorporates a graduated use of open-ended and closed-ended questions as well as other techniques for supporting students as they learn a new skill without *giving them the answers* or doing the task for them. It is based on Vygotsky's notion of the *zone of proximal development*, or "the distance between the actual developmental level as determined by independent problem solving and the level of potential development as determined through problem solving under adult guidance or in collaboration with more capable peers" (Vygotsky, 1978, p. 86).

The kinds of activities involved in scaffolding may include:

- Enhancing the student's interest in the task.
- Simplifying the task by reducing the steps or making them more explicit.
- Providing direction to help the student focus on the goal.
- Helping the student see discrepancies between his or her product and the desired product.
- Reducing frustration and risk.
- Giving feedback (e.g., by summarizing progress and explicitly noting behaviors that contribute to success).
- Assisting internalization, independence, and generalization to other contexts (i.e., by helping students become less dependent on cues and prompts from the coach) (Bransford, Brown, & Cocking, 2000; Hogan & Pressley, 1997; Larkin, 2001).

Here's how a coach might provide scaffolding for a student who doesn't know how to begin a writing assignment.

STUDENT: My science assignment is to write about some technological innovation from the last 15 years that has changed my life. I don't have a clue about how to do this.

COACH: What do you think the first step is?

STUDENT: First, I have to decide what to write about. I use a ton of technology, but I don't know which ones were invented in the last 15 years.

COACH: How about if we brainstorm a list of possible innovations first? And then what might you do?

STUDENT: Then I could look them up on the Internet to find out when they were invented?

COACH: That's a possibility. But if it's a long list, is there a way you could keep from having to look up every item?

STUDENT: I could show it to my science teacher and ask him which ones came out in the last 15 years.

COACH: Would your science teacher answer that question for you?

STUDENT: Nah, he'd probably tell me to look them up on my own.

COACH: So what's another way to narrow down the list?

STUDENT: Let's see. I could guess or ask my dad. He'd probably know.

COACH: You could do that. But how about looking over the list and eliminating the ones you're not interested in?

STUDENT: Good idea.

COACH: OK, let's summarize the steps in beginning to write a paper. First, we make sure we understand what the assignment is. Then we brainstorm possible ideas to write about. Then we narrow down our choices, both by making sure they fit the assignment rules and by finding something we're interested in. Does that make sense?

STUDENT: Yeah. OK, let's start brainstorming. Wait. I don't know how to do that.

COACH: Brainstorming means coming up with as many ideas as you can without critiquing them until you've generated a pretty complete list.

STUDENT: OK, let's see. I use a smartphone, I play video games, and I go on the Internet. I think that's it.

COACH: Are you sure?

STUDENT: I think so—it's actually a smaller list than I thought.

COACH: How about if you think about a typical day—both a school day and a weekend day—and think about what you usually do? Take last Sunday, for instance. What did you do from the moment you got up in the morning to when you went to bed that involved technology? And you may want to think about what you *did* with that technology. I would guess, for instance, that you do many different things with a smartphone, and you might want to think about the technology involved in each thing.

STUDENT: (*With assistance from coach, expands his list and then chooses a few that are of greatest interest to him.*)

COACH: OK, so tell me what brainstorming means, and give me an example of another kind of assignment where you might use it.

STUDENT: Brainstorming means coming up with as many ideas as you can for something without judging them until you're done. I could use it for my next physics project, where I'm supposed to come up with a labor-saving device that uses one of the simple tools.

COACH: Wow—you gave a nice, succinct definition of brainstorming, and you even thought of how you could apply it to another assignment!

Notice how the coach alternated between asking open-ended questions and providing more explicit instructions depending on what the student needed. Sometimes the open-ended question was sufficient to lead the student to define a step in the process; at other times, the student's answer showed he was narrowing his choices prematurely. Note also how the coach summarized the steps in the process. Because the ultimate goal is for the student to be able to perform this whole process by himself, this summary facilitates the process. The next time the student has a similar assignment, the coach might say, "Do you remember the steps we went through with the technological innovation paper you had to write?" If the student can't retrieve the steps, the coach could help him create a list or checklist that he could use.

Providing Clear Instructions or Directions

In most of their interactions with students, coaches use all the communication skills we've discussed to help students understand themselves—how they learn best, how they accomplish tasks, how they motivate themselves—and make decisions and commitments. Sometimes, however, coaches do provide direct instruction. For example, coaches may teach students how to study for tests, how to write papers, how to plan long-term projects, or how to take notes. We have created teaching routines for these skills, and they are included in Appendices 11–16.

There are some general guidelines coaches should keep in mind as they prepare an instructional sequence for students. Some of these, listed next (from Hofmeister & Lubke, 1990), are just good teaching strategies recommended for use with all students. Others are directed for use with students with executive skills weaknesses. Remember: These are students who have weak working memory, poor organizational skills, difficulty creating a plan or sequence of steps to follow, and short attention spans. They become easily overwhelmed or quickly frustrated if they find directions to be complex, lengthy, or confusing. With this in mind, good teaching involves:

1. Stating the goal of the lesson up front (e.g., "Today I'm going to walk you through a process for planning a long-term project").
2. Focusing on one step or one thought at a time and avoiding digressions.
3. Avoiding ambiguous terms or phrases: These students often have trouble understanding figures of speech, so if you use them—and it's difficult not to—look at their facial expressions for signs of confusion. If the signs are there, explain what the expression means.
4. Presenting material in small steps and giving explicit, step-by-step directions.
5. Modeling the skill or process you are teaching. One effective way to do this is to "think aloud" as you progress through the skill to be mastered or the task to be accomplished. For instance, if a student is truly lost in terms of understanding what an assignment is asking her to do, you might say, "Here's how I would think about this assignment if someone had given it to me to do . . . " Then describe the thought process you would go through as you attempt to understand the assignment and create a game plan for it.
6. Providing multiple examples to illustrate the point you are trying to make whenever you can.
7. Stating instructions positively. Tell students what *to do* rather than what *not to do*. Also, avoid opinions, preferences, and personal biases. Instructions are factual statements about actions to be performed.
8. Checking for understanding frequently. Ask questions to monitor students' comprehension or have them repeat, paraphrase, or summarize what they have just heard. Reteach immediately when it is clear that the students do not understand.
9. Not trying to teach too much at once and not spending too much time in didactic presentations. When working with students individually, talk for no more than a couple of minutes before involving them in some way.
10. Modeling the skill you've taught, then using guided practice (scaffolding, getting the students started, giving them hints along the way, providing incomplete models) and giving the students the opportunity to practice independently.
11. Assuming that the students you coach will not remember anything that they *hear* in sufficient detail to apply it on their own. Any skill that you think is important for them to learn should be turned into a set of written directions or—even better—a checklist of steps to be followed.

Specific Praise

Praise is a powerful way to shape behavior, but there is a sharp distinction between effective and ineffective (or even damaging) praise. When we praise children for traits over which they feel they have no control ("You're so smart!" "What a pretty girl you are!"), the information we're giving them is not particularly useful because they don't know what they have to do to stay that way. On top of that, particularly in the case of telling someone how smart they are, we run the risk of them avoiding challenging tasks in the future for fear they won't succeed and, therefore, will stop working toward staying smart. The best kind of praise specifies what the student has done that's praiseworthy.

Effective praise (1) is delivered immediately after the display of positive behavior; (2) specifies the particulars of the accomplishment (e.g., "You got out your assignment book without me having to ask you"); (3) provides information to the student about the value of the accomplishment (e.g., "I can see you're learning to remember to use the strategies we've been talking about"); (4) lets the student know that he or she worked hard to accomplish the task (e.g., "I can see you put a lot of time and thought into this writing assignment"), and (5) orients the student to better appreciate his or her own task-related behavior and thinking about problem solving (e.g., "I like the way you used brainstorming to think of a lot of ideas before zeroing in on the best one.").

A general rule of thumb is that for every critical or corrective statement directed toward a student, he or she should receive three positive statements. In fact, there is substantial research indicating that just using praise in this way can by itself lead to significant positive behavior change. This is often difficult to accomplish with students who seem to be bent on just trying to "get by." For this reason, we often recommend reinforcing *improvement* or approximations of good behavior (e.g., "It looks like you hung in there a little longer with your math homework last night than you did with the last math assignment you had").

Sometimes with teenagers praise can be tricky. Above all, it has to be genuine. Students with a history of school failure or learning problems have either received very little praise regarding schoolwork or perceived the praise they did receive as hollow. As a result, their internal "radar" tells them when someone is just trying to make them feel good without actually identifying anything specific to feel good about. Coaching, fortunately, lends itself to many opportunities for genuine praise. Furthermore, by praising executive skills, we're increasing the likelihood that students will continue to practice these effortful skills. Here are some examples:

- "Hey, you got here right on time. Good time management skills!"
- "It looks like you were able to use that checklist to help you remember everything you needed to bring home from school."
- "I can see you were angry at me, but it looked like you worked hard to control your emotions."
- "For the last three nights, you've followed your homework schedule just the way your wrote it out. I think your task initiation skills are really coming along."

Additional Resources for Module I

Some YouTube videos that illustrate communication skills are:

- Paraphrasing: *www.youtube.com/watch?v=xrbXMaiR_Ww&feature=related*
- Reflecting listening: *www.youtube.com/watch?v=7AxNI3PhvBo*
- Scaffolding: *www.youtube.com/watch?v=pXl7PP3bBKE&feature=related*

- Effective praise: *www.youtube.com/watch?v=g_ySoJttPoA www.youtube.com/profile?user=TeacherTalkTV&feature=iv&annotation_id=annotation_288029#p/u/2/FNF-NxAz8AzM*

For a more in-depth discussion about the use of scaffolding, open-ended questions, and clear instruction, consult Fisher and Frey's excellent resource *Guided Instruction: How to Develop Confident and Successful Learners* (2010).

MODULE II: EXECUTIVE SKILLS

In order to coach at an advanced level, coaches must have a thorough understanding of how executive skills develop, the critical role of these skills in school performance, and their own role in fostering skill development. Chapter 1 provides an overview of these concepts, and coaches may find it useful to share this information with parents, with teachers, and with students themselves so that they likewise understand the purpose of coaching and what it can accomplish.

So how does coaching help students develop executive skills? There are elements of the coaching process that naturally facilitate executive skills development, as addressed in Table 3.5 (p. 50). These elements combine to form a basic framework for successful executive skills building.

Students are likely to sign up for coaching as a means to a specific end result, for example, to improve school performance. However, the ultimate goal of coaching is always to improve executive functioning to the point where students acquire the self-management skills they need to be successful on their own without relying on a coach. Toward this end, it may be helpful for coaches to, at some point in the coaching process, conduct an executive skills assessment exercise with students to help them identify their own executive skills strengths and weaknesses and consider strategies they can use to strengthen their own executive skills weaknesses. During the information-gathering phase of coaching, coaches often use the Executive Skills Semi-Structured Interview—Student Version to help them understand the executive skills strengths and challenges of the students with whom they will be working. Although some students may be ready at the outset for a discussion of executive skills, for others it is best to wait until they have experienced some success from coaching before having that conversation. When that point is reached, students can complete the Executive Skills Questionnaire—Student Version (in Appendix 4, p. 176) to facilitate the discussion.

Once the questionnaire is completed and executive skills strengths and weaknesses are identified, coaches can then discuss with students how they are able to use their executive skills strengths to improve school performance and how their weaknesses impede school success. Students can be invited to create interim goals to address problems they encounter in school because of specific executive skills weaknesses. Here's what that discussion might look like:

COACH: OK, Clarisse, you've now taken the Executive Skills Questionnaire, and you've identified a couple of executive skills weaknesses: task initiation and emotional control. Can we talk a bit about how each of these might get in the way of your ability to do as well in school as you would like?

CLARISSE: Well, the emotional control piece affects me in a couple of ways. Sometimes when I've had a fight with my boyfriend or one of my girlfriends is upset about something, I get hung up on that and have a hard time paying attention in class. And I also tend to freeze when taking tests, especially when I know I haven't studied as hard as I should have.

COACH: So you're saying that your emotions interfere with your ability to pay attention in class if you're upset about something and may affect test performance, at least when you feel you haven't studied enough. [Note the use of paraphrasing.]

CLARISSE: Yeah, and I guess it can sometimes make it hard for me to concentrate on homework too.

COACH: It sounds like it can get in the way in a lot of different situations. Would you say this happens often?

CLARISSE: Not much lately actually. Things have been pretty calm with my friends and boyfriend—and thanks to coaching, I've been studying more for tests.

COACH: How about the other weakness then—task initiation?

CLARISSE: That can be a problem. Not with daily homework, but with longer term assignments. With daily stuff, it goes pretty quickly. In fact, I think the hard part about task initiation is that the task often looks like it's going to take me forever to do, and I think, "I can't face that right now. I'll do it later." And then I can't put it off any longer and I end up pulling an all-nighter or at least staying up really late to get it done.

COACH: So the biggest problem with task initiation is with large assignments then?

CLARISSE: Yeah, especially when there's any kind of writing involved. That seems to be the hardest for me.

COACH: When you go to college, a lot of classes you take are likely to use term papers as a major part of your grade. What do you think about coming up with a way to tackle this problem now so that you've already worked it out before you go to college?

CLARISSE: Ugh! I don't even want to think about it, but I suppose you're right.

COACH: I think we can come up with something. Remember we talked before about rating *effortful* tasks using a 1 to 10 scale?

CLARISSE: Writing papers is *definitely* a 10 for me!

COACH: So how could we change the task to make it feel more like a 3?

CLARISSE: Negotiate with my English teacher so I only have to write a paragraph instead of an essay?

COACH: Cute. But then you'd have to negotiate that with every teacher who gives you a writing assignment. But how about that—what is there about having to write only a paragraph that makes it seem more manageable?

CLARISSE: I could do it quickly . . . OK, I can see where you're heading with this. I can break the paper down into very small pieces so no one piece takes too long.

COACH: Would that do it? If you made a plan to start the paper by writing the first two paragraphs and no more, would that help?

CLARISSE: I have another idea. Maybe I could start by jotting down as many ideas for the paper as I can come up with. That to me is easier than writing a couple of paragraphs and I remember you said that the easier you make the first step, the easier it is to start.

COACH: That's a great idea—and then you have some idea of the material you're working with, so writing that first paragraph or two would be easier.

CLARISSE: OK! I have an English paper due in 3 weeks, so maybe I can try this out on that.

COACH: Sounds good. Keep in mind that what you're doing here is not only figuring out a way to make it easier to write a paper but also a strategy that might help you improve your difficulties with task initiation. It might give you ideas for handling other tasks that you keep wanting to put off.

In this example, the coach used open-ended questions to help Clarisse figure out a strategy for improving task initiation. With the right questions and reminders, Clarisse was able to come up with a strategy on her own. But if that hadn't worked out, the coach might have had to make more direct suggestions—or to help Clarisse engage in some brainstorming (discussed later in Module IV: Problem Solving). Notice how at the end of the discussion the coach pulled it back to executive skills development. This helps Clarisse see that there may be ways to generalize from the specific task she's focusing on now to other situations in which task initiation might be an issue.

Additional Resources for Module II

For more information about executive skills, the following references may be helpful:

- *Executive Skills in Children and Adolescents: A Practical Guide to Assessment and Intervention, Second Edition* (Dawson & Guare, 2010).
- *Smarts: Are We Hardwired for Success?* (Martin et al., 2007). This book offers readers additional information about how to understand their own executive skills profile and to make adjustments in their work to better match their executive skills strengths and weaknesses.
- *Executive Function in the Classroom: Practical Strategies for Improving Performance and Enhancing Skills for All Students* (Kaufman, 2010).

MODULE III: DOCUMENTING COACHING EFFECTIVENESS

With the emphasis in today's schools on evidence-based practice, being able to document that coaching is an effective intervention is important for two reasons. First, it proves that the coach's time is well spent. This is important when the coach is a member of the school staff because if there's no evidence the intervention works the coach is likely to be shifted to other responsibilities. But it's also important when the coach is hired by parents because it shows that the expense is justified.

The ultimate measure of efficacy is whether the students being coached achieve their long-term goals. But coaches can't wait until college acceptance letters start arriving or students graduate from high school to assess efficacy. There are two other sources of data that coaches can use to assess success: interim goals and the daily plans that students make.

Interim Goals as Outcome Measures

Students typically set marking period goals, often in the form of report card grades. These are easy outcome measures. If a student has set as a goal earning a B– or better in all classes, the report card at the end of the marking period will indicate whether he met his goal. And if the student fell short, that can be quantified too—if he earned a B– or better in four out of five classes, then the student was 80% successful in meeting his goal.

Based on the goal and graphing information presented in Table 3.1 (p. 34), Figure 4.1 shows what graphs might look like for the first two examples.

Using Daily Plans as Measures of Progress/Success

In every coaching session, we ask students to make plans for the next day. For students who are working toward a single proscribed goal (e.g., pass in 80% of math assignments), their daily plan may involve only a single task. This can be depicted in graph format by graphing the percentage of tasks accomplished per week, as shown in the first graph in Figure 4.1.

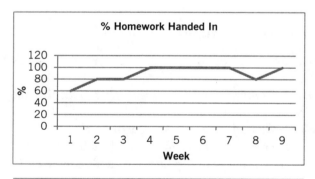

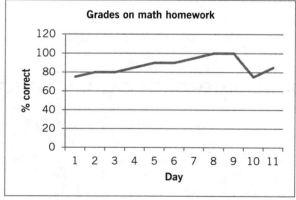

FIGURE 4.1. Graphing interim goals.

Very often, however, students will list multiple tasks they expect to accomplish before the next coaching session. The easiest way to chart their performance is to graph the percentage of tasks they accomplished on a daily basis. Such a graph might look like Figure 4.2.

Why is graphing important? Because it is a concrete measure of accomplishment. For students who have experienced a lot of school failure, it may be the first time they have any clear evidence of task completion or goal attainment. Coaches and students also maintain a written record of the daily plans made, using either the Daily Coaching Form provided in this manual or one developed by the coach and student that meets their specific needs, but reviewing those daily plans does not give the same succinct, visual feedback about success as a graph. Graphs can either be done by hand on graph paper or on the computer using an Excel spreadsheet, whichever is easier for the coach and student.

Other Forms of Record Keeping

Three other forms of data collection or record keeping can be used in coaching: goal attainment scaling, checklists, and scoring rubrics.

Goal Attainment Scaling

This methodology was first developed to evaluate community mental health services (Kiresuk & Sherman, 1968), but has since been adapted to address behavioral goals in a school setting (e.g., Coffee & Ray-Subramanian, 2009; Hunley & McNamara, 2010). As such, it is perfectly suited to coaching, which has goal setting as a core element, because it allows goal attainment to be quantified. The steps involved in goal attainment scaling, as applied to coaching, are:

- *Step 1:* Coach and student define the goal the student wants to work on.
- *Step 2:* Coach and student specify five outcome levels, beginning with the expected outcome level (given a value of 0). Other levels are specified as either somewhat more or less than expected (+1, –1) or much more than expected (+2, –2).
- *Step 3:* On a daily or weekly basis, the coach and student determine how well the goal

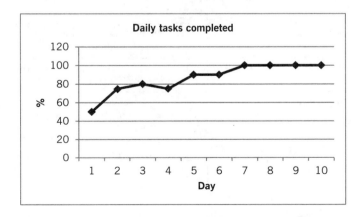

FIGURE 4.2. Graphing.

has been met, and the results are then graphed so that progress can be easily monitored over time.

   To illustrate, a goal attainment scale for a student who has trouble remembering to bring home everything needed to complete homework assignments is shown in Figure 4.3. A graph depicting the data collected using the goal attainment scale in Figure 4.3 might look like Figure 4.4. Another example, addressing a different executive skills weakness, is shown in Figure 4.5. A blank Goal Attainment Scale Form is included in Appendix 17.

   While goal attainment scaling appears to be a fairly simple and straightforward way of quantifying goals, there are some common mistakes that people make when using this method. As detailed by Coffee and Ray-Subramanian (2009), the most common errors include creating overlapping intervals (e.g., Billy makes 5–10 mistakes on his in-class math assignment; Billy makes 3–5 mistakes on his in-class math assignment), leaving gaps between intervals (e.g., specifying every other interval), and creating unequal intervals (e.g., Sam calls out 1–3 times during music class; Sam calls out 4–10 times during circle time), which provides misleading data about progress. Additionally, each goal should address only one behavior (i.e., do not include homework completion *and* accuracy rates in the same goal). Finally, the goals should be as specific as possible. Coffee and Ray-Subramanian recommend using SMART goals—that is, goals that are specific, measurable, attainable, realistic, and timely or tangible.

Checklists

Checklists are used whenever a student has a multistep routine that he or she follows to accomplish a specific task. For instance, Mindy has trouble remembering to bring to school with her every day the things she needs to get through the day. She and her coach can create a checklist of all the things she might need to bring with her. An example of such a checklist is shown in Figure 4.6.

Level of attainment	Behavior
–2 (much less than expected)	Carrie remembers everything she has to bring home for homework 1 day out of 5
–1 (somewhat less than expected)	Carrie remembers everything she has to bring home for homework 2 days out of 5
0 (expected outcome level)	Carrie remembers everything she has to bring home for homework 3 days out of 5
+1 (somewhat more than expected)	Carrie remembers everything she has to bring home for homework 4 days out of 5
+2 (much more than expected)	Carrie remembers everything she has to bring home for homework 5 days out of 5
Monitoring schedule	Monitor: _____ daily X _____ weekly _____ other (specify): _____

FIGURE 4.3. Goal attainment scale for working memory.

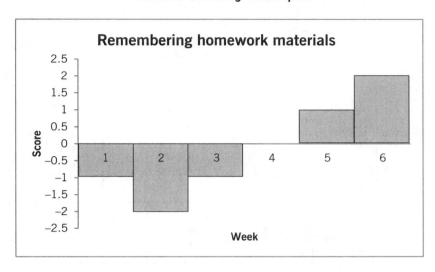

FIGURE 4.4. Remembering homework materials.

Level of attainment	Behavior
−2 (much less than expected)	Kendrick is reprimanded by biology teacher for off-task talking more than 5 times during biology lab
−1 (somewhat less than expected)	Kendrick is reprimanded by biology teacher for off-task talking 4–5 times during biology lab
0 (expected outcome level)	Kendrick is reprimanded by biology teacher for off-task talking 3 times during biology lab
+1 (somewhat more than expected)	Kendrick is reprimanded by biology teacher for off-task talking 1–2 times during biology lab
+2 (much more than expected)	Kendrick is reprimanded by biology teacher for off-task talking 0 times during biology lab
Monitoring schedule	Monitor _____ daily _____ weekly X_____ other (specify): twice weekly during bio labs

FIGURE 4.4. Goal attainment scale for off-task talking (response inhibition).

Date: _____

Item	Mon.	Tues.	Wed.	Thurs.	Fri.
Homework folder					
Textbooks					
Notebooks					
Gym clothes					
House keys					
Other:					
Percent items remembered					

FIGURE 4.6. Example of a daily school checklist.

The items Mindy has to remember to bring may vary from day to day, but the list prompts her to think about each item, decide whether she needs it, and check it off the list once she makes sure she has it in her purse or backpack. This checklist allows her to calculate the percentage of items recalled each day, which can then easily be graphed, as described previously, for a concrete measure of accomplishment.

Another commonly used checklist is a proofreading checklist, which students use after writing a paper. A number have been developed, but the most widely used is the COPS method (Schumaker, Nolan, & Deshler, 1985). Guided by this checklist, students read through their paper and check for (1) **C**apitalization, (2) **O**verall appearance (e.g., spacing, legibility, complete sentences, paragraph indentation), (3) **P**unctuation, and (4) **S**pelling.

Scoring Rubrics

Scoring rubrics is a tool that lists a set of criteria that describe a piece of work and provide gradations of quality, from "excellent" to "poor." In this way, rubrics link qualitative assessment to a quantitative rating system that allows one to judge a piece of work more objectively and to measure progress toward improvement. When assigning papers, projects (both group and individual), and demonstrations, many teachers include a scoring rubric to guide students in creating their work. In the context of coaching, rubrics are most useful in helping students judge how well they perform a given task that cannot be quantified easily.

An example of a scoring rubric that might be used to help students improve how they study for tests is shown in Figure 4.7. A blank Rubric Form is included in Appendix 18.

Rubrics can also be used to assist students in their goals to improve organization (e.g., notebooks, desk, backpack, locker; also, organization in writing assignments or long-term projects) as well as effort and task persistence. They can also be used to help students learn to control frustration or other emotions that interfere with their academic success. An example of such a rubric is shown in Figure 4.8.

	Criteria				
Element	4	3	2	1	Value
Amount of time spent studying	Met goal of _____ hrs. _____ min. spent studying.	Spent at least 75% of committed time studying.	Spent at least 50% of committed time studying.	Spent less than 50% of committed time studying.	
Number of study sessions	4 or more study sessions (1 per day) before exam.	3 study sessions.	1–2 study sessions.	Didn't study.	
Prestudy preparation	Went to extra help sessions with teacher.	Used detailed study guide and/or practice tests.	Skimmed notes to determine what would be on test.	Didn't prepare for studying in advance.	
Variety of study techniques	Used 3 or more different study methods.	Used 2 different study strategies.	Used one study strategy.	Didn't study.	
				Total points earned:	

FIGURE 4.7. Studying for tests rubric.

	Criteria				
Element	4	3	2	1	Value
Getting along with teachers	Did not lose my temper* with any of my teachers. *Losing temper means making an angry, impolite response or comment in class.	Lost my temper in 1–2 classes this week or with one teacher 1–2 times.	Lost my temper in 3–4 classes or with one teacher 3–4 times this week.	Lost my temper 5 times or more this week.	
Completing homework without frustration	Did not "lose my cool"* with any homework assignment. *Losing cool means engaging in an angry rant or refusing to complete an assignment.	Lost my cool with 1–2 assignments.	Lost my cool with 3–4 assignments.	Lost my cool with 5 or more assignments.	
Getting along with football coach	Did not lose my temper* with football coach. *Losing temper means making an angry, impolite response or comment; may be nonverbal (e.g., gesture, facial expression).	Lost temper 1–2 times.	Lost temper 3–4 times.	Lost temper 5 or more times.	
				Total points earned:	

FIGURE 4.8. Managing frustration rubric.

ADDITIONAL RESOURCES FOR MAKING RUBRICS

The following websites offer useful tips on creating rubrics and/or include examples of rubrics:

- *rubistar.4teachers.org/index.php* (free tool)
- *www.makeworksheets.com* (fee-based tool)
- *www.teach-nology.com* (fee-based tool)

A helpful resource for creating 5-point scales to address emotional control is Buron and Curtis (2003).

MODULE IV: PROBLEM SOLVING

Very often in the course of coaching, students present with problems that they feel unable to solve themselves. In many cases, coaches can help simply by asking students open-ended questions to help them discover they had the solution within their grasp all along. Examples are presented in the following dialogues.

> STUDENT: I lost my assignment sheet, and I've done it so many times my world cultures teacher won't give me a replacement!
>
> COACH: Is there another way you could get the assignment sheet without asking the teacher?

> STUDENT: I promised my math teacher I'd stay after school for help, but then I realized I have a play rehearsal and they're going to be practicing the one scene I'm in!
>
> COACH: What's your priority—and would you like help figuring out how you can talk to the teacher or the director of the school play?

> STUDENT: I'm in deep trouble. I bombed my earth science test even though I thought I knew the material, and now I'm in danger of failing for the marking period.
>
> COACH: Do you think there's something your teacher would be willing to do to help you make up for the bad grade?

These are all examples of how open-ended questions can be used to promote problem solving. In each case, the coach did not solve the problem for the student, but asked questions to help the student figure out a likely solution or a path to a good solution. Notice that the coach did not say things like, "I'd be glad to talk to your world cultures teacher and ask for another copy of the assignment sheet"; "The priority is obviously math. Do you want me to explain this to your drama advisor?"; or "Do you want me to ask your science teacher if you could retake the test?" In all these scenarios, the problem presented is not the coach's to solve and, therefore, the coach should not offer to be the solution. There may be times when a student needs help negotiating with a teacher for an accommodation, such as the chance to retake a test or to earn extra credit. However, when a coach assists with this kind of negotiation, some ground rules should be established and the entire process well thought out. Later we present an example of when this might be a feasible option and how it might progress.

There are times, however, when a single open-ended question or even a simple suggestion from a coach is not going to solve the problem posed. In these cases, a more formal problem-solving process is in order. Coaches can use the Problem-Solving Worksheet (in Appendix 16, p. 204), guided by the following steps (adapted from Dawson & Guare, 2010, pp. 105–106):

1. Talk with the student about what the problem is. This generally involves three steps: (a) empathizing with the student or letting him or her know you understand how he or she feels ("I can see that makes you really mad" or "That must be really upsetting for you"); (b) getting a general sense of what the problem is ("Let me get this straight—you're upset because your English teacher told you that the topic you really want to write about is off limits); and (c) defining the problem more narrowly so that you can begin to brainstorm solutions ("You'd like to be able to approach your English teacher and argue your case").

2. Brainstorm solutions. Together with the student, think of—and write down—as many different potential solutions to the problem as possible. You may want to set a time limit (like 2 minutes) because this sometimes speeds up the process or makes it feel less like an open-ended task. Don't criticize the solutions at this point because this tends to squelch the creative thinking process.

3. Ask the student to consider all the solutions and select the one he or she likes best. Decision making may be facilitated by having the student circle the top three to five choices and then narrow the list down further by talking about the pluses and minuses associated with each.

4. Ask the student whether he or she needs help carrying out the choice.

5. Talk about what will happen if the first solution doesn't work. This may involve choosing a different solution or analyzing where the first solution went wrong and fixing it.

6. Praise the student for coming up with a good solution (and then praise again after the solution is implemented).

This is a standard problem-solving approach that can be used for all kinds of problems, including interpersonal problems as well as obstacles that prevent students from getting what they want or need. Sometimes the best solution will involve helping students figure out ways to overcome the obstacles, while at other times it will involve helping the students come to terms with the fact that they cannot have what they want.

After you've used the process (and the worksheet) with the student for a number of different kinds of problems, he or she may be able to use the worksheet independently. Because your goal is ultimately to foster independent problem solving, you may want to have the student fill out the Problem-Solving Worksheet alone before seeking your help, if needed. Eventually, the student will internalize the whole process and be able to solve problems "on the fly."

Negotiating Solutions to Problems

There are times when the best solution to a problem will involve students having to negotiate with the person with whom they are having a conflict or disagreement. There are two ways to help students do this: (1) coaching them through the process to prepare them to negotiate with the adult in question; or (2) acting as a mediator to help the student and the adult reach a "negotiated settlement."

In the following dialogue, we illustrate both approaches using the case of the student who bombed an exam despite studying and wants to find a way to bring her grade up.

STUDENT: I'm in deep trouble. I bombed my earth science test even though I thought I knew the material, and now I'm in danger of failing for the marking period.

COACH: Do you think there's something your teacher would be willing to do to help you make up for the bad grade?

STUDENT: I don't know—like what?

COACH: Well, I can think of several possibilities. One might be to allow you to retake the test to bring your grade up—maybe for partial credit. Another might be to give you an extra-credit assignment to complete. Or maybe your teacher could let you suggest another way to demonstrate that you've learned the material.

STUDENT: I don't know. Ms. Welsh has never said anything about any of those possibilities. I suppose I could ask her.

COACH: You sound pretty skeptical. Would it help to talk through the conversation you might have in advance so you have a better idea of what you want to say beforehand?

STUDENT: Yeah, but how would I start?

COACH: I think you'd start by asking to make an appointment with her to discuss your grade on the last test. When you meet with her, you should begin by explaining what you did to study for the test and why you think you did badly. You don't want to make it look like you just blew it off and now want her to give you a second chance.

STUDENT: No way I blew it off! I studied for at least 3 hours—and I thought I understood the material, but I think I focused on the wrong stuff.

COACH: OK, so you tell her that. And then what?

STUDENT: I tell her I really can't afford to fail this class and can she tell me how I can bring my grade up?

COACH: That's one possibility. Teachers usually are focused on having students master material rather than just working for grades. Is there a different way you could ask for help?

STUDENT: Well, I could say that now that I've taken the test I have a better idea of what's most important to learn and could I retake it?

COACH: Do you think she'll find your request reasonable?

STUDENT: I have no idea—but I really did study hard. I made flash cards for key terms and memorized the three kinds of rocks and how they differ. I just wasn't prepared to be asked what kind of land forms or geographic features are associated with each kind of rock.

COACH: I think the more detail you give her about how you studied, the better she'll appreciate the work you put in. And then if you explain exactly how you missed the mark, she may agree to let you retake the test. Chances are it will only be for partial credit though.

STUDENT: I could live with that. I just can't deal with an F.

Although this is the preferred way to coach a student to approach a teacher, there may be times when both the coach and the student know that the teacher has a reputation for being rigid regarding grading rules. In many cases, it's best for the coach to help the student learn to accept the rules and to try to do better the next time. But in some cases, particularly those involving students with attention disorders or learning disabilities, the coach may feel that the student is being unduly penalized for a problem caused by the disability. In this case, it is reasonable for the coach to offer to accompany the student to the negotiation session to help the student advocate for him- or herself.

When a coach and student agree that it would be best for the coach to join the student when meeting with the teacher, they should plan in advance how they want to manage the session, similar to the prior dialogue, only with an added discussion regarding what the coach will and will not do during the session. In general, the student should lead the discussion, with the coach coming in as needed to clarify something the student has said that might be confusing. Adding to the prior scenario, the student and coach agreed that the coach would accompany the student to the meeting. Here's how the dialogue might go:

TEACHER: (*looking at coach*) So what's this about? I understand Tina wasn't happy with her grade on her last test.

COACH: I think Tina wants to explain her concerns.

STUDENT: Ms. Welsh, I feel terrible about failing the test. I studied for 3 hours and I even made flash cards and quizzed myself to make sure I learned the material, but I guess I studied the wrong material. Some of your questions really threw me for a loop.

TEACHER: Well, maybe you learned something about the process and will do better the next time.

STUDENT: The problem is that I did badly in the beginning of the marking period, and for the last few weeks I've been working hard to make up for lost time. If you check, you'll see that I've handed in all my homework and lab reports on time and my previous two quiz grades were pretty good. But I'm still trying to figure out what's important and what's not important to study. Now that I know what you're emphasizing, do you think it would be possible for me retake the exam?

TEACHER: I don't have a policy about retaking tests. It seems like it wouldn't be fair to other students.

COACH: I'm working with Tina because she has a learning disability and she has some difficulty differentiating between essential and nonessential information when studying.

Her IEP allows her "test accommodations as needed," and it seems like this might be a reasonable way to give her some practice in learning the skill of knowing what to study. If that's not possible, is there some other way she could demonstrate that she has learned the material that would also enable her to bring her grade up?

TEACHER: Well, I guess I could allow her to retake the test. I couldn't give her full credit, but I'm willing to average the two grades together.

TEACHER: (addressing Tina) For the next test, I'm planning on offering a study session after school. Would you be willing to come to that? I think it would help you know where to put in your time studying.

STUDENT: That would be excellent! I keep thinking that if I could figure out what's important I could make much better use of my time.

In this situation, when it became apparent to the coach that the teacher was not really understanding why Tina struggled with studying, she decided to intervene on Tina's behalf. When the session was over, she would do well to debrief with Tina and perhaps talk with her about how she might advocate for herself in the future. She could talk with Tina about how she might use her IEP to access reasonable accommodations, such as study guides, pretest study sessions with the teacher, and testing accommodations (e.g., opportunity to retake tests for full or partial credit). Further discussion of coaching as part of a special education plan is presented in the next section.

As stated, in most cases it's preferable to coach students in advance for how to negotiate with a teacher but have them approach the teacher by themselves. However, in the following situations, accompanying the student to the negotiation meeting may be in order:

- When the student's disability impedes his or her ability to communicate effectively. This would apply particularly to students with language-based learning disabilities, where they have trouble organizing and retrieving language.
- When the student has trouble managing emotions or controlling temper in anxiety-provoking or emotionally charged situations.
- When the teacher is seen by the student as particularly intimidating and likely to be unwilling to listen to the student's request even if it seems reasonable to both the student and the coach.
- When the student is asking for something unusual and it is likely that the student may need help making his or her case in order for the teacher to consider the accommodation.

An intermediate step between accompanying the student to the negotiation session and having him or her approach the teacher alone would be for the coach to contact the teacher in advance of the session and explain what the student is hoping to accomplish as a result of the negotiation. If the coach explains that the goal of the session is not only to come to some agreement about a reasonable solution to a problem but to teach the student to advocate for him- or herself, the teacher may be more willing to assist in the process.

MODULE V: SECTION 504 PLANS, SPECIAL EDUCATION, AND RTI

Students with executive skills weaknesses receive school-based services, including coaching, through two primary vehicles: special education and Section 504 plans. Each of these are defined briefly next. Coaches, particularly those who work *outside* the school system (e.g., through private contracts with the family), are often put in the position of having to advocate on the student's behalf that the student must be provided with a coach in order to achieve academic success. Psychologists and private evaluators also are frequently called upon to make a case that a school district must provide a coach within the school for a student whom they have evaluated and determined to have executive skills weaknesses that require direct intervention.

Section 504

Both 504 plans and special education are governed by laws and regulations that specify who is eligible for services and what kinds of services. Section 504 is a civil rights law that prohibits discrimination against individuals with disabilities. It is designed to ensure that children with disabilities have access to the same education as those without disabilities. The law requires school districts to provide a free appropriate public education (known as FAPE) to students who "have a physical or mental impairment that substantially limits one or more major life activities." A physical or mental impairment may include an attention disorder, a specific learning disability, or a traumatic brain injury, all of which are likely to impact executive functioning. The term "major life activity" as stated in the law (34 C.F.R. 104.3(j)(2)(11) refers to "functions such as caring for one's self, performing manual tasks, walking, seeing, hearing, speaking, breathing, learning, and working." This list was expanded in the amendments act (Americans with Disabilities Amendments Act of 2008) to include "eating, sleeping, standing, lifting, bending, reading, concentrating, thinking, and communicating." The website *www2.ed.gov/about/offices/list/ocr/index.html* is an excellent resource for a more in-depth discussion of this law.

The services covered under Section 504 are typically accommodations and modifications provided in the regular classroom and designed to enable children with disabilities to benefit from classroom instruction. Examples of these include allowing extended time on tests or alternative test methods, modified homework assignments, allowing for breaks (so children with ADHD, for instance, can get up and move around or leave the classroom temporarily), and modified grading procedures (e.g., weighing daily work higher than tests for students who test poorly). Students who qualify for services under Section 504 may also be eligible for supplementary services and/or special education or related services. Typically, however, students who qualify for special education do not need a 504 plan because their services are provided through special education.

Special Education

Special education is intended for children with an educational disability that adversely affects educational performance and requires specialized instruction to correct. Helping students learn to become organized, to manage time effectively, or to do the planning required to complete long-term projects or to juggle multiple assignments at once very often requires individualized instruction that would warrant special education.

Special education has traditionally involved a comprehensive evaluation to determine whether students have an educational disability that would qualify them for special education services. The most common disabilities are learning disabilities, emotional or behavioral disorders, a speech/language handicap, mental impairment or mental retardation, autism (including Asperger syndrome), and "other health impaired," such as ADHD or another medical condition that might affect learning.

A number of steps are involved in accessing special education services for students, and coaches who are employed directly by parents would do well to become knowledgeable about the special education laws and procedures in their state. Table 4.1 outlines the basic process to access special education under the Individuals with Disabilities in Education Act of 2004 (the

TABLE 4.1. Steps in the Special Education Process

Step	Description
1	Student is identified as possibly needing special education and related services (either the parent of a child or the school system may initiate a request for an initial evaluation to determine whether the student has a disability).
2	Child is evaluated. This must occur within 60 calendar days from the time parental consent for evaluation is obtained. The evaluation must include a variety of assessment tools to gather relevant functional, developmental and academic information about the child, including information from the parent.
3	Eligibility is decided. This decision is made by a special education team that consists of the child's parents and a group of qualified professionals, including the child's teacher, an administrator, and other relevant specialists.
4	Child is found eligible for services. Children who are eligible for special education services must both have a disability and be in need of specialized instruction in order to make adequate educational progress.
5	IEP meeting is scheduled. An IEP, an individualized education program, describes the plan that will be developed for the child. This meeting must take place within 30 days of the date eligibility was determined.
6	IEP meeting is held, and the IEP is written. The IEP must include, among other things, the following elements: (1) a statement of the student's present levels of academic performance; (2) a statement of measurable annual goals, including academic and functional goals (i.e., goals associated with activities of daily living); (3) a description of how the child's progress toward meeting the annual goal will be measured; and (4) a statement of the special education and related services that will be provided to the student as well as program modifications or supports.
7	Services are provided.
8	Progress is measured and reported to parents on a quarterly basis.

most recent revision of the federal special education law). (For a more extensive discussion of the special education process, see the website of the National Dissemination Center for Children with Disabilities: *www.nichcy.org/Pages/Home.aspx.*)

Schools are accustomed to providing specialized instruction in content area subjects, such as reading, math, and written language. However, a case can be made that students whose executive skills weaknesses are so profound that they are failing classes or achieving substantially below their potential (based on report card grades) will require specialized instruction in executive skills in order to make adequate progress. In this case, a coach is the ideal vehicle for providing that specialized instruction.

Writing IEP Goals to Address Executive Skills Weaknesses

Good IEP goals do three things: (1) They specify what behaviors the student will perform; (2) they depict the conditions under which the behavior will occur; and (3) they specify the level of performance expected. Examples of IEP goals for the student with executive skills weaknesses for which coaching would be a reasonable intervention strategy are as follows:

- Given a verbal reminder from the teacher, the student will hand in completed homework assignments 90% of the time.
- With assistance from a coach, the student will use a long-term project planning sheet to develop timelines and subtasks for all long-term projects.
- The student will use a scoring rubric to evaluate and maintain notebook organization on a weekly basis in all subjects in which notebooks are graded for organization.

An excellent resource for IEP development is *The IEP from A to Z: How to Create Meaningful and Measurable Goals and Objectives* (Twachtman-Cullen & Twachtman-Bassett, 2011).

Response to Intervention

Succinctly described, RTI "is a school-based system designed to identify and meet children's needs through increasingly more focused and intensive levels ('tiers') of assessment and intervention" (Hunley & McNamara, 2010). We have written about how executive skills development can be facilitated within this model (Dawson & Guare, 2010), and readers are referred to that book for a broader overview of how executive skills can be supported within a three-tiered model. Coaching is primarily designed as a Tier 2 and Tier 3 intervention, but there may be a place for classwide coaching at Tier 1 as well. (See Chapter 6 for a discussion of classwide peer coaching interventions that also qualify as a Tier 1 intervention.)

Universal Level

The universal level encompasses systems-level or classroom-level supports directed at *all* students and designed to meet the needs of *most* students. As we have written previously, we believe there are support systems that can be incorporated into daily classroom instruction and procedures that, if implemented, will reduce the need for Tier 2 and Tier 3 interventions and, therefore, reduce the need for a coaching intervention. These are identified in Figure 4.9 in the form of a checklist that can be used to determine whether the classroom provides reasonable supports for students with executive skills weaknesses.

A key feature of our academic coaching program is to have students engage in goal setting, often for the purpose of learning time and task management skills, particularly as needed in the context of homework. Thus, a universal application of coaching would be to have students make a daily homework plan in which they establish a schedule for nightly homework activities. A Daily Homework Planning Form that teachers can use for this purpose is included in Appendix 9 (p. 186).

Targeted Level

The targeted level, or Tier 2, is designed to meet the needs of the 10 to 15% of the student population for whom universal supports are insufficient. Group coaching is an example of a Tier 2 intervention. This model was implemented by Merriman (2010) with a group of 50 at-risk middle school students. Some of these students were identified as educationally handicapped, but all were referred because of chronic problems completing homework, which led to poor

Managing classroom assignments	Ensure students: • Start promptly • Complete on time • Hand in when done	
Managing homework	Ensure students: • Write down assignments in assignment book • Understand assignments • Bring home necessary materials to do homework • Hand in assignments on time	
Managing materials	Ensure students: • Keep desks organized • Keep notebooks organized • Maintain organizational systems	
Planning/time management	Help students: • Break down long-term assignments into subtasks and timelines • Follow timelines • Make daily homework plans	
Behavior management	• Post classroom rules • Review rules frequently • Model and practice rule following	
Promoting problem-solving/independence	• Build in choice or self-directed study in assignments • Encourage goal setting • Use conflict mediation • Teach problem solving for both social and academic problems	

FIGURE 4.9. Checklist of classroom supports for Tier 1 classrooms.

report card grades. Students were assigned to either group coaching or an after-school "homework center." Both groups met after school for 42 minutes 4 days a week, Monday through Thursday. During each session, the homework center students were monitored by two teaching assistants, who ensured that students worked on their nightly homework but did not provide academic support. Students assigned to the group coaching condition were divided into smaller groups, with no more than 10 students per group. Coaches, who were school psychologists, explained the intervention to the students, and then helped them set long-term and short-term goals as well as homework completion objectives. In each session, these students reviewed the previous day's goals and plans and made plans for the day, using a coach monitoring form similar to that provided in this manual. At the end of each session, students began their homework while the coach met individually with them to discuss progress and to refine goals if necessary. Each coach met individually with each student for about 5 minutes once a week. On Mondays, coaches shared with students the previous week's homework completion rates, and students logged these data on their own individual preformatted spreadsheet graphs.

The study found that both interventions (coaching and homework center) were effective in increasing homework completion rates; however, the level of effectiveness varied depending on student needs. For students with disabilities, the homework center approach was more effective, whereas for nondisabled students with homework problems, the group coaching intervention was more effective. This suggests that group coaching would be an effective Tier 2 intervention, but may not be the most effective way to address the homework problems of students with disabilities. It should be noted that although homework completion rates improved for both groups, grade point averages did not. This suggests that how the goals are defined may be critical to outcomes. If the desired outcome of a coaching model is improved report card grades, then this should be built into goal identification and progress monitoring.

Intensive Level

This level is reserved for the 1–7% of students with chronic or more severe problems. Interventions at this level are highly individualized, and to be most effective, their design usually involves a collaborative effort from parents, teachers, and the student. Figure 4.10 provides an example of a coaching intervention for a student with significant executive skills weaknesses.

The individual coaching programs in this book can all be considered Tier 3 interventions. These include coaching for academic success, as described in Chapter 3, as well as the peer coaching variation of this model, described in Chapter 6. The social skills peer coaching program described by Plumer in Chapter 7 is another example of a Tier 3 intervention.

Making Decisions Regarding Eligibility for Tier 2 and Tier 3 Interventions

Good intervention design incorporates the following elements: (1) a goal statement; (2) a description of the intervention procedure; (3) the length of time the intervention will be implemented; (4) the criterion for success; and (5) the measurement procedure. By carefully defining the success criteria, decisions can be made regarding the most appropriate tier for any given student. If the success criteria are met, the student remains at that tier level, with the intervention faded gradually. If the success criteria are not met, the intervention is either altered to make improvements at that tier level or the student is placed in the next higher tier.

Behaviors of concern: Mike forgets assignments, forgets to bring materials home, and forgets to hand in assignments. He also has trouble managing his time and breaking down long-term projects into subtasks and making and following timelines. Problems are severe enough that Mike has failed several classes and is in danger of not earning enough credits to pass for the year.

School's responsibility: To assign a coach to work with Mike on strategies to improve recall, organization, planning, and time management.

Coach's responsibility: To meet with Mike for the last 15–20 minutes of school every day in order to (1) review all homework assignments, including daily homework, upcoming tests, and long-term projects or papers; (2) break down long-term assignments into subtasks and develop timelines; (3) create a study plan for tests; (4) make a homework plan for the day; and (5) monitor how well the plan is followed and track assignment completion. The coach will also check in with teachers at least weekly (on Friday) to track any missing assignments and to double-check long-term assignments. Coach will e-mail parents on Friday informing them of any missing assignments.

Teachers' responsibility: To provide baseline data to determine current level of performance (e.g., percent assignments handed in on time) and to make sure Mike has ample time to write down his assignments at end of day and/or make sure website homework postings are current and explicit. Teachers will also respond by noon on Friday to coach's request for feedback about missing assignments.

Parents' responsibility: Mike will be allowed to spend Friday evening and Saturday with friends as long as homework assignments for the week have been handed in. Criterion will be determined from baseline performance. Parents will download e-mail from coach on Friday and have a feedback session with Mike before weekends plans are made.

Mike's responsibility: Mike will attend coaching sessions consistently and will participate in setting goals and making plans for homework completion.

FIGURE 4.10. Sample intensive-level student support plan.

This may be best illustrated through a case example:

Charmaine is unable to complete long-term projects independently. She begins them late and leaves out segments of the assignment, and the work she does is of poor quality (not well organized with insufficient detail). She fails to hand in the project at all 20% of the time and hands in assignments late 50% of the time. The average grade she earns on the assignments she hands in on time is C– to D. With loss of credit for late assignments, the average grade earned on these is D– to F.

Charmaine's school employs a problem-solving team to make decisions regarding interventions. The level of support provided by her classroom teachers (i.e., at Tier 1) includes breaking down long-term assignments for students into subtasks, with timelines and interim due dates assigned. Because Charmaine fairly routinely fails to meet these due dates and to hand in her long-term projects on time, the problem-solving team meets and defines a set of criteria for success as a first step in deciding an appropriate intervention:

1. Charmaine will hand projects in on time 80% of the time, with 80% of elements on the scoring rubric included.
2. Charmaine will earn grades of C– or better.

The problem-solving team decides Charmaine would qualify for a Tier 2 intervention—a small-group coaching program in which Charmaine will attend coaching sessions 4 days a week right after school to make plans for project completion. All students assigned to the coaching program have similar problems, which allows the coach to teach the planning/organizational skills necessary for project completion. Unfortunately, despite communication with Charmaine's parents and their willingness to have her stay after school, her attendance is sporadic, resulting in only minor improvement in project completion. Thus, the success criteria are not met. The problem-solving team meets again and decides to assign Charmaine an individual coach, who will meet with her during her daily study hall. She is now getting more direct assistance in the time and task management skills necessary to carry out long-term assignments, and this level of intervention meets with more success. After the initial success, a fading procedure is determined, with input from Charmaine. Figure 4.11 shows the RTI Progress Monitoring Form employed by Charmaine's team. A blank version of this form is included in Appendix 19 (p. 208).

CONCLUSION

In this chapter, we provided readers with a fairly comprehensive description of the kinds of skills and knowledge that coaches need in order to work at an "expert" level. We encourage readers to use the practice exercises (pp. 135–149) to try out the skills described and to check their responses against those provided in the answer key (pp. 150–158). These exercises can serve not only as an opportunity to practice but also as a "self-assessment" to help readers determine their progress toward skill mastery. Readers who feel they need more practice are encouraged to follow up by using the resource materials listed throughout the chapter.

Student's Name: _Charmaine_

Tier level	Intervention	Start date	Review date	Criterion for success	Measurement procedure	Outcome	Next step
1	Teachers break down assignment into subtasks with interim due dates.	10/1	12/1	Projects handed in on time 80% of the time, with 80% of elements on scoring rubric included; grade of C– or better.	Calculate percentage of projects handed in on time, percent elements included, and average project grade.	40% projects handed in on time, 60% project elements included; average grade: D.	Move to Tier 2.
2	Small-group coaching; meet daily, Mon–Thurs after school with others with same problem; make daily work plans for project completion.	12/2	1/20	Projects handed in on time 80% of the time, with 80% of elements on scoring rubric included; grade of C– or better.	Calculate percentage projects handed in on time, percent elements included, and average project grade.	60% projects handed in on time, 70% project elements included; average grade: D+. Attendance at coaching sessions is sporadic.	Move to Tier 3.
3	Individual coaching; meet daily during study hall to provide guided assistance in how to make work plans; use study hall time 2–3 days a week to work on projects.	1/23	3/3	Daily plans followed 80% of time. Projects handed in on time 80% of the time, with 80% of elements on scoring rubric included; grade of C– or better.	Calculate and graph percentage of daily goals met. Calculate percentage projects handed in on time, percent elements included, and average project grade.	80% projects handed in on time, 85% project elements included; average grade: C.	Remain in Tier 3 but fade coaching sessions (daily to every other day to twice a week to once a week) based on meeting criteria.

FIGURE 4.11. Example of a completed RTI Progress Monitoring Form.

CHAPTER 5

Setting Up a School-Based Academic Coaching Program

As we stated earlier, coaching can be provided on an ad hoc basis, initiated by a student assistance team or a trained school staff member—for example, the school psychologist, guidance counselor, or school administrator—to identify individual students who would benefit from coaching and match them with coaches based on student preferences and availability of adults, such as teachers, guidance counselors, or aides, to act as coaches. To have a greater impact, however, we believe that coaching can become institutionalized, making it one of an array of interventions offered to students who are struggling academically, whether they are on an IEP or not. This chapter suggests a process for creating a coaching program at the middle or high school level. In the first part, we describe a coaching program with adults as coaches. We then discuss how this approach can be modified to use peers as coaches.

SETTING UP AN ADULT COACHING PROGRAM

For a coaching program to be successful, a dedicated coach coordinator is a necessity. Realistically, this is not a full-time position, but the person who takes it on will add it to his or her job responsibilities. Staff who might logically perform this role include a school administrator (e.g., a vice principal), a school psychologist or guidance counselor, or a special education coordinator (although this may be problematic if coaching is made available to students who do not qualify for special education). Table 5.1 lists the steps a coach coordinator will follow in setting up a coaching program, each of which is discussed next.

Step 1: Soliciting Potential Coaches

Coaches can be identified in one of two ways: either the coach coordinator (along with input from school administrators) can personally invite individuals within the school to become coaches,

TABLE 5.1. Steps in Setting Up an Adult Coaching Program

Step	Task
1	Solicit potential coaches.
2	Provide training for coaches.
3	Identify students who may benefit from coaching.
4	Interview students and invite them to participate.
5	Notify parents.
6	Match students to coaches.
7	Participate in the goal-setting session and help establish the daily coaching schedules.
8	Check in weekly with each coach to assess the process.
9	Arrange for periodic group case consultation meetings with coaches.
10	Evaluate coaching effectiveness.

or they can announce the coaching program to the faculty as a whole and ask for volunteers. In the first instance, the coordinator has more control over the process because this allows for a "prescreening" of potential candidates. The drawback, however, is that potential candidates—people who might be interested in participating—may be overlooked. A combination of the two approaches is likely to yield the best results. A script for soliciting volunteers that might be read at a faculty meeting is as follows:

"Our school is establishing a new program called 'coaching' to provide academic support to at-risk students, helping them to stay on top of their coursework and pass their classes. The job of a coach is not to offer tutoring but rather to help students with the time and task management demands required for academic success (also called executive skills). We are looking for faculty members willing to volunteer their time—as little as 10 to 15 minutes a day—to work with individual students to help them make daily homework plans. We will provide whatever training is required and offer logistical support to match you with a student with whom you can work compatibly. We will also arrange for ongoing group consultation to give those who volunteer to be coaches opportunities to meet and share ideas and experiences.

"We know that teachers are incredibly busy, but we have good evidence that coaching is an effective intervention and that it can help at-risk students stay in school and underachieving students stay on top of their work and improve their grades. Because students' participation in coaching is voluntary, we know that these kids are motivated to make it work. We think this will be a fun and rewarding way to bring teachers and students together to help them stay in school and be successful. If you would like to volunteer for this, please let me know or put your name on the sign-up sheet."

The coach coordinator may also want to make available to potential coach candidates a description of what the job entails. A handout describing job responsibilities and the coaching process is included in Appendix 20 (p. 209). Individuals who agree to act as coaches should also be asked how many students they are willing to work with at any given time. Although aspects of the process can be streamlined or automated—for instance, coaches, teachers, and parents can communicate via e-mail rather than direct contact—volunteers should understand that each student will require between 45 and 60 minutes of their time per week.

Step 2: Providing Training for Coaches

The intensity of the training depends on the background of the people providing the service. For skilled teachers, it may be a simple matter of giving them a copy of Chapter 4 and asking them to read it through so they understand the process and the skills involved. If more intensive training is warranted (e.g., with paraprofessionals or community volunteers), then devoting a training session to each of the training modules in Chapter 4 may be necessary. The practice exercises at the end of the book (pp. 135–149) can be incorporated into the training sessions.

In all cases, however, the coach coordinator should review all the coaching forms and record-keeping procedures with coaches so that they understand how to use them. If the coach coordinator participates in the goal-setting session with each coach–student pair, decisions about what goals to set and how to track success can be made at that time (thus requiring less expertise on the part of the coaches themselves).

Step 3: Identifying Students Who May Benefit from Coaching

Students can be identified using a number of methods:

1. Solicit nominations from staff, including teachers, administrators, guidance counselors, school psychologists, the 504 plan coordinator, and special education teams.
2. Contact teacher assistance teams and let them know the service is available for students who are brought to their attention.
3. Identify at-risk students based on early markers that signal academic problems. Sometimes eighth-grade teachers and administrators compile a "student watch list," identifying those who may struggle with the upcoming transition to high school. The advantage of this approach is that an intervention can be put in place preemptively, *before* these students experience failure in a new school setting.
4. Use report card grades or other school performance data, such as absences, school tardiness, and discipline referrals (e.g., detentions) to identify students at risk of school failure or adjustment problems.

The second part of this process involves identifying those at-risk students who will be good candidates for coaching. Individuals who might respond well to coaching include:

1. Students with failing grades whose ability markers, such as standardized achievement test scores, indicate that classroom performance is not commensurate with their skills and abilities.
2. Students who did well in elementary school, where more teacher support was provided, but who show a gradual drop-off in middle school or in the transition to high school. These trends suggest that students have not kept pace as the demands for executive functioning increase. Their ability to learn is intact and they have the foundational skills to perform, but they need help developing lagging executive skills.
3. Students who have been explicitly identified—by, for example, a psychologist or neuropsychologist—as having weak executive skills. (These professionals now commonly incorporate an assessment of executive functioning in their comprehensive evaluations.)
4. Students who have been identified by teachers as "lazy" or "unmotivated," labels that are often used to describe those who, in fact, have weak or delayed executive skills.

Although we always believe coaching is most likely to be successful when students participate voluntarily, at the middle school level coaching programs can be set up such that at-risk students can be assigned to work with a coach with the goal of improving school performance or passing classes. Just as some schools assign students with failing grades to attend an after-school homework club, we believe they could also assign students to work with a coach to set goals to improve some aspect of school functioning. In fact, coaching at this level may work best when it is combined with an after-school homework club. We also know of middle schools where group coaching is incorporated into an end-of-day routine in the resource room, where students are helped to create homework plans and engage in other time and task management tasks (such as creating timelines for long-term assignments).

Step 4: Interviewing Students and Inviting Them to Participate

At the high school level, we recommend approaching students individually and inviting them to work with a coach. The script provided in Chapter 3 (p. 27) can be used as a guide for this purpose. Students should not be coerced to participate, although it is reasonable to stress the benefits of coaching as well as the relatively brief time commitment required. Points to stress might include the following: (1) Coaching has been shown to help students improve both their grades and study habits; (2) it can require as little as 5–10 minutes per day once the process is up and running; (3) the student, and not the coach, is in charge of setting goals, and in the beginning the process usually involves setting small goals that can be achieved with only a little extra effort from the student; and (4) the coach can help troubleshoot or mediate when problems arise in particular classes. Sometimes students find the thought of coaching appealing if it means they can "get their parents off their back." The coach coordinator may want to offer to meet with both the student and the parents to work out an agreement that if the student faithfully attends coaching sessions and meets the goals on a fairly consistent basis, the parents will stay in the background when it comes to monitoring homework or other aspects of school performance.

Some students may be more willing to work with a coach if they can do it with a friend. In this arrangement, the coach meets with both students together at the same time every day. Although this may mean a little more work for the coach because communication with both students' teachers will be necessary, as the coaching progresses, it may be possible for the students to take on more and more of the coaching responsibilities themselves, an approach we sometimes call "reciprocal coaching."

Students who are not sure they want to commit to coaching may be persuaded to at least give it a try for a short period of time. Ideally, they should be encouraged to continue for at least half a marking period so that midterm grades can be used as a marker of success. However, if the coach coordinator senses a lack of motivation, it doesn't make sense to push the issue. At this point, the coach thanks the students for considering the offer and encourages them to return if they change their mind.

Step 5: Notifying Parents

Because coaching involves a change in students' daily schedule, once they agree to participate, the parents should be informed—via letter or e-mail—of the service and their permission obtained. A sample permission letter is provided in Appendix 21 (p. 210). The coach coordinator should also provide parents with contact information if they have additional concerns or questions about the process. Coaching for special education students will likely involve a change in their IEP. Thus, parental notification and permission must be obtained, and the change should be noted in the IEP.

Step 6: Matching Students to Coaches

Students are likely to be particular about the coach they work with. Thus, when assigning coaches, students should first be asked whom they might like to be paired with. If they name people who have not volunteered for coaching, the coach coordinator may want to approach these individuals and let them know they've been requested as coaches. This may be all it takes to persuade people to volunteer.

The coach coordinator can also share with students a list of potential coaches and ask them to select one or two with whom they might like to work. Although it may be tempting to try to match students and coaches based on compatible personality traits or shared interests (and this may indeed be a good place to start), we have seen improbable relationships work well because the student and coach connected in a way no one would have predicted. Thus, rather than trying to make a science out of the matching process, the coach coordinator might consider a couple of steps that we recommend. First, take cues from the student. If the student's first meeting with a coach goes well and the coach and student appear compatible, then the pairing works. We have found that even chronic underachievers, such as students with ADHD, will work hard for teachers if they like them. In these cases, teachers themselves end up as powerful reinforcers for students. Coaches can do the same for the students they coach if the chemistry is right.

Second, the coach coordinator can explain to both students and coaches that the first phase of coaching should be considered a trial period, and that when this time is up (e.g., 2–3 weeks into the process) the coordinator will meet with each party separately to assess progress and to make any necessary changes, including finding a different coach. Knowing that changes can be made—that within a relatively short period of time there is an "escape hatch" or an opportunity to correct any problems—may persuade tentative students to buy into the process.

It is possible that the number of students interested in coaching exceeds the number of coaches available. In this case, students can be placed on a waiting list. Alternatively, students can be randomly assigned to either a coach or a waiting list, which may set up a natural experiment that will ultimately provide additional information about coaching effectiveness (e.g., a comparison study of report card grades of students receiving coaching vs. those on the waiting list).

Step 7: Participating in the Goal-Setting Session and Helping Establish the Daily Coaching Schedules

Once coaches and students are matched, the next step is to hold the initial goal-setting session. Although experienced coaches can conduct these sessions themselves, in the early stages of establishing a coaching program it may make sense for the coach coordinator to meet with both the student and coach and lead this session. Chapter 3 provides detailed instructions for how this session progresses. Appendices 5 and 6 (pp. 178–183) contain long-term and interim goal-setting forms.

Once long-term and interim goals have been established, the coach and student determine how success will be measured. Sections in both Chapter 3 (pp. 34–35) and Chapter 4 (Module III, pp. 69–76) provide guidance for this. As noted in Chapter 3, with middle school students, the focus should be on interim goals (either weekly or marking period goals) rather than long-term goals.

Finally, the coach and student identify a time every day (or at least 4 days a week) when they can meet to make daily plans and assess progress. The coach coordinator should make a note of the meeting time and place, and keep a master list to help monitor the coaching program. A Coach Coordinator Master List is included in Appendix 22 (p. 211).

Step 8: Checking In Weekly with Each Coach to Assess the Process

Coaching works because students make a public commitment to pursue the goals they set. In a sense, a coaching program works for the same reason—because coaches make a public commitment to volunteer their time. In addition, just as students benefit from the attention they receive from coaches, coaches benefit from the recognition and support they receive from the coach coordinator. Although the check-in may be brief and casual, it should occur weekly, and the coach coordinator would do well to maintain ongoing records both to evaluate the process and to provide documentation to help justify to administrators the time and effort involved in maintaining a coaching program. A Coach Coordinator Weekly Monitoring Form, which can be used to track the program, is provided in Appendix 23 (p. 212).

Step 9: Arranging for Periodic Group Case Consultation Meetings with Coaches

As coaches continue their participation in the program, they are likely to acquire experience that would be beneficial to share with other coaches. They may also encounter problems or have questions about how to proceed. To share information and brainstorm solutions, the coach coordinator should organize occasional case consultation meetings. These meetings should be informal and optional. However, as issues arise at the weekly check-in, the coach coordinator may want to invite individual coaches to attend and share their experiences with the group, focusing on successes and things they have learned about the process. Coaches should also be invited to discuss problems they have encountered, and the group may be asked to offer advice or brainstorm possible solutions. If common issues or problems emerge, the coach coordinator may want to arrange for more formal inservice training to address them. For instance, if a number of students are struggling with how to study for tests, then a case consultation meeting could be devoted to good study strategies and a brief review of what the research says are the most effective ways to study for tests. Coaches should also be invited to suggest specific topics for discussion at future case consultation sessions.

The first case consultation meeting should occur fairly early in the coaching process, ideally within 2–3 weeks of the initial session with students. As coaching progresses, the group can establish the frequency and length of the meetings.

Step 10: Evaluating Coaching Effectiveness

By conducting weekly check-ins, at which the coach coordinator asks coaches to estimate the percentage of daily goals their students meet, an ongoing assessment of the process is possible. Report card grades can also serve as a measure of coaching effectiveness, particularly if grades during coaching can be compared with those earned before coaching. We also recommend that at the end of each marking period the coach coordinator meet with the coaches as a group and with the students as a group to obtain feedback from both about how the process has gone and how it could be improved. These discussions will no doubt produce qualitative rather than quantitative data, but the results can nonetheless be compiled, in either narrative or list form. Coach Feedback Forms included in Appendix 24 (p. 213) can be used for this purpose.

Both coaches and students are more likely to feel that the time they put into volunteer activities is worthwhile when they see the payoff (e.g., improved student performance). Often, however, effective programs die out even when the payoff is evident because the work of those participating is not appreciated. For a coaching program to gain longevity, care and nurturing by the coach coordinator is critical. Finding ways to celebrate success, make participants feel part of a social network, and provide tokens of appreciation (e.g., certificates or other small awards) are just some of the ways coach coordinators can let participants know that their work and time are valued.

SETTING UP A PEER COACHING PROGRAM

We believe that the school-based coaching program described previously can, under the right conditions, be equally effective using peer coaches. In Chapter 7, Pamela Plumer describes a peer coaching program to support social skills development using fourth-grade students as coaches, and we have implemented her model successfully with fifth-grade students. In addition, we have successfully implemented social skills coaching programs using peers as coaches at the middle and high school levels. In our experience, peer coaches were able to help peers with autism spectrum disorders learn complex social skills. Using procedures such as modeling, rehearsal, prompting, shaping, and fading, coaches were able help peers learn to listen, stay on topic, read the feelings of others as well as their own, and use these skills across the school day. Peer coaching of executive skills can be equally effective because there is a clear template to follow, the executive and academic skills issues confronting students will be familiar to peer coaches, students are often more receptive to help from their peers, and the selection criteria for coaches will reflect their own strengths in executive skills.

The steps to follow in setting up a peer coaching program are identical to the steps to establish an adult coaching program (see Table 5.1). The process differs, however, as described next.

Step 1: Soliciting Potential Coaches

Potential coaches can be identified through existing school groups such the National Honor Society or Junior National Honor Society, student council, or peer mediation programs, if available. Although not universally true, students who are members in these groups tend to have better self-regulation, which is a marker for executive skills. In addition, their academic achievements and goals testify to relatively strong executive skills. Peer coaches will have the following characteristics:

- They indicate a desire to coach and to help other students learn.
- They are empathetic.
- They are confident without being condescending or arrogant.
- They lead others by example and through encouragement of others' efforts.
- They take pleasure in the accomplishments of others.
- They have the ability to teach by questioning rather than directing.

We suggest that potential coaches consider these characteristics and that the coach coordinator interview each candidate. Once the program is stably implemented, a peer coach coordinator serves this function.

The peer coach coordinator's introduction to coaching (Step 1 in the previous section) is essentially the same as that for the adult coach coordinator.

Step 2: Providing Training for Coaches

The training for student coaches has the components of more intensive training referred to previously. Potential coaches should first be given a copy of Chapter 4 to read, and the coach coordinator should schedule a question-and-answer session. For those students who are still interested, training consists of sessions on each of the training modules along with the practice exercises. As part of this training, the students are paired in role-play dyads, with each one alternately taking the role of coach and student. During these role plays, the coach coordinator circulates among the candidates to give pointers and answer questions. If there is an adult coaching program in the school, an added component for peer coach training can be a brief apprenticeship, with the peer coach observing the adult coach for two daily sessions and then taking the role of the coach and having the adult coach observe and "coach the coach." Another difference in the peer coaching model is that either an adult coach or the coach coordinator will always participate in the initial goal-setting session to assist the peer coach in working with the at-risk student to establish his or her long-term goals and ensure that these are realistic. We do not see this as a role for the peer coach unless he or she is experienced in this process and has been determined by the coach coordinator to be capable. Once the long-term goals have been set, the peer coach will meet with the student on a daily basis.

Step 3: Identifying Students Who May Benefit from Coaching

The procedures for this step are the same as for adult coaching.

Step 4: Interviewing Students and Inviting Them to Participate

The information provided in this step remains essentially the same as for adult coaching. Additionally, however, students have the option of choosing to work with an adult coach or a peer coach because for some the peer coach may be more appealing. This is especially true for students who may have had conflicts with teachers or who have more difficulty with adult authority.

Step 5: Notifying Parents

This step is essentially similar to that for adult coaching. If a student has chosen coaching in part so that the parents will "back off," parents may want to know what reliability checks have been built into the peer coaching process, how the coaches will be supervised, and so on. Providing parents with information about the types of students selected as coaches, along with their training and ongoing supervision, will be reassuring. Given their experiences with their own children, they may readily see how peer coaches might be more acceptable and have more influence than adults.

Step 6: Matching Students to Coaches

The first step in the matching process is to determine whether the student prefers to work with a peer or an adult. If the student chooses a peer, then the coach coordinator can show them the list of student coaches available to determine whether there is a particular coach with whom they would like to work. Toward this end, the Getting to Know You survey (provided in Appendix 1, pp. 165–166) could be a useful tool for coaches to complete, and ultimately for students to review in order to make more informed decisions about whom they might like to work with. If the student expresses no preference for a particular coach, the coach coordinator has both student and coach profiles available as one factor in the matching process. It can also be helpful for the coach coordinator to know about the coaches' particular academic interests or strengths because this could aid the coaching process if the student is struggling in a particular subject area. At the same time, it is important to note that coaching is a different process from academic tutoring in a subject area; if a student also has this need, additional tutorial services will be needed. One of the major advantages of using peer coaches is that it decreases or even eliminates the detrimental issues of shortage of coaches, waiting lists, and so on. In addition, with peers working together, there is an increased likelihood that they will be familiar with and be able, in some cases, to creatively use communication technology to enhance the coaching process.

Step 7: Participating in the Goal-Setting Session and Helping Establish the Daily Coaching Schedules

As noted, this is another area where adult and peer coaching may diverge, at least in the short run. The goal-setting process is key to successful coaching. Hence, we believe it is important for the person most familiar with and practiced at coaching (i.e., the coach coordinator) to participate in this process with both adult and peer coaches in the early stages. Beyond that, in order for the peer to have additional practice in goal setting, he or she can be "apprenticed" to an adult coach as an observer and then as a coach with the adult observing. This is another juncture at which the focus student can be given the option of continuing with the adult or transferring to the peer. As with adult coaches, peer coaches will need to develop an understanding of how success will be measured and tracked using the resources provided in this manual. After this, the student and the peer coach will specify their daily meeting times, location, and so on. If the peer coach group is large, the coach coordinator is unlikely to have the time to oversee all of them. A solution is to have adults who are familiar with coaching act as advisors for a group of peer coaches.

Step 8: Checking In Weekly with Each Coach to Monitor and Troubleshoot

As with goal setting, this check-in process with peer coaches is an important component to ensure the integrity of the process, to reinforce the coach for the work he or she is doing, and to make decisions about whether the coach needs additional training.

Step 9: Running Group Supervision/Case Consultation Sessions for Coaches

In our experience with peer coaches working on social skills, these sessions are quite important in the first few months, when coaches are relatively new to the process. To help focus their attention or jog their memory on key areas, the coach advisor will find it useful to run through a list of typical issues that arise in coaching (e.g., students missing appointments or not completing work they committed to, problems with a particular teacher) as well as any issues the coaches may have, such as needing more specific information about study skills, test-taking strategies, and so on. As noted, if there are recurring concerns about a particular area, it will be helpful to schedule more formal training sessions to address these. This is also an important time to solicit suggestions from coaches about any changes to the coaching protocol based on their experiences. Scheduling these sessions can be difficult for adults and coaches given their other responsibilities, but the success of the program depends on these meetings. Coaches can go to their advisors with immediate problems, but the first of these group meetings should take place in within the initial 2 weeks of the program, with a follow-up 2 to 3 weeks later. After this, monthly or bimonthly meetings should suffice.

Step 10: Evaluating Coaching Effectiveness

The procedures for this section are the same as for adult coaching, and the same Coach Feedback Forms (in Appendix 24) can be used as part of the evaluation process.

The role of the coach coordinator assumes greater importance when working with the peer coach component, primarily because this requires closer support and supervision. In many cases, however, the advantages to using peers as coaches outweigh the disadvantages because they represent an untapped resource. Whereas many high school teachers are stretched thin with demands on their time, students are often looking for meaningful extracurricular activities that will give them a chance to learn new skills and to give back to their school community. Students who see themselves as future teachers as well as those who want to prepare themselves for leadership positions of any kind will benefit from what coaching has to teach them about working collaboratively with others to achieve meaningful goals.

CONCLUSION

This chapter provides two models for setting up a schoolwide coaching program. We fully recognize that this is an effortful and labor-intensive process that requires commitment and perseverance on the part of the individuals who take this on and that benefits from support and encouragement on the part of school administrators. For those readers who are interested in pursuing this model but are not sure they have the skills, time, or expertise, we suggest they ease into it gradually. Taking on a few individual coaching "clients" of their own for practice is the best way to get started. A second preliminary step would be to set up a "study group," ideally for continuing professional development credit, to consider this and possibly other model interventions for meeting the needs of at-risk students. We have known study groups in schools to use our other books on executive skills as the focus for year-long reading and discussion, and we believe this text would be well suited to this approach as well. An outcome of such a group might be to identify a natural coach coordinator as well as teachers interested either in coaching themselves or helping to support the establishment of a peer coaching program.

UNIT III

SPECIAL APPLICATIONS

CHAPTER 6

Classwide Peer Coaching

In classrooms, academic instruction and behavior/social management, along with all other aspects of classroom functioning, are typically teacher mediated. Teachers decide on instructional content and strategies, establish rules and expectations for behavior and social interactions, and act as surrogate frontal lobes for their students. However, there is a substantial body of evidence indicating that peers working with each other can significantly impact academic achievement and instruction, behavior management, and social interactions and can serve as a powerful adjunct to the work of teachers.

The potential power of peer-mediated interventions is particularly evident when one considers the ages and educational levels of the children who have benefited from the various models available. The effectiveness of these interventions has been demonstrated at all grade levels, from kindergarten to high school, and across all ability levels, from children with significant educational handicaps to typically achieving children. These models are versatile in that they can be used to address both individual student needs and classroomwide needs. These interventions are variously known as peer tutoring, peer-mediated interventions, and peer coaching (Brewer, Reid, & Rhine, 2003; Greenwood, Delquadri, & Carta, 1997; Utley, Mortweet, & Greenwood, 1997).

In this chapter, we review the advantages offered by peer coaching, different models that are available, critical features shared by the models, and supporting evidence. We also describe examples for peer coaching of executive skills on an individual and a classwide basis. Later, in Chapter 7, Pamela Plumer describes her adaptation of our original coaching model for use in a peer coaching format to help improve social interactions and behavioral regulation.

ADVANTAGES OF PEER COACHING

At a time when teachers are confronted with ever-increasing expectations and requirements, well-organized peer coaching can free up a teacher for more academic activities, including extra help for students in need, by decreasing management or organizational demands. We also know that timely response monitoring and feedback are critical to learning. In a class of 20–25 children, this is a difficult task for an individual teacher. Peer coaching provides increased individual attention, response monitoring, and immediate feedback. Thus, ongoing and individualized instruction is much more feasible. When each student and the peer play both roles (i.e., coach and coached), learning is reinforced. With classwide coaching, students are continuously serving as models for one another. As students get older, they are more likely to respond to peer than adult feedback. Additional advantages include the following:

- In inclusive classrooms, teachers can address a broad range of learning needs and simultaneously engage all students.
- Collaboration among students enhances positive social interactions.
- Volume of academic responding is significantly increased.
- Mastery and fluency with newly learned material are increased.

MODELS OF PEER COACHING

In peer coaching, two different models are typically described. In the individual model only two students are paired together, whereas in the classwide model all students participate in the process.

Characteristics of individual models include the following:

- There are dyads or, at most, triads of students.
- Assignment can be skill based or random.
- The direction of instruction can be one directional or reciprocal.
- Content and format are typically provided by the teacher, responses are specific and observable, and the degree of structure is controlled.
- Coach presents items or expectations, evaluates peer's performance, and provides feedback and points. Coach may model the response if needed.

As noted in the next chapter, Pamela Plumer describes her peer coaching model, in which one student is coached by a peer. She describes in detail how this procedure operates and, in the particular application that she developed, the target behaviors involved in peer interactions. However, the format of her model can readily be adapted to address other areas, particularly executive skills. She discusses such applications in her chapter, and hence we do not consider individual models any further here, focusing instead on classwide models.

Characteristics of classwide models include the following:

- The class is typically divided into two teams, with each team accumulating points. In most, but not all, examples, the teams compete with one another. However, the prize for the winning team typically involves the opportunity to choose a reward that the whole class can benefit from, such as a class party.
- Students are further divided into dyads or triads, most typically the former.
- Assignment can be random or based on student choice or ability. If assignment is skill based, the stronger student typically leads off in the actual coaching session.

- The direction of instruction or coaching is reciprocal.
- Content and format are initially provided by the teacher. Content and responses are specific and observable, and the degree of structure is controlled.
- In the classwide model designed to address academic areas, the coach presents items or expectations, evaluates the peer's performance, and provides feedback and points. The coach may model the response if needed.

EVIDENCE OF EFFECTIVENESS

In the areas of academic instruction, such as math, reading, and spelling, an Educational Resources Information Center review reported no fewer than 25 studies published in various journals showing classwide peer tutoring as superior to more typical forms of teacher-led instruction in improving the academic outcomes of students (Greenwood, Arreaga-Mayer, Utley, Gavin, & Terry, 2001). Among the most significant evidence is a 12-year longitudinal study by Greenwood and Delquadri (1995), which compared students who did not receive classwide peer tutoring with those who did. The groups involved both at-risk and not-at-risk students. For students in the classwide peer tutoring condition, findings included improved engagement during instruction, improved achievement, reduced numbers of students needing special education, and decreased numbers of students dropping out of school by the end of 11th grade (Greenwood, Maheady, & Delquadri, 2002). Maheady, Mallette, and Harper (2006) note that across all the studies reviewed both students without and students with disabilities demonstrated significant improvements in academic performance as a result of peer-mediated learning.

PEER COACHING AND EXECUTIVE SKILLS

It is evident from the studies just cited that peer tutoring, peer coaching, and peer-mediated instruction, when applied in academic areas such as reading, math, and spelling, can offer significant benefits to students and teachers. Students show impressive achievement gains in these areas, and there are indications that, through the process of coaching one another, students improve their own levels of mastery. Peer coaching provides a level of individual and reciprocal attention that teachers in regular classrooms are not able to provide, and the systematic, ongoing measurement and timely feedback available with these models satisfy an essential condition for effective learning that, like individual teacher attention, is difficult to provide in today's classrooms.

We particularly like the classwide application of these methods because all students are participants and, once learned, the method can be applied to address a number of different objectives. Moreover, relevant to the present book, students become active participants and decision makers in their own learning, which, indirectly at least, facilitates the development of executive skills.

But are there classwide peer coaching approaches that more directly address executive skills? Although not synonymous with executive skills, the capacity for self-regulation or self-management of behavior is dependent on the development of good executive skills. If executive skills such as response inhibition, emotional control, sustained attention, planning, and time management, among others, are weak, then self-regulation or self-management suffers. Conversely, improvements in executive skills in these areas are reflected in improved self-regulation and a decreased need for external monitoring and management. If one of the primary goals of education is to help students become independent and self-sufficient learners, then the ability to manage their own behavior is one key to self-sufficiency (Rafferty, 2010). Imagine independent work time in a classroom where a teacher does not need to routinely prompt students to remain on task, return to their seats, begin their work, or restate task directions. Or imagine an end to the school day where the classroom and individual student areas are organized and students have collected and packed the materials that need to go home, again without constant monitoring and reminding. Teachers monitor and coach students to develop these skills because they are a prerequisite for learning, and to the extent that students learn to self-monitor, teachers can devote more time to teaching and learning rather than to behavior management.

Along with self-monitoring as a component of independent learning in students, a second and equally critical skill is the capacity to set and reach goals. In Chapter 2, we noted the extensive empirical research that supports the value of goal setting in promoting high levels of performance in both adults and children. We also noted that the goals serve four primary purposes:

- They direct behavior (toward task-relevant and away from task-irrelevant behavior).
- They energize.
- They encourage persistence.
- They motivate people to discover and use task-relevant knowledge and skills.

In our work on executive skills, we have identified goal-directed persistence as a central element in the development of executive skills. Throughout childhood, we want children to move beyond what Barkley refers to as context-dependent attention, where behavior is determined by current situational variables, and toward goal-directed persistence, where our current behavior is determined by its relevance to the achievement of a future goal. Although this capacity for goal-directed persistence does not reach its full capacity until we are in our mid-20s, creating the means for children to work on this skill over an extended period of time will enhance their capacity for decision making and self-regulation of behavior, promote achievement of academic, behavioral, and social goals, and aid in the development of executive skills. Using the components of classwide, reciprocal peer coaching and self-monitoring, we believe that the process of goal setting can be introduced and practiced in regular classrooms in early elementary school and that, as a result, children will show an increased development in goal-directed persistence and in the other executive skills needed to achieve a goal.

In helping children to develop executive skills, we have identified seven essential steps:

1. Identify a behavior to be learned or a specific problem behavior to be addressed.
2. Set a goal.
3. Outline the steps that need to be followed to meet that goal.
4. Whenever possible, turn the steps into a list, a checklist, a visual cue such as pictures, or a short set of rules to be followed.
5. Supervise the child as he or she follows the steps.
6. Evaluate the program's success and revise if necessary.
7. Fade the supervision.

It can be seen that, once a behavior to be learned has been identified, goal setting dictates the first step in the process and the reason why other executive skills are brought into play. Thus, planning and prioritization, time management, working memory, sustained attention, and so on, are skills that will be used to help accomplish the goal. When this process is introduced into the classroom and children learn to work with one another on achieving their goals, executive skills develop.

The steps for implementing this model in the classroom include the following:

1. Introduce the idea of goals and goal setting.
   - Define what a goal is and solicit examples from the students.
   - Discuss why people set goals and why this is important.
   - Discuss the process of how to reach a goal, including deciding on the steps and making a plan, and the importance of practice.
   - Discuss time and how long it should take to reach a goal.
   - Discuss reasonable and unreasonable goals and give examples of each.
   - Discuss how students can remember what their goal is and how to keep track of their progress.
2. Introduce the idea of keeping track of and measuring progress toward a goal and the concept of self-monitoring.
   - Give examples of different ways to see the goal and determine progress toward the goal. Use a board game example.
3. Introduce the idea of coaching.
   - Have students give examples of coaching in their lives.
   - Talk about a teacher as a coach.
   - Talk about them working with each other as coaches and solicit examples of how they have done this.
   - Relate coaching to accomplishing a goal.
   - Describe how students will be coaches for each other and give examples.
4. Discuss how goal setting, self-monitoring, and coaching will be carried out on a daily basis and what tools are needed, and give an example modeling it with a student.

In the next section, we outline a model that utilizes self-monitoring and reciprocal peer coaching as a method for learning executive skills and addressing academic, behavioral, or social skills objectives in the regular classroom.

CLASSWIDE PEER COACHING MODEL

In this section, our objective is to present teachers a method that will help children become more self-directed learners over time. Self-directed learning requires self-regulation of behavior, which in turn requires the ability to self-monitor and set goals. And, as we noted previously, the capacity for self-regulation of behavior depends in large part on the development of executive skills. The activities featured here focus on the development of executive skills through self-monitoring and goal setting. Although we understand that teachers play the role of "surrogate frontal lobes" by lending children their executive skills, we also believe that children can develop executive skills through experience and practice in the classroom and thus become more independent, self-directed learners. We also believe that, through reciprocal peer coaching, students can learn these skills through continuous practice, as both coaches and "players" serve as ongoing models for one another.

We have selected two classroom activities to help students learn and practice self-monitoring and goal setting. The first involves a paper-and-pencil task with the aim of increasing automaticity in the retrieval of math facts. All students initially work on a math facts problem sheet for a specific amount of time. Following this, the teacher collects and corrects each paper, establishing a baseline for each student. The teacher briefly meets with students individually and asks them to set a goal for the number of problems they think they can improve on by Friday. This is a student-determined goal for which they will have daily practice time with their coach. The second activity involves coaching and self-monitoring of behaviors during an independent work time in the classroom. The objective is for students to coach each other on and to self-monitor "good independent-work behaviors," that is, behaviors that lead to efficient and accurate completion of independent classwork without constant teaching monitoring. Although this can be a teacher-determined goal, it can also be a student-determined goal by soliciting from the class suggestions about behaviors that are necessary for productive, independent work time. This involves students in the goal-setting process, increases their awareness of what behaviors are important, and, because they have contributed, increases their motivation. The activities and the procedures are designed so that first- or second-grade children can carry them out on a classwide basis.

If teachers so opt, different activities can be chosen (e.g., behavior during morning meeting, clean up personal space and pack up at the end of the day, spelling words instead of math facts). The current examples were chosen for demonstration purposes and because they are procedures that have been successfully implemented, in modified form, in public school classrooms. We encourage teachers and administrators interested in peer coaching and peer tutoring for academic progress to consider the *Together We Can!* program (Greenwood et al., 1997), an excellent resource for implementation of peer tutoring in the classroom. For teachers who want to work on behavior management, we recommend *The Good Student Game* (Babyak, Luze, & Kamps, 2000). We also encourage teachers to modify or design their own scoring sheets and to select behaviors that they want students to work on.

These methods can be readily adapted to older students. As students advance through the grades, their time horizons lengthen. Hence, they may want to have longer term goals. If so, we recommend that teachers work with students to establish subgoals, that they help students create specific plans for achieving these goals, and that students articulate concrete activities or behaviors that will occur daily to enhance progress toward the goal and that these behaviors be monitored and rated both by the student and by peer coaches. These recommendations are based on research and clinical experience with goal setting that indicate the following:

- Goal attainment is more likely with proximal as opposed to distal goals.
- Complex goals are more likely to be achieved when subgoals are specified.
- If the goal is time limited, a timeline and benchmarks are necessary for success.
- Goal attainment is more likely if the activities or behaviors needed to achieve the goal are specific, observable, and measurable.
- Goal attainment is more probable if students make a public commitment to the goal and know that a coach will check on their progress.

Teaching Goal Setting, Reciprocal Coaching, and Self-Monitoring

In each of the following sections, we describe how to implement these procedures in the classroom and indicate the forms and score sheets that will be needed. To introduce goal setting, coaching, and self-monitoring, the teacher engages the class in the following discussion using scripts such as those presented next.

Goal Setting

"This week we're going to talk about goals and goal setting. You all set goals already but you may not know it. When you say, 'When I grow up I want to be . . . ,' that's setting a goal.

"Goals are something people want to get better at or to change. One of my goals might be to learn how to swim. So, if that was my goal, what would I need to do to learn how to swim? Could I do it in this room? ["No!"] What do I need? ["A pool!"] OK, now I'm at the pool. Should I just jump in? ["No!"] Why not? ["Because you can't swim!"] How am I going to learn then? [If no response, teacher can ask,] Do I need someone to help me? ["Yes!"] [If they haven't picked up on the swim attire issue yet, teacher can say,] OK, I'm at the pool and you told me that's where I need to be and that I need someone to help me and my helper or coach is here. I'm standing at the edge of the pool in my jacket, jeans, and sneakers. Can I jump in? ["No!"] Why not? ["Because you don't have your bathing suit on!"]

"OK, so now I have a pool, a bathing suit, and a coach. Now my job is to follow the directions of my coach. Will I learn everything there is to learn in one lesson? ["No!"] During my lesson, my coach is going to tell me some things to do that will get me on my way and I will do them. At the end of the lesson, my coach will tell me what I need to practice before I come to my next lesson and I tell my coach I will do that.

"I go to the pool three times before my next lesson and I practice. If I have friends with me and they know how to swim, I can ask them to watch me and tell me how I look. When I go back for my next lesson, my coach sees that I improved on the things she gave me to practice. What do you think would happen if I didn't do that? Would I get better? ["No!"] Will you get better at anything if you don't practice? ["No!"] So, like we said before, everybody has things that they want to do better. Can you tell me some things you practiced and got better at? [Examples might include bike riding, skateboarding, and swimming].

"School is a place for learning and your goal, and my goal for you, is to learn how to do things like read, spell, do math, pay attention, and listen to directions. This week we're going to work on setting goals and practice how to get to them. We're going to set some goals together as a class and you're going to set some individual goals for yourself."

Reciprocal Coaching

"Today we're going to talk about coaching. Having a coach helps you to improve in lots of different ways, like the other day when we talked about swimming. Coaches can help us to reach our goals. In our classroom, I'm the coach for everybody but because there are 21 of you and only one of me, I need some mini-coaches, and you all will get to be a coach. When you're the coach, you will help your partner reach his or her goal.

- "When you're the coach, you're like me—a teacher.
- "Your partner is the student.
- "When you switch, you become the student and your partner is the coach.
- "Good coaches do these things:
    1. They encourage their student.
    2. They help their student when he or she isn't sure what to do.
    3. They never make fun of or tease the student.
    4. Like teachers, peer coaches rate how their student did in practice.
    5. Coaches always try to be fair and honest when they rate their student's behavior.

"Here's how it will work. Every Monday, each of you will take a number out of this hat. Once you all have a number, we'll begin making partners. The people with the number 1 and the number 2 will be partners, the people with the number 3 and the number 4 will be partners, and so on until everyone has a partner. Partners will be together for the week and will coach each other on the goals we talked about. Partners will write their names together on the chart here. [See Appendix 30, p. 222, for a blank Class Roster for Teams and Coaches.]

"After the names are on the chart, the first five pairs will be the orange team and the next five pairs will be the purple team. Each day I'll announce when the coaching time is going to start. Since you are not always sitting with your partners, when I announce the coaching time one of the partners will need to move to the other. You'll take turns moving. On Monday, the student whose name is first in the partner pair will move to the partner. On Tuesday, the second person in the partner pair will move and so on for the week. Every Monday your partners and teams will change.

"Now, let's talk about teams and what it means to be on a team. Whenever you have teams, one team is going to lose and one is going to . . . ["Win!"] We're going to change the people on the teams every week. Each one of you will be on a team that loses sometimes and one that wins sometimes. The winning team for the week will get to choose what the class treat [e.g., popcorn party, extra recess] is on Friday and both teams will get the treat. Everyone will clap for the effort of the winning team and everyone will clap for the effort of the losing team. Just like good coaches, good teams:

- "Always congratulate each other for trying or working hard.
- "Never make fun of the other team.
- "Never tease team members.
- "Remember that they can win next time if they didn't win today."

Note: The characteristics of good coaches and good teams should be posted in the classroom where all children can see them, and they should be reviewed and read aloud by the students at the beginning of each coaching session.

Coaching Yourself (Self-Monitoring)

"Remember, when you have a goal, something you want to get better at, you practice. Sometimes when you practice, if your coach isn't around, you kind of coach yourself. You kind of talk to yourself, tell yourself whether you think you did a good job or not. To give you some practice being a coach for yourself, you're also going to rate yourself when you're practicing with your coach. Then you and your coach will compare your ratings."

Since the primary objectives in coaching and self-monitoring are accurate appraisals and correspondence between coach and self-ratings, we have adopted an idea from the CWPASM model (Mitchem, Young, West, & Benyo, 2001) that the teacher randomly observes coaching partnerships and if the pair's rating matches the teacher's rating, the pair is awarded a bonus point. In addition, as in the CWPASM and Plumer models, if the ratings do not match, it is the coach's score that is accepted.

Math Goal Setting

To begin the process, the classroom teacher needs to establish a baseline in an academic task for each student, for example, administering a timed test of 100 random addition facts. The directions are to begin when the examiner says "Go" and to stop when the signal is given (5 minutes later). Facts must be done in order from left to right, top to bottom. Upon reviewing the tests, the teacher determines patterns of facts repeatedly missed. Later, when conferencing with students individually, the teacher can review the test with them, complimenting them on the correctly answered facts and then moving to areas of weakness and helping the students set a goal to improve. The teacher then asks the students their estimate of how many more facts they could get correct in a week, and this becomes their goal.

Teacher Demonstration

To introduce the process to a group, the teacher can use whatever group presentation tools are available: SMART Boards, overhead projectors, and so on. The teacher creates a practice sheet of 20 facts and projects it onto a classroom wall before class. He or she then selects a student to assist in this demonstration in class. The assistant will be the "student" and the teacher will be the coach. The teacher explains that the student will have 1 minute to do as many facts as possible, providing exact instructions for the process the student is to follow: name and date on paper; begin at the left, moving across to the right and completing each fact until you arrive at the end of the row; progress to the facts on the next row, until time is up. After asking the student if he or she has any questions about completing the fact sheet, the teacher says "Begin" and starts the timer. At the end of 1 minute, the teacher announces "Time's up," and the coach then corrects the fact sheet, circling errors. The coach compliments the student on correct answers: "Wow! You got 13 correct!" "Great job on the first row!" Next, the coach guides the student through making corrections. For each incorrect response the coach has the student say and write the two addends and the sum, reinforcing the correct response. The coach talks positively with the student as this process continues until corrections have been made. The coach takes out the daily score sheet and rates the student, and then the student rates the coach. (See Appendix 25, p. 217, for a blank Score Sheet for Math Facts Goal) The teacher then asks the class to tell something they saw and asks if they have any questions.

Two-Student Demonstration

After this teacher–student demonstration, two students volunteer to do the same role-play procedure using paper and pencil, with a simple fact sheet prepared in advance. The teacher compliments the student and the coach on correct behaviors (e.g., "I like how you remembered. . . ."). The students switch roles, so they each have a turn to be the student and the coach. The teacher does this with several different pairs, praising the behaviors that he or she wants to see repeated.

Whole-Class Demonstration

In this approach, the teacher selects partners and has them move into place with materials ready. The teacher monitors the room, praising, giving feedback, and reinforcing students for good performances in peer tutoring: "I like how you told Jerry he did a great job." "You did a wonderful job making corrections!" The teacher may award extra bonus points to teams as an incentive to keep up the good work.

Reporting Points/Clean Up

The teacher keeps this step brief. Each team calls out their scores so they can be recorded by the teacher. (See Appendix 30, p. 222, Class Roster for Teams and Coaches.) All materials are returned to their folders. Timers are returned to the basket on the teacher's desk. Students return to their personal seats.

Daily Practice

Each Monday through Thursday, after the math focus lesson, the teacher will indicate that it is time for students to work on their math facts goal. Students will get their math goal folders, which contain four practice sheets (one for each of the first 4 days of the week), scoring sheets, and a pencil. The student who is the mover for that day also gets a timer from the basket on the teacher's desk. From the time the teacher gives the signal to move, students will have 15 minutes to get their materials, time each other for 1 minute, work on corrections, complete their self- and coach ratings, report their scores to the teacher, return all materials, and return to their own seats.

Independent Work Behavior Goal Setting

When beginning to establish protocols for independent work time, the teacher must focus on what behaviors he or she would like to reinforce: listening to/following directions, staying in seat, focus on the job, completion of task. A group discussion is an effective way to involve students and to have them help set the goals.

   1. The teacher begins by saying to the students that his or her job is to teach and their job in school is to learn. The teacher then asks, "What makes it easier for you to get your work done?" Responses may include being quiet, no distractions, and listening. Through questions and examples of situations, the teacher elicits these key behaviors from the class:

  a. Listening/following directions.

  b. Staying in seat.

  c. Focus on the task.

  d. Finish the job.

 2. The teacher explains that students will be coaching each other and monitoring independent work behavior using a score sheet. Prior to outlining these skills, the teacher has first made an overhead projection or readied a SMART Board with a copy of the Score Sheet for Independent Work Time (see Appendix 26, p. 218, for a blank version). A blank score sheet is included in the Appendix). The teacher then explains the basics of record keeping, as follows:

  a. Write names/dates for the peer tutors.

  b. Give descriptors for the coaching jobs—including the rating scale for each job.

  c. Mark the score sheet and add up a total score for each student.

 3. The teacher gives examples and nonexamples of independent work time behavior. The teacher instructs students to give a thumbs-up for examples of good independent work behavior or a thumbs-down for nonexamples.

- *Example:* Mrs. Brown notices Abbi and Kim are getting their work done quietly at their seats. She observes them writing down scores upon completion of their work. They finish by putting their materials away where they belong.
- *Nonexample:* Ms. Lodge speaks to several partners about being out of their seats. These students are visiting with one another, talking about a recent movie they had all seen.

 4. The teacher models independent work behaviors. He or she selects a couple of pairs to role-play situations in which students are supposed to be engaged in coaching. In a low voice, the teacher asks a student to leave her seat or chat with her neighbor. After 2 minutes, the teacher questions the students on what they saw. The class discusses whether they witnessed the desired skill set. The teacher conducts this exercise a few more times until he or she thinks the students understand.

 5. The students practice independent work behaviors. Students pair up and work on independent work with all the necessary materials (including scoring sheets). The teacher mills around the groups, complimenting good independent work behaviors.

- "I like how you listened to the directions."
- "You are doing a great job staying on task."
- "Great job staying in your seat."
- "Thanks for working so quietly."
- "You did a fine job on your scoring sheet."

 6. When this first session is over, the teacher collects the score sheets and praises the positive behaviors he or she witnessed.

Daily Practice

Ideally, the coaching procedure is used during at least one independent work time per day. The teacher signals that an independent work time is about to begin and that coaches should move to their partners. He or she asks one student to review "good independent work behaviors" and then starts a timer for 10–15 minutes. In this case, the partner pairs are simultaneously monitoring each other. The teacher gives out any task directions, asks whether there are any questions, and lets the work time continue until the timer rings. At that point, the teacher directs the students to rate themselves, rate their partners, compare ratings, report the pair's score to the teacher and return to their seats. The teacher records each pair's scores on a class roster (see Appendix 30 for a blank form).

As we have noted, these examples were chosen because similar programs have been successfully implemented in regular classrooms. Additional score sheets for morning meeting (Appendix 27, p. 219) and an end-of-the-day clean-up and pack-up routine (Appendix 28, p. 220), as well as a blank form (Appendix 29, p. 221) that readers can use to adapt these strategies to fit other classroom routines or behaviors of concern are included at the end of the book.

CONCLUSION

Peer-mediated instruction, known also as peer tutoring or peer coaching, has a proven track record for enhancing academic and behavioral outcomes for students in regular classrooms. It allows for increased teacher focus on academics, active engagement and collaboration among all students, and increased academic output and mastery. Studies have demonstrated the superiority of academic outcomes when peer coaching is compared with more traditional methods of teacher-centered instruction.

In this volume, we have focused on coaching as a methodology not only for academic success but also for the development of executive skills. We believe that one of the primary goals in our educational system is, or should be, the development of students as independent, self-directed learners. In order to achieve this, students need well-developed executive skills. As a strategy, classwide peer coaching with a self-monitoring component speaks directly to this outcome by actively involving students in the use of executive skills to achieve academic and behavioral goals on a daily basis. Moreover, this intervention can be introduced at an age when students are just beginning the learning process, thus allowing for practice and mastery over time and in a way that benefits the instructional process for teachers and learner outcomes for students. In this chapter, we have provided a methodology that we hope will help teachers to begin this process and students to enhance their independence and self-direction.

CHAPTER 7

Peer Coaching for Social Skills Development

PAMELA PLUMER

Not only does coaching appear to be an effective strategy for addressing the academic needs of individuals with executive functioning weaknesses, but recent research has provided initial support for its role in addressing the social difficulties for this population as well (Plumer, 2007; Plumer & Stoner, 2005). Specifically, a peer coaching intervention package has been developed as a daily intervention for elementary-age students experiencing social difficulties often associated with executive functioning weaknesses. This chapter provides information about the research supporting the peer coaching intervention as well as details about how to implement the program in a school setting. Finally, the peer coaching manual is included at the end of the chapter for use in schools.

As the authors of this book have previously described, executive functions are necessary not only for academic success but also for developing and maintaining social relationships. Children with executive functioning weaknesses in the areas of response inhibition and emotional control are likely to experience negative social interactions during their school day. "Thinking before acting," maintaining emotional control, and remaining flexible during play are crucial skills for navigating social relationships. Because executive functioning deficits have not been identified as a distinct disorder, most research on executive functioning weaknesses has focused on children with identified disabilities, such as ADHD and autism. Recent studies have illustrated the relationship among executive function weaknesses, ADHD, and social difficulties. For instance, researchers found a significant but modest correlation between early disinhibition in preschool children and later ADHD symptoms and social difficulties in third grade (Gewirtz, Stanton-Chapman, & Reeve, 2009). Miller and Hinshaw (2010) found that measures of early execu-

Pamela Plumer, PhD, is a school psychologist in an elementary school in Northampton, Massachusetts. She also facilitates a support group in which she utilizes coaching strategies in advising graduate students throughout the dissertation process.

tive functioning weaknesses in preadolescent girls predicted social functioning and academic difficulties in adolescence. In a 2008 review of the peer difficulties of children with ADHD, McQuade and Hoza noted that more research examining the relationship between executive functioning and social impairment in children is essential because (1) this area of study has been widely overlooked and (2) the research that does exist is conflicting (Biederman et al., 2004; Clark, Prior, & Kinsella, 2002; Diamantopoulou, Rydell, Thorell, & Bohlin, 2007).

Although more research is needed, there is evidence that weak executive function (e.g., behavioral inhibition) skills interfere with social relationships. Barkley (1997) has stated that difficulty with behavioral inhibition appears to be the main force behind the behavior problems of children with ADHD. These children have difficulty preventing themselves from responding impulsively as well as stopping an ongoing response. These intrusive behaviors often lead to social difficulties, particularly with peers. Children who have difficulty inhibiting their behaviors often interrupt conversations, try to solve problems in an aggressive manner, and have poor conversational skills, which may be related to their difficulty valuing future social consequences over immediate ones (Barkley, 1997). Social problems experienced by children with ADHD have led some researchers to suggest that disturbed peer relations could be considered a defining characteristic of the disorder (Landau, Milich, & Diener, 1998; Landau & Moore, 1991; Whalen & Henker, 1991), while their social impairments have also been described as intervention resistant (Hinshaw, 1992). Children who have difficulties with behavioral inhibition, such as those with ADHD, often experience high levels of peer rejection (Landau et al., 1998). Additionally, some research has found that children with ADHD "were categorized as victims, bullies, and bully/victims significantly more often than were children without ADHD" (Wiener & Mak, 2009, p. 116). Because of the pervasive nature of these social difficulties, intervention methods specifically targeting these problems are needed.

Although numerous interventions exist that successfully address the problem behaviors of children with behavioral inhibition difficulties, most research has focused on academic and behavioral interventions. Most often, when children experience difficulties with social interactions in school, they receive support through social skills training, which often focuses on areas such as cooperation, assertion, responsibility, self-control, and empathy (Elliott & Gresham, 1993). Although social skills training interventions are frequently implemented to improve social functioning, a 2007 review (de Boo & Prins) of six social skills intervention studies found that only four studies (Antshel & Remer, 2003; Frankel, Myatt, Cantwell, & Feinberg, 1997; Miranda & Presentacion, 2000; Pfiffner & McBurnett, 1997) demonstrated positive effects and could be noted as having experimental empirical status. As the authors noted, "A 'well-established' intervention for the serious and persistent social problems in children with ADHD is not available and the development of such an intervention is sorely needed" (de Boo & Prins, 2007, p. 14). A recent study provided initial evidence for improving the social skills of children with ADHD, particularly those with weak pragmatic skills, through the use of a school-based social skills program that included strategies to promote generalization of skills (Corkum, Corbin, & Pike, 2010).

A number of factors limit the use of traditional social skills interventions when working with children with ADHD. Many traditional approaches to social skills interventions fail to match the intervention to the specific type of social skills problem that a student is experiencing (Gresham, 2002). Quite often, interventions are implemented in a "one-size-fits-all," packaged approach without first considering the specific social skills difficulties of the child. Research indicates that the types of social problems exhibited by children with ADHD are likely the result of performance rather than skills deficits (Barkley, 1997; Landau et al., 1998; Loney & Milich, 1982). In regard to social problems of children with ADHD, Barkley (1997) states "the problem, then, for those with ADHD is not one of knowing what to do, but one of doing what they know when it would be most adaptive to do so" (p. 244).

Barkley's statement illustrates a second criticism of social skills training programs: that the interventions fail to take place at the point of performance, an important element when working with children with ADHD (DuPaul & Stoner, 2003). Interventions for children with behavioral inhibition deficits are most effective when they focus on the performance of a particular behavior at the place and time the behavior occurs (DuPaul & Stoner, 2003). Although social skills training programs train children with ADHD to exhibit appropriate social behaviors, this training often occurs distant from the actual point of performance. Interventions that involve intervening at the point of performance are likely to help children with ADHD enhance social skills performance. Also, when intervening at the point of performance, interventions occur in naturalistic environments, such as playgrounds, in contrast to many social skills training programs that take place in small, pull-out groups.

Students who have social problems with their peers often experience these negative interactions during unstructured free-time activities, when teacher involvement is less available, which makes point-of-performance intervention difficult. When considering how to intervene during times such as recess, one method that has been successful uses peer involvement. In a review of peer-mediated social skills interventions, Elliott and Gresham (1993) found that using peers as intervention agents is cost effective because it minimizes the amount of time an adult needs to be working with the target student. Successful peer-based interventions have been documented for decades (Mathur & Rutherford, 1991). Using peers as intervention agents increases the possibility of intervening at the point of performance for children experiencing social problems. Additionally, using peers instead of adults as intervention agents for social problems is a naturalistic strategy. A student working with his or her peers to address specific problems during social activities is a more subtle approach to a school-based intervention than having the student work with an adult during unstructured, free time. Peers have been successfully used as intervention agents when working with children with ADHD in several school-based studies (Broussard & Northup, 1997; DuPaul, Ervin, Hook, & McGoey, 1998; DuPaul & Henningson, 1993; Mitchem et al., 2001; Rutherford, DuPaul, & Jittendra, 2008). Directly addressing the social problems of children with ADHD, Hoza, Mrug, Pelham, Greiner, and Gnagy (2003) found initial positive results of an intervention for improving the friendships of school-age children with ADHD using peer "buddies" as part of a summer program. Interventions that use peers as intervention agents in schools are highly desirable because they address the problems of time demands and lack of resources that currently exist in many school systems.

AN ALTERNATIVE SCHOOL-BASED INTERVENTION: PEER COACHING

Plumer and Stoner (2005) developed a peer-based intervention specifically to address the research gaps in school-based, naturalistic interventions for the social problems of children with ADHD. In a pilot study, the authors investigated the effects of a peer coaching package in combination with classwide peer tutoring (CWPT; Greenwood et al., 1997) on the peer social behaviors of students with ADHD. On the basis of the accurate prediction that generalized results of CWPT alone were not likely because CWPT is primarily an academic intervention, the authors included a peer coaching intervention combined with CWPT and investigated the effects of the combined interventions. The peer coaching intervention included correspondence training, contingent rewards for desired behaviors, and self-monitoring, and was based on the work of Dawson and Guare's (1998) first coaching manual. The intervention addresses the three key issues discussed previously. First, the intervention was individualized and specifically targeted the social behaviors the students were experiencing. Second, it occurred at the point of performance during times when there was little teacher involvement. Third, the intervention involved a peer coach as part of the process. Plumer and Stoner's peer coaching intervention is discussed in greater detail later in this chapter. Briefly, however, the intervention involved a pair of students (one peer coach and one focus student with ADHD) setting a daily social goal for the focus student. The peer coach then observed the focus student's behavior while the focus student attempted to achieve his or her goal during unstructured free time, such as recess. The students then met after the goal was attempted in order to rate the focus student's behaviors. Both students received rewards based on their weekly performance, and the entire process was supervised by an adult participant, who conducted weekly meetings with the peer coaching pair.

In the Plumer and Stoner (2005) pilot study, a multiple-baseline across-subjects design was implemented with three students in grades 3 and 4. Results of direct observations of positive peer social behaviors suggested the peer coaching package was a promising intervention for addressing peer social problems of children with ADHD. However, conclusions about the effectiveness of peer coaching could not be determined because the intervention was combined with CWPT. Further research was then conducted to determine the effects of the peer coaching intervention by itself on the positive social behaviors of children with ADHD (Plumer, 2007). A single-subject, ABAB design was used with three elementary-age students in grades 3 and 5. Results suggested that the peer coaching package led to improvements in positive social behaviors during recess for two of the three students.

Peer coaching has been implemented not only with individual peer coaching pairs but in a group format as well, with the coaching procedures utilized as a way to generalize social skill strategies taught in weekly groups. Up to this point, nine peer coaching pairs have participated in the peer coaching activities, and all participants, including the adults involved, have indicated that the peer coaching activities are considered socially valid. Additionally, the adults found the intervention to be cost-efficient. Teachers and students appreciated that the intervention took little time to implement throughout the day and yet seemed to produce positive results.

The rest of this chapter describes the peer coaching intervention in detail, including suggestions for implementation in schools. Although the research supporting peer coaching has focused on children with ADHD, the intervention appears to be useful in elementary-age children with weak executive functioning skills, particularly behavioral inhibition, that appear to be interfering with their social relationships.

WHAT DOES PEER COACHING INVOLVE?

In basic terms, peer coaching involves a team of two students—one the coach and one the focus student—who meet each morning to set daily social goals for the focus student. These goals are recorded on the Daily Goal Form (Appendix 33, p. 225). Guided by the laminated reminders of the peer coaching steps, which are kept in their desks, the peer coach reminds the focus student of his or her goal before the period in which the goal is to be achieved. Ideally, many goals take place during unstructured times such as recess or lunch. During that period, the focus student works on his or her goal while the peer coach checks in to see how the focus student is doing. At the end of the period, the students get together and rate how they think the focus student did in achieving his or her goal. The peer coaching process is overseen by an adult supervisor, who checks in with the students at least once per week. At the end of each week, the students meet with the adult supervisor to discuss what occurred during the week and plan for the next week. They also receive rewards based on their weekly performance. Up to this point, all peer coaching pairs have been in grades 3 through 5, with success experienced at each of those grade levels.

WHO MIGHT BENEFIT FROM PEER COACHING?

All students who have thus far participated in peer coaching have been children who have experienced difficulties in the area of behavioral inhibition as well as social difficulties. Some have often engaged in disagreements during unstructured free-play times, while others have been socially ostracized partly because of their lack of behavioral inhibition. Children who are good candidates for peer coaching are those with whom other children can work successfully. Although peer coaching involves an adult supervisor, many of the steps are conducted by the peer pair only. Children who are frequently oppositional may not be appropriate candidates for a focus student because the best interests of the peer coach are also a responsibility. As Dawson and Guare have indicated, it is crucial that the student chosen for coaching is a willing participant. The following is a list of characteristics of children who may benefit from the peer coaching intervention.

- A child who plays basketball at recess and has a difficult time controlling his or her temper when fouled. A goal may include remaining calm when fouled.
- A child who tends to interrupt conversations when he or she becomes excited. A goal may be to participate in conversations without interrupting.
- A child may chase other students around the playground without them wanting to be chased. A goal could be to chase only those children who want to play chase.
- A child often argues with another child during unstructured times such as recess. A goal could be to avoid arguing with that particular child.
- A child sometimes has a difficult time choosing an activity and sticking with it. The goal could be to choose a specific activity ahead of time.
- A child is feeling like he or she is not liked by many children and is trying to find someone to play with at recess. A goal could be for the student to establish recess plans with specific children before going to recess.

The intervention is intended to be quite flexible and individualized to the needs of the focus student. Therefore, the intervention should address specific difficulties the focus student is experiencing, particularly at times when teacher attention is limited.

WHO WOULD MAKE AN IDEAL PEER COACH?

Because peer coaching is intended to be implemented during unstructured times, choosing an appropriate peer coach is crucial to the success of the intervention. The most important factor that both children in the coaching pair should understand is that the peer coach is on the focus student's side, like a coach and a teammate. As can be explained to the participants, with this intervention the focus student has an extra set of eyes and ears (the peer coach) to help in achieving his or her goals.

The adults working with the focus student should choose an appropriate peer coach, a student who often demonstrates appropriate behaviors inside and outside of school. The peer coach should be tolerant and not afraid to take a stand when he or she sees others being treated unfairly. When first learning about the peer coaching activities, some teachers have voiced concern that the peer coach may take advantage of his or her position and act more like a boss and less of a teammate. To date, this has not been a problem. Not one student has complained that his or her peer coach was behaving in an overly assertive manner.

Another concern when using peers as intervention agents is that the peer coach may feel overloaded with responsibility, or may feel peer pressure as a result of spending time with a socially undesirable student. These outcomes have not been encountered up to this point. In contrast, an interesting anecdotal result was revealed from one peer coaching pair when the focus student stated that "everyone" wanted to be his peer coach, providing further evidence that the activities were viewed positively by both participants as well as their classmates.

Throughout all of the trials of peer coaching thus far, teachers have chosen appropriate peer coaches to participate in the activities. Once a potential peer coach has been identified, the adult supervisor should speak with the focus student and family to make sure they approve of the recommended peer coach and with the potential peer coach and family to obtain permission to participate. Once approval is obtained, the supervisor should then communicate with the families of both participants to ensure that everyone understands the nature and goals of the intervention.

Because the students need to speak to each other at least three times throughout the day (once to set the goal, once as the goal is about to be attempted, and once to rate the focus student's performance), it is often easier for them to be from the same class. However, it is possible for children to have coaches outside of their classrooms if they participate in classes/social activities together in which the target behaviors can be observed. For instance, Tommy, a third-grade student, set goals that take place during recess, which is for both third- and fourth-grade students. Tommy could thus have a peer coach from fourth grade, as long as their teachers provide time for them to meet at the beginning of the day, before recess, and directly after recess. Up to this point, peer coaching as described in this chapter has involved peer coaching pairs from the same classrooms.

DO THE FOCUS STUDENT
AND THE PEER COACH HAVE TO BE FRIENDS?

Although the coach should be a friendly, compassionate, and kind individual, it is not necessary that the children have considered each other as "friends" before the intervention. However, it is important that they are "friendly" with each other. In some cases, the students have participated in the intervention in a straightforward manner, interacting when needed but largely maintaining separate social lives. In contrast, there have been some pairs in which the focus student has been included in the social circle of the peer coach, and the students became closer friends throughout the experience. The purpose of the intervention is not necessarily to forge a friendship between the peer coach and the focus student, but it certainly would be a welcomed side effect.

HOW MUCH "COACHING" IS THE RESPONSIBILITY OF THE PEER COACH?

Peer coaches in this model function differently than coaches in the model described by Dawson and Guare. As elementary school children, peer coaches are not expected to regularly develop ideas on their own without adult support. The adult supervisor plays a major role in the coaching process and is largely responsible for presenting information and suggestions to the coaching pair. Additionally, the adult supervisor should help the students understand the link between the focus student's daily behavior and long-term social goals. While the supervisor often provides suggestions for how the focus student could behave in order to reach his or her goals, the peer coach can also provide suggestions and guidance before or during social situations. However, the peer's main responsibility is to remind the focus student of his or her goal and provide positive reinforcement. The peer coach is not expected to teach specific skills or provide instruction beyond what is reasonable for elementary-age children. The peer coach is there to support the focus student at the point of performance, and the adult supervisor is also there to help guide the coaching process. With that said, there have been some very successful peer coaching pairs, particularly among older elementary students, in which the peer coach was quite capable of providing suggestions and support to his or her partner.

WHAT IS THE ROLE OF THE ADULTS IN THIS PROCESS?

A strength of the peer coaching intervention is that it occurs in the moment, or close to the point of performance in real-life social situations. The intervention also includes a method for providing social skills training or practice through working with an adult supervising the process. The adult supervisor is a critical component of the peer coaching intervention. One could even consider that the intervention includes two coaches: the peer coach and the adult supervisor. While a benefit of the peer coaching package is that it involves students working together during times when teachers are less present, an adult must be closely involved with this process. The role of the adult supervisor is to check in with the students, perform treatment integrity checks (see Appendix 39, p. 231, for a useful guideline), and lead weekly meetings. The supervisor is responsible for working with the students' teachers to determine reasonable rewards that are provided once per week. Quite often, these rewards are provided in the classroom. The supervisor could be a counselor, psychologist, principal, paraprofessional, or any other school staff member who is able to check in with the students on a regular basis.

At the conclusion of each week, the supervisor meets with the peer coaching pairs to discuss their scores for the week and deliver possible rewards. At that time, the supervisor also completes letters to the families of both the focus student and the peer coach to inform them of their children's weekly performance. The supervisor can also perform a treatment integrity check to ensure the intervention is being implemented as planned. The meetings typically last 20–30 minutes and are often conducted during nonacademic times, such as lunch. It is preferable that the weeks of the intervention run Monday to Friday, but school schedules are difficult to arrange and sometimes weeks have ranged from Tuesday to Tuesday, for example. During these weekly meetings, the supervisor can provide examples for goals for the week and lead a discussion about problems the focus student encountered during the week. Ideally, the supervisor will come to know the students well and will have a good understanding of the difficulties experienced by the focus student. The adult supervisor's role of meeting with the students, performing random treatment integrity checks to ensure the students are following the procedures, and helping to coordinate rewards should take about 30–45 minutes per week.

The teacher's role in the peer coaching process is first to select an appropriate peer coach. Second, he or she must view the peer coaching process as an important part of the students' day and help dedicate about 5–10 minutes per day for the activities. The teacher also can help provide time for rewards to be administered.

WHAT DOES THE TRAINING INVOLVE?

Prior to the implementation of peer coaching, the supervisor meets with each peer coach–focus student pair to conduct the training procedures, which can be found in the manual. The training typically last 45 minutes to 1 hour and can be conducted in one or two sessions. A three-ring binder with the materials provided in the manual is provided to the student participants, and can be kept in a private area of the focus student's classroom. The supervisor informs the students that even though the focus student was chosen to participate in this study as the student with goals, everyone—including the supervisor and peer coach—experiences problems in various areas. Once the purpose of the intervention has been discussed, the students then practice the activities, including developing goals and rating sample performances.

HOW ARE GOALS CHOSEN?

As seen in the following manual, the peer coaching pair can choose daily social goals but are expected to participate in this process with adult supervision. The students spend time talking with the supervisor about appropriate goals. To open this discussion, it is often helpful to have the focus student think of his or her own goals. The peer coach and the supervisor may also make suggestions, although the focus student ultimately needs to agree to the list of suggested goals. The students record the suggested goals and keep a copy in their binder so they can refer to it during the week. They can choose a different goal each day or choose the same goal on multiple days if the focus student is having a difficult time meeting it. However, once a goal has been achieved, it should not be repeated too often. The adult supervisor should help ensure the students are choosing appropriate goals. Because the purpose of the intervention

reward basket. The adult supervisor should determine whether the focus student is able to wait 1 week until he or she receives a reward for his or her performance. Some children may need rewards more frequently, whereas for others the rewards may be faded over time. Ideally, the focus student will depend less on the reward as a motivator over time, and the motivation will become more intrinsic.

CAN THE INTERVENTION BE APPLIED TO A GROUP FORMAT?

The peer coaching is intended as an individualized intervention; however, this process has also been successful when implemented in a group format. A school counselor may have a group of students working on social skills and behavioral inhibition. The counselor could implement a particular program and focus on specific skills. As a variation on a typical social skills group, the group could include two or three peer coaching pairs. The students could then practice their skills in the group, and the weekly peer coaching goals could focus on the skills learned that week. This group format has been successful with a group of elementary-age students experiencing difficulties with behavioral inhibition and their typically functioning peer coaching partners.

Variations of this intervention could also be successful if introduced in a universal manner. One message emphasized in the peer coaching intervention is that everyone could use support in some area of his or her life. One child may need help controlling his temper during a football game at recess, another student may need help remembering to raise his hand before speaking in class, and another student may need help remembering to check her punctuation before handing in a writing assignment. A teacher could choose to have every student in his or her class participate in the coaching process. Every student could have a partner, and the students could rate each other. A goal of the peer coaching process is for students to become comfortable with the idea of helping each other in a variety of ways with limited adult support. Therefore, universal implementation of similar strategies would be a way to encourage students to work together and support each other.

HOW TO EVALUATE
WHETHER THE INTERVENTION IS SUCCESSFUL

Determining social growth is challenging to measure, particularly during a busy school day with limited resources. Studies of peer coaching have used direct observations of positive social behaviors with the Peer Social Behavior Code of the Systematic Screening for Behavior Disorders (Walker & Severson, 1992), but conducting the observations requires a significant amount of time and resources. Although direct observations during unstructured times such as recess are preferred, rating scales can also be utilized, such as the Social Skills Improvement System Rating Scales (Gresham & Elliot, 2008) or the School Social Behavior Scales, Second Edition (Merrell, 2002). Teacher and student interviews are helpful in judging the efficacy of the intervention. Adults implementing the intervention may also wish to include peer sociometric status ratings for the student participants. The adult supervisor should complete treatment integrity checks (see Appendix 39) in order to determine whether the intervention is being implemented as intended. At the very least, the adult supervisor should be able to note whether the focus student's weekly score is improving over time.

FINAL NOTES

When determining whether an intervention is worthwhile, it is important to consider the potential benefits in comparison to the amount of time and effort required to produce those results. Based on the initial research of peer coaching thus far, it appears that the potential positive results are worth the time and effort. All of the adult and children participants in peer coaching have found the intervention to be socially valid. Further research should continue to investigate the effects of peer coaching on the social interactions of children with executive functioning weaknesses; but current research provides initial support for its implementation in schools for children experiencing social difficulties.

The following manual is provided to school professionals for their personal use. The forms referred to in the manual can be found in the appendices. The manual can be used during the training process, and the forms can be used throughout the peer coaching process.

PEER COACHING MANUAL

Introduction to the Peer Coaching Process

Peer coaching is a process that was developed in order to have students help each other achieve goals in school. Sometimes students have a difficult time getting along with their peers or staying on task throughout the day. It is difficult for teachers to constantly monitor their students' social behavior, whether in class or especially during free-time activities, like recess or lunch, when less supervised social interactions are likely to occur. Some students could benefit from a peer helping them pay attention to how they are getting along with their peers. With peer coaching, two students from the same classroom work—one the coach, the other the focus student—together during the day. The peer coach and the focus student pick a daily goal at the beginning of each day, and the peer coach helps the student to achieve that goal. By providing reminders and feedback, and watching to make sure goals are achieved, the peer coach acts as an extra helper so the student can achieve his or her goal. At the end of the week, if the student has done well in achieving the established daily goals, he or she receives a reward for the hard work. The peer coach also receives a reward for helping the student throughout the week. While the two students work alone most of the week, they will have an adult supervisor working with them and helping them with the different steps of the process.

Participants

Peer coaching involves three key participants: the peer coach, the student working toward daily goals (focus student), and the adult supervisor. The peer coach and the focus student are both chosen by the classroom teacher. It is very important that both students agree to participate and are interested in the peer coaching process.

Adult Supervisor

The adult supervisor is responsible for training the students in the peer coaching process, and works with the students every week to make sure the process is working well. The supervisor does not have to be the teacher in the students' classroom.

Student Working toward Daily Goals

The student working toward daily goals, or focus student, is chosen because he or she is having difficulty getting along with peers at school. The goal of peer coaching is to increase the number of positive social interactions and decrease the number of negative social interactions that the student has throughout the day. The student's goal is to monitor his or her own behavior in order to earn a reward each week, and the peer coach is there to provide support and help the student achieve these goals.

Peer Coach

The peer coach is a student who gets along well with the students in his or her class and will work well with the focus student in the peer coaching process. The peer coach is seen as responsible and reliable by his or her teacher. The peer coach should also be enthusiastic and positive about the coaching process and interested in helping the focus student to succeed. The role of the peer coach is to help the focus student set social goals and to provide regular feedback. The peer coach and focus student check in with each other on a daily basis to guide success.

Training

The first step in the training process is a meeting between the supervisor and students, which will last approximately 1 hour. In this meeting, the supervisor discusses the information presented previously and provides students with the peer coaching binder, which contains the process information and other materials they will need.

The students also are informed that the supervisor is available any time during the week for any help they may need. Also, they will choose another adult whom they can contact for help if the supervisor is not available. It is the supervisor's responsibility to inform the students' teachers about what they will be doing.

After the training, the students will start the peer coaching process in their classroom. On the first day, the supervisor is present to help with all of the steps. Thereafter, only the two students are involved. The supervisor meets with the students together once a week to assess how the process is working, discuss social goals, and administer rewards. The supervisor should also occasionally observe the students throughout the week to ensure that peer coaching is going well.

Introduction to Peer Coaching

At the beginning of the training session, the supervisor provides the students with an introduction to peer coaching and explains the roles of the different participants. The supervisor should emphasize that the focus student and the peer coach will be working *together*, and the role of the peer coach is not to tell the student what to do. Rather, they are to work together to devise goals, and the peer coach is there to remind the student of the goal and provide positive feedback throughout the day.

Determining Daily Goals

After introducing the process and discussing the roles, the supervisor helps the students establish some initial daily goals that are appropriate for the student.

> *Example of a daily goal:*
> Sam sometimes has a hard time getting along with Colby during recess. They get into arguments, especially during basketball. Sam's daily goal is to invite Colby to play on his basketball team during recess and not argue with him during the period.

The initial list of sample daily goals is included on the Sample Goal Form (see Appendix 38, p. 229) in the binder.

Directions for the Peer Coaching Process

The forms that accompany this manual describe the peer coaching process for both students. The peer coach's form is called Peer Coaching Steps for the Peer Coach (Appendix 31, p. 223), and the form for the student working toward a daily goal is called Student's Daily Goal Steps (Appendix 32, p. 224). Laminated copies of these forms are kept in the students' desks. Copies are also included in the peer coaching binder. Both students use the Daily Goal Form (Appendix 33, p. 225).

At the beginning of the day, the two students meet to decide on a daily goal. They then write the daily goal on the top of the Daily Goal Form in the peer coaching binder. At the beginning of the period when the goal is to be achieved, the peer coach looks at the Daily Goal Form with the student and reminds him or her of the goal. During that period, the peer coach again reminds the student of the goal, and lets the student know whether he or she is doing a good job trying to achieve the goal. At the end of the period, the students complete the rating section of the Daily Goal Form. The peer coach circles his or her score first and covers the answer. The student then circles his or her rating.

Rating System

As indicated on the Daily Goal Form, 4 points is considered honors; 3 points, satisfactory; 2 points, needs improvement; and 1 point, unsatisfactory. The following are definitions for the categories:

- Honors
  - The target student does not experience any difficulties reaching his or her goal.
- Satisfactory
  - The student has one or two minor difficulties reaching his or her goal. Minor difficul-

ties include arguing with a peer or breaking a rule of a group game, as it relates to the daily goal.

- o The student may receive one or two warnings from the supervising teacher or feedback from his or her peer coach.
- o The student quickly displays appropriate behavior following the warnings or feedback.
- Needs improvement
  - o The target student has several (three or more) problems working toward his or her goal (including arguing with peers or breaking rules of games, as they relate to the daily goal).
  - o The student may receive several warnings from the supervising teacher about his or her behavior or feedback from the peer coach, and he or she quickly displays appropriate behavior following the warnings or feedback.
- Unsatisfactory
  - o The student has three or more problems working toward his or her goal. Any serious rule violations relating to the daily goal, such as hitting another student, would result in an unsatisfactory score.
  - o The student's behavior *does not change* in response to teacher warnings or feedback from the peer coach.

If the scores are within 1 point of each other, the student receives the peer coach's score for his or her "points for the day." If both students circle the same number, a bonus point gets added to the score they circled. If their scores are 2 or more points from each other, the student receives a score of 1 for that day. The students then record the points for the day, transfer this information to the Weekly Goal Table (Appendix 35, p. 227), and close the binder.

Rewards

At the end of each week of peer coaching, the students may earn rewards for their performance. Both students receive a reward if the focus student earned a certain point average throughout the week. The students compile a list of three possible weekly rewards and complete the Reward Menu (Appendix 34, p. 226) during the training session. The weekly scores are based on the average score for the week, rounded to one decimal place. The point ranges are the following: Reward 3: average of 3.0–3.9 points; Reward 2: average of 4.0–4.9 points; Reward 1: 5 points. The Reward Menu is completed during the training and finalized once the students' teachers approve of the rewards.

During the peer coaching process, at the end of the week, the students calculate their average score for the week on the Weekly Goal Table. The supervisor may help the students calculate this score if necessary. Once the students determine which reward they have earned, they show the supervisor the average score and indicate which goal they have achieved. The supervisor completes the information on the Letter to Family . . . forms (Appendix 36, p. 228, and Appendix 37, p. 229) and sends the letters home with the students at the end of the week. The supervisor works with the students and their teachers to ensure that the reward is delivered each week as earned.

Practice Exercises

Once the roles and the steps of the intervention have been explained to the peer coach and focus students, and they have compiled a list of social goals and have completed the Sample Goal form and the Reward Menu, they practice the peer coaching steps. They use social goals that were generated for the Sample Goal Form and complete the Daily Goal Form. The supervisor provides students with sample scores, and they then determine the number of points earned for each day. They also practice calculating the average score for the week. The supervisor asks them questions about the steps of the process for each sample goal. When they are able to provide the correct steps, complete a Daily Goal Form, and transfer the score to the Weekly Goal Table without mistakes, the training is concluded.

CHAPTER 8

Parting Thoughts

Let's step back and take a longer view of the coaching process. We have used a variety of terms to describe what and how coaching helps young people develop. We've talked about coaching as a strategy for helping students learn *self-management* and *self-regulation* and for empowering them to become *self-regulated learners*. The tools we teach them to use include *self-monitoring, self-instruction, self-talk*, and *self-evaluation*.

But the culmination of coaching coincides with the end goal of effective education in general: to enable students to achieve the broader independence or autonomy that they will need to function successfully in their world beyond high school. This ability to function autonomously is called *self-determination*. An accepted definition of self-determination is as follows:

> Self-determination is a combination of skills, knowledge and beliefs that enable a person to engage in goal-directed, self-regulated, autonomous behavior. An understanding of one's strengths and limitations together with a belief in oneself as capable and effective are essential to self-determination. When acting on the basis of these skills and attitudes, individuals have greater ability to take control of their lives and assume the role of successful adults in our society. (Field, Martin, Miller, Ward, & Wehmeyer, 1998, p. 2)

Coaching, as we have described it in this text, has the potential to foster self-determination in students. Although the process may focus on setting goals and making daily plans to achieve those goals, good coaches are going well beyond teaching goal setting and planning. They are helping students understand themselves. This occurs through (1) the structured interviews coaches conduct with students at the beginning of the process to help identify long-term goals and areas of academic challenge and (2) the surveys and questionnaires students complete as they progress through coaching. But it also occurs through coaches' ongoing interactions with students as the coaching process unfolds. By helping students problem solve, by giving them a means to gather data to assess progress, by acting as cheerleaders as they begin to experience success, and by reflecting with them on what it took for them to be successful, coaches are helping to instill self-confidence, positive attitudes, and a sense of personal efficacy that will propel students forward onto the path they choose for themselves once coaching ends.

We have cited quantitative studies that document coaching effectiveness in the short term as a strategy to improve grades, increase homework completion and accuracy rates, and address social skill weaknesses. Qualitative studies, however, provide the most compelling evidence of the effectiveness of coaching in helping students achieve self-determination. Parker and Boutelle (2009) interviewed a group of college students who had worked with coaches over a number of semesters and who scored high on an objective measure of self-determination. They identified key themes emerging from these interviews that answered three critical research questions:

1. Why do students engage and disengage from coaching?
2. How do students define coaching compared with other services?
3. What are student perceptions of the benefits and limitations of coaching?

The student responses to these questions are so congruent with our own experiences that we feel compelled to summarize their findings here. (Readers are encouraged to read the article for a more comprehensive understanding.)

REASONS FOR BEGINNING AND ENDING COACHING

Students reported that they believed coaching could help them achieve greater academic success, and they focused on executive skills in particular as in need of improvement. Several identified time management as a key skill they wanted to work on, while another pursued coaching to improve organizational skills. Students also indicated that coaching helped them achieve meaningful goals and cited this as a reason to continue with the process.

Supporting our coaching model goals, students indicated that they discontinued coaching when they felt they had begun to internalize the process. One student commented, "I guess after three semesters of coaching, you're sort of at a point when going to the coach isn't hopefully all that necessary because you already know what it is you need to be doing and you should be working . . . " (p. 208).

COMPARING COACHING WITH OTHER SERVICES

The students in Parker and Boutelle's study distinguished coaching from other supports and services in a number of ways. They described it as highly personalized because coaches quickly came to understand the students they were coaching and the strategies that worked best for them. They also focused on how coaches encourage decision making and problem solving over offering directives or advice. The authors noted, "Unlike didactic models such as tutoring or strategy instruction, coaches' use of questioning techniques elicited goals, plans and strategies *from* the students. Students reported that coaches posed questions to activate their executive function skills" (p. 210). In contrast to other services these students received in the past, they "described coaching as a collaborative relationship in which they worked with their coaches as active, equal partners to determine the goals and outcomes of the coaching work." They also discussed how, through coaching, they were able to generalize the goal attainment skills they were learning to other nonacademic aspects of their lives. Finally, they were now using "self-talk" to begin to coach themselves. One student said, "'Well, now there's sort of this nagging voice in my head . . . it's a voice that's just reminding me, Charles, you need to do this other stuff . . . and Charles, stop that'" (p. 211).

BENEFITS AND LIMITATIONS OF COACHING

The students in Parker and Boutelle's study identified a number of benefits of coaching that clearly will produce long-lasting change. They described coaching as a process to help them "clarify and accomplish academic and life goals, develop more accurate and positive degrees of self-awareness, and experience a better quality of life" (p. 211). The self-awareness included improving their "understanding of how they achieved goals, beginning with a recognition and acceptance of the executive function challenges they faced when pursuing those goals" (p. 211). Finally, they reported attitude changes, including the ability to reduce stress, improve relationships with others, and experience the increased confidence that comes with goal attainment.

Students' descriptions of limitations to the coaching process tended to be somewhat idiosyncratic. One student reported that a deepening depression, which she was addressing with a therapist, prevented her from attending coaching sessions, while another reported forgetting some sessions. A third complained that the process did not produce results fast enough. Others felt the goal-setting aspect was difficult because they weren't ready to set goals for themselves, and one expressed frustration that coaching was less didactic than he wanted.

We recognize that, while this article featured college students, our manual focuses more on adolescents and teenagers in elementary, middle, and high school settings. Nonetheless, it seems fitting to conclude this text by giving voice to students who have experienced coaching. By making coaching available in one or more of the forms we describe here to children below the college level, we believe students can be better prepared for college or whatever life goals they set for themselves after high school graduation. With this book, we extend an invitation to dedicated professionals working in schools and clinics to bring coaching to a wider audience of young people. Yes, executive skills take time to develop. However, with assistance from skilled and knowing coaches, we believe those skills can become habits of mind that will serve students well as they pursue their life goals no matter when the process begins.

PRACTICE EXERCISES

MODULE I: COMMUNICATION SKILLS

Exercise 1. Paraphrasing

Read the statements below and then write a reasonable paraphrase. Remember: The paraphrase should capture the information as briefly as possible using different words. Suggested responses are included at the end of the chapter so that you can compare your answers with a model.

1A

STUDENT: I was all set to do my homework last night following the schedule we made out, and then my friend Suzy texted me that she thought her boyfriend was breaking up with her, and so, of course, I had to call her, and we ended up spending about 45 minutes talking about it. I couldn't let her deal with that by herself!

Paraphrase: _____

_____

_____

1B

STUDENT: I'm supposed to go to my wrestling practice right after school, but Mr. Chase is holding a study session for my economics midterm exam. I'm not doing well in that class and I feel like I really need to go to that session, but my wrestling coach will kill me for missing a practice.

Paraphrase: _____

_____

_____

On-the-Job Practice

Try out paraphrasing in "the real world"—either on the job or with family members. How did it work? Was it easy or difficult? What is the most difficult aspect of paraphrasing?

_____

_____

_____

_____

Exercise 2. Reflective Listening

Read the following student statements and then write a good "reflective listening" response—remember to focus on the *feelings* the student is expressing and pick out the most important ones. Suggested responses can be found at the end of the chapter.

2A

STUDENT: I am *so* backed up! I kept putting off my English paper, and I have two tests to study for. And then my mom went and volunteered me to babysit for my little cousins. That's going to take up the whole day on Saturday, and I really can't afford to give up that much time!

Response: _____

_____

_____

2B

STUDENT: My soccer coach never plays me. I go to every single practice and I work really hard. If I'm lucky, he'll put me in for 2 minutes at the end of the game if our team is ahead and he knows we're going to win. It's not like we're a professional team—it's even JV soccer! [*Note:* This is not an academically relevant comment, but when students form relationships with academic coaches, they often bring up other topics. It is obvious that this student is preoccupied with this event. By reflecting his feelings, the student may be able to move on from that experience and focus on the coaching session.]

Response: _____

_____

_____

On-the-Job Practice

Try out paraphrasing in "the real world"—either on the job or with family members. How did it work? Was it easy or difficult? What is the most difficult aspect of reflective listening?

_____

_____

_____

_____

Exercise 3. Open-Ended and Closed-Ended Questions

Answer the following questions to show an understanding of the uses of open- and closed-ended questions in the coaching process.

3A

In what situations would a coach use open-ended questions? _____

_____

_____

3B

In what situations would a coach use closed-ended questions? _____

_____

_____

3C

Write two examples of open-ended questions:

_____

_____

3D

Write two examples of closed-ended questions:

_____

_____

On-the-Job Practice

Practice using open- and closed-ended questions either on the job or with family members. List your questions below. Did you feel you used the right kind of questions in these situations? Explain why.

_____

_____

_____

_____

_____

_____

_____

Exercise 4. Scaffolding

4A

After reading the scaffolding scenario below, use the following list to check off which strategies the coach used in working with the student. Underline where the activity appears in the dialogue and label it with the first letter of the activity (indicated in **boldface** in the list).

Scaffolding activity	Coach used this strategy
Enhance the student's interest in the task	
Simplify the task (reduce steps, make them more explicit)	
Provide direction	
Indicate discrepancies between the student's work and the desired product	
Reduce frustration and risk	
Give feedback	
Assist internalization/generalization	

STUDENT: My science assignment is to write about some technological innovation from the last 15 years that has changed my life. I don't have a clue about how to do this.

COACH: What do you think the first step is?

STUDENT: First, I have to decide what to write about. I use a ton of technology, but I don't know which ones were invented in the last 15 years.

COACH: How about if we brainstorm a list of possible innovations first? And then what might you do?

STUDENT: Then I could look them up on the Internet to find out when they were invented?

COACH: That's a possibility. But if it's a long list, is there a way you could keep from having to look up every item?

STUDENT: I could show it to my science teacher and ask him which ones came out in the last 15 years.

COACH: Would your science teacher answer that question for you?

STUDENT: Nah, he'd probably tell me to look them up on my own.

COACH: So what's another way to narrow down the list?

STUDENT: Let's see. I could guess or ask my dad. He'd probably know.

COACH: You could do that. But how about looking over the list and eliminating the ones you're not interested in?

STUDENT: Good idea.

COACH: OK, let's summarize the steps in beginning to write a paper. First, we make sure we understand what the assignment is. Then we brainstorm possible ideas to write about. Then we narrow down our choices, both by making sure they fit the assignment rules and by finding something we're interested in. Does that make sense?

STUDENT: Yeah. OK, let's start brainstorming. Wait. I don't know how to do that.

COACH: Brainstorming means coming up with as many ideas as you can without critiquing them until you've generated a pretty complete list.

STUDENT: OK, let's see. I use a smartphone, I play video games, and I go on the Internet. I think that's it.

COACH: Are you sure?

STUDENT: I think so—it's actually a smaller list than I thought.

COACH: How about if you think about a typical day—both a school day and a weekend day—and think about what you usually do? Take last Sunday, for instance. What did you do from the moment you got up in the morning to when you went to bed that involved technology? And you may want to think about what you *did* with that technology. I would guess, for instance, that you do many different things with a smartphone, and you might want to think about the technology involved in each thing.

STUDENT: (*With assistance from coach, expands his list and then chooses a few that are of greatest interest to him.*)

COACH: OK, so tell me what brainstorming means and give me an example of another kind of assignment where you might use it.

STUDENT: Brainstorming means coming up with as many ideas as you can for something without judging them until you're done. I could use it for my next physics project, where I'm supposed to come up with a labor-saving device that uses one of the simple tools.

COACH: Wow—you gave a nice, succinct definition of brainstorming, and you even thought of how you could apply it to another assignment!

4B

Imagine that you are coaching a student with very weak working memory. She routinely forgets to bring home materials that she needs to complete her homework, she often forgets to put them in her backpack after she does her homework, and unless the teacher prompts her individually to hand in her homework, she often forgets to do that. List the steps you might follow to scaffold the task in order to help her learn to remember everything she needs to do.

1. _____

2. _____

3. _____

4. _____

5. _____

On-the-Job Practice

Describe a situation in which you created a scaffold for a student with whom you work. This should be a situation in which, without your help, the student wouldn't have been successful, but the help you provided gave the student the minimal clues necessary for him or her to be successful.

_____

_____

_____

_____

_____

_____

Exercise 5. Clear Directions

To practice the art of providing clear instructions, write the directions for getting from your work site to your home. It may be helpful to start by drawing a map and then use that map to write the sequence of moves someone must make to travel from your work site to your home.

Map

Directions to my house: _____

_____

_____

_____

_____

_____

_____

_____

_____

_____

On-the-Job Practice

After working with a student or teaching a class, complete the following checklist, checking off which instructional element you incorporated into the lesson. It should be noted that not all elements are essential 100% of the time in order for a lesson to be effective. But if you left out any steps, can you think of a way you might have included them in your instructional sequence?

Instructional element	Present (+) or absent (−)
Goal of lesson stated	
Focused on one step at a time without digressions	
Avoided ambiguous terms or phrases	
Material presented in small steps, with explicit step-by-step directions	
Skill was modeled	
Multiple examples provided to illustrate the skill	
Instructions stated positively (i.e., not in the form of prohibitions)	
Frequent checks for understanding used	
eaching session was brief	
Provided opportunity for guided practice	
Provided written checklist or visual aid to accompany oral lesson	

Exercise 6. Specific Praise

For each of the following situations, write a statement that incorporates at least some of the elements of effective praise:

6A

Student reports that she actually studied for a history test for more than 1½ hours and used some of the strategies talked about in coaching. Always in the past, she couldn't get herself to study more than a half-hour, which she did by skimming her notes.

_____

_____

6B

Student made an appointment with his biology teacher to discuss his poor test grade. The biology teacher talked with the coach and told her that he was impressed with how well the student controlled his emotions during the meeting.

_____

_____

6C

Student agreed to count the number of times he talked out in math class by making checkmarks on an index card. He brings the card in the next day showing that he cut in half the number of talk-outs from the day before.

_____

_____

MODULE II: EXECUTIVE SKILLS

Exercise 7. Strengths and Weaknesses

To personalize your understanding of executive skills, we recommend that you complete the Executive Skills Questionnaire—Adult Version, in Appendix 3. After doing so, answer the following questions:

1. List below your two to three highest scores, which represent your executive skills strengths, and your two to three lowest scores, which represent your executive skills weaknesses.

Executive skills strengths   Executive skills weaknesses

_____   _____

_____   _____

_____   _____

2. Describe three aspects of your job where you are able to use your executive skills strengths:

_____

_____

_____

3. Describe three tasks that are part of your job that you find challenging because of your executive skills weaknesses:

_____

_____

_____

Now think about how you might use a coach to work on improving your ability to carry out one of those tasks. We'll give you an example to use as a model for creating your own coaching plan.

Coaching Plan

Executive skills weakness: organization
Job task you find challenging because of your executive skills weakness: keeping my desk surface clear
How could you use a coach to help you address this problem? 1. Make a plan with the coach for cleaning off my desktop bit by bit (i.e., not all at once—that would be too overwhelming!) 2. Meet with the coach daily to define the task for the day—e.g., sort materials into two piles (keep/discard); put books or other materials away where they belong (e.g., on bookshelves, return to owner); file a certain number of papers per day until job is finished. 3. Once the desk is clean, make a new plan with the coach for maintenance (e.g., clean off desk before leaving in afternoon, with daily check-in by coach to ensure follow-through) 4. Make plan to fade coaching—every other day, twice a week, once a week, etc.

Exercise 8. Coaching Plan

Using the prior model, take one of the job tasks you find challenging because of an executive skills weakness and develop a coaching plan to address the problem.

Coaching Plan

Executive skills weakness:
Job task you find challenging because of your executive skills weakness:
How could you use a coach to help you address this problem? 1. 2. 3. 4.

MODULE III: DOCUMENTING COACHING EFFECTIVENESS

Exercise 9. Creating Goal Attainment Scales

Create two goal attainment scales. The first one should address the problem of handing in assignments after the due date. The second should address an executive skills weakness of your own choosing. Select a problem behavior that a student is likely to have as a result of a weakness in one of the 11 executive skills discussed in this manual.

Goal Attainment Scale
Behavior: Handing in Assignments after the Deadline

Level of attainment	Behavior
−2 (much less than expected)	
−1 (somewhat less than expected)	
0 (expected outcome level)	
+1 (somewhat more than expected)	
+2 (much more than expected)	
Monitoring schedule	Monitor: _____ daily _____ weekly _____ other (specify): _____

Goal Attainment Scale

Behavior: _____

Level of attainment	Behavior
–2 (much less than expected)	
–1 (somewhat less than expected)	
0 (expected outcome level)	
+1 (somewhat more than expected)	
+2 (much more than expected)	
Monitoring schedule	Monitor: _____ daily _____ weekly _____ other (specify): _____

Exercise 10. Graphing Interim Goals

Select three interim goals from Table 3.1 and label the vertical and horizontal axes for each one.

Goal selected: _____

Goal selected: _____

Goal selected: _____

Exercise 11. Checklists

Create a checklist that might help a student remember everything he has to do for a daily class, such as math, in which he needs to remember things like handing in homework, writing down assignments, etc.

Element	Checked (✓)

Exercise 12. Scoring Rubrics

Create a scoring rubric (using the Rubric Form in Appendix 18 or one of your own design) for one of the following: (1) improving the quality of note taking; (2) managing performance anxiety (e.g., speaking up in class, doing an oral presentation in front of the class, or controlling test anxiety); (3) keeping a science notebook organized.

MODULE IV: PROBLEM SOLVING

Exercise 13

The student you are coaching complains to you that the cooperative learning group she is working with does not work well together and she's worried that it will affect the final project grade, which will affect her own report card grade. Group members are fighting with each other, one person is not doing any work, and one student is dominating the group, which inhibits other group members from participating. Using the following worksheet, imagine walking through a problem-solving process with this student and answer all but the last two questions with reasonable responses that might result from that process.

Problem-Solving Worksheet

What is the problem?
What are some possible things I could do to solve the problem?
What will I try first?
If this doesn't work, what can I do?
How did it go? Did my solution work?
What might I do differently the next time?

MODULE V: SPECIAL EDUCATION

Exercise 14. IEP Goal

Using the IEP goals provided in the chapter as examples (p. 83), write an IEP goal that includes the three criteria for each of the following problems:

14A

Student routinely forgets to bring home necessary materials to complete homework (e.g., worksheets, textbooks, workbooks, notebooks).

_____

_____

_____

14B

Student routinely underestimates how long an assignment will take and leaves it to the last minute or hands it in late.

_____

_____

_____

14C

Student makes careless mistakes or leaves out questions when taking tests, leading to low or failing grades.

_____

_____

_____

Exercise 15. Coaching within an RTI Framework

A reasonable progression for coaching within an RTI framework is to move from classroom supports at Tier 1 to group coaching at Tier 2 and individual coaching at Tier 3. Using this chapter's scenario with Charmaine as a model, describe what an intervention might look like at all three tiers for the following academic problems:

15A

Student routinely earns failing grades on tests, primarily because she doesn't study.

Tier 1: _____

_____

_____

Tier 2: _____

_____

_____

Tier 3: _____

_____

_____

15B

Student hands in homework late because she loses materials and/or forgets to bring it home at the end of the day.

Tier 1: _____

_____

_____

Tier 2: _____

_____

_____

Tier 3: _____

_____

_____

PRACTICE EXERCISES ANSWER KEY

Exercise 1A

Paraphrase: *You were planning to do your homework but then your friend was in crisis and you felt you had to be there for her.*

Exercise 1B

Paraphrase: *Sounds like you have a conflict—you want to go to Mr. Chase's study session but it comes at the same time as your wrestling practice.*

Exercise 2A

Response: *It sounds like you're feeling pretty overwhelmed by your schoolwork—and maybe a little annoyed at your mother for volunteering you to babysit without checking with you first.*

Exercise 2B

Response: *You're pretty angry at your soccer coach for only playing you for such a short time.*

Exercise 3A

When you want students to think more deeply and to use their own executive skills to make plans or solve problems.

Exercise 3B

When you want students to commit to making a plan or when you want to pin them down about exactly what they intend to do. Closed-ended questions may be necessary with students with poor cognitive flexibility (such as Asperger syndrome).

Exercise 3C

1. *How are you going to fit in writing a paper this weekend when you've got so much else to do also?*
2. *What study strategies are you planning on using to prepare for your midterm in U.S. history?*

[*Note:* If you struggled with this, look at the examples of open-ended questions provided in Chapter 4.]

Exercise 3D

1. *How long a break are you planning on taking after you get home from school before you start your homework?*
2. *Did you use the checklist we made before you left school to make sure you brought home what you needed for homework?*

Exercise 4A

Scaffolding activity	Coach used this strategy
Enhance the student's **I**nterest in the task	✓
Simplify the task (reduce steps, make them more explicit)	✓
Provide **D**irection	✓
Indicate discrepancies between student's work and desired product	
Reduce frustration and risk	✓
Give **F**eedback	✓
Assist internalization/generalization	✓

STUDENT: My science assignment is to write about some technological innovation from the last 15 years that has changed my life. I don't have a clue about how to do this.

COACH: <u>What do you think the first step is?</u> [F]

STUDENT: First, I have to decide what to write about. I use a ton of technology, but I don't know which ones were invented in the last 15 years.

COACH: <u>How about if we brainstorm a list of possible innovations first?</u> [D] And then what might you do?

STUDENT: Then I could look them up on the Internet to find out when they were invented?

COACH: That's a possibility. <u>But if it's a long list, is there a way you could keep from having to look up every item?</u> [S, F]

STUDENT: I could show it to my science teacher and ask him which ones came out in the last 15 years.

COACH: Would your science teacher answer that question for you?

STUDENT: Nah, he'd probably tell me to look them up on my own.

COACH: So what's another way to narrow down the list?

STUDENT: Let's see. I could guess or ask my dad. He'd probably know.

COACH: You could do that. <u>But how about looking over the list and eliminating the ones you're not interested in?</u> [I]

STUDENT: Good idea.

COACH: <u>OK, let's summarize the steps in beginning to write a paper. First, we make sure we understand what the assignment is. Then we brainstorm possible ideas to write about. Then we narrow down our choices, both by making sure they fit the assignment rules and by finding something we're interested in.</u> Does that make sense? [S]

STUDENT: Yeah. OK, let's start brainstorming. Wait. I don't know how to do that.

COACH: Brainstorming means coming up with as many ideas as you can without critiquing them until you've generated a pretty complete list.

STUDENT: OK, let's see. I use a smartphone, I play video games, and I go on the Internet. I think that's it.

COACH: Are you sure?

STUDENT: I think so—it's actually a smaller list than I thought.

COACH: <u>How about if you think about a typical day—both a school day and a weekend day—and think about what you usually do? Take last Sunday, for instance. What did you do from the moment you got up to when you went to bed that involved technology? And you may want to think about what you *did* with that technology.</u> I would guess, for instance, that you do many different things with a smartphone, and you might want to think about the technology involved in each thing. [D]

STUDENT: (*With assistance from coach, expands his list, and then chooses a few that are of greatest interest to him.*)

COACH: <u>OK, so tell me what brainstorming means and give me an example of another kind of assignment where you might use it.</u> [A]

STUDENT: Brainstorming means coming up with as many ideas as you can for something without judging them until you're done. I could use it for my next physics project, where I'm supposed to come up with a labor-saving device that uses one of the simple tools.

COACH: <u>Wow—you gave a nice, succinct definition of brainstorming, and you even thought of how you could apply it to another assignment!</u> [F]

Exercise 4B

1. *Identify the problem (e.g., "It looks like several times a week you forget to bring something home that you need for homework").*
2. *Ask student if she has any ideas for ways she could remember everything.*
3. *If she has trouble answering that question, either suggest they brainstorm together different possibilities or ask if she'd like you to make several suggestions to see which one fits.*

4. *Select one idea and make it concrete. For example, if she decides to make an end-of-day checklist, the next steps would be: (a) Ask her to think about all the categories of materials that should go on the checklist; (b) ask her the best place to keep the checklist (e.g., on her smartphone, on an index card in her purse, or in a special spot in her folder or notebook; and (c) ask her how she will remember to get out her checklist before going home.*
5. *Ask her to critique her plan or strategy and improve it—e.g., What might get in the way of making this work? Could the obstacles be removed? How else might we make it better?*

Exercise 6A

You studied for 90 minutes—way more than you've ever studied before. And you used several different study strategies. That's great task persistence.

Exercise 6B

Your biology teacher told me you handled yourself really well when you talked with him about your test grade. I think you're getting better at controlling your emotions in difficult situations.

Exercise 6C

Look at that! You obviously worked hard to reach your goal of raising your hand before speaking in class.

Exercise 9

Goal Attainment Scale
Behavior: Handing in Assignments after the Deadline

Level of attainment	Behavior
−2 (much less than expected)	*Corey hands in late more than 30% of assignments*
−1 (somewhat less than expected)	*Corey hands in late 21–30% of assignments*
0 (expected outcome level)	*Corey hands in late no more than 20% of assignments*
+1 (somewhat more than expected)	*Corey hands in late between 5 and 19% of assignments*
+2 (much more than expected)	*Corey hands in late less than 5% of assignments*
Monitoring schedule	Monitor: _____ daily _X_____ weekly _____ other (specify):_____

Exercise 10

Examples of Interim Goals

Goal	How will it be measured?	Horizontal axis	Vertical axis
Complete 80% of homework assignments 4 days out of 5.	Graph percentage of homework completed daily.	*Weeks*	*% Homework completed*
Complete math homework with 80% accuracy 4 days out of 5.	Graph percentage accuracy daily.	*Days*	*% Items correct*
Study at least 30 minutes for all Spanish quizzes.	Graph number of minutes spent studying for each quiz.	*Quizzes (listed by date)*	*Number of minutes studied*
Earn grades of 80 or better on all science quizzes and tests.	Graph test and quiz grades.	*Quizzes/ tests (listed by date)*	*Grades earned*
Attend math class 9 days out of 10.	Graph number of math classes attended weekly.	*Weeks*	*Number of days math classes attended per week*
Hand in all English homework on time.	Graph percentage of English assignments handed in on time per week.	*Weeks*	*% Assignments handed in on time per week*
Participate in French class.	Keep tally sheet during class; graph number of times hand raised per class.	*Days*	*Number of times hand raised to participate*
Keep biology notebook organized and up to date.	Create a scoring rubric with a 1–5 scale; along with coach, rate the notebook at each coaching session; graph daily score.	*Days*	*Rubric score*
Bring P.E. clothes to every gym class.	Graph number of days per week student brings clothes to class.	*Weeks*	*Number of days brought clothes to class*
Arrive to first-period class on time.	Graph percentage of days per week on-time arrival.	*Weeks*	*% Days on-time arrival*
Attend after-school math help sessions at least twice a week.	Graph number of math help sessions attended per week.	*Weeks*	*Number of math help sessions attended*
Break down long-term projects into subtasks, with timelines.	Complete long-term project planning form; graph percentage of steps completed on time.	*Project (listed by date)*	*% Steps completed on time*

Exercise 11

Element	Checked (✓)
1) Hand in homework	_____
2) Write down homework assignments	_____
3) Pack in backpack:	_____
a. assignment book	_____
b. math textbook	_____
c. math worksheet	_____
d. calculator	_____
4) Complete math homework	_____
5) Put finished homework in backpack	_____

Exercise 12

Skill assessed: *Improving note taking*

Element	Criteria				Value
	4	3	2	1	
Inclusion of key concepts	*Compared with master copy, included at least 80% of key concepts*	*Compared with master copy, included at least 60% of key concepts*	*Compared with master copy, included at least 40% of key concepts*	*Compared with master copy, included less than 40% of key concepts*	
Relevant details tied to key concepts	*Included 6–8 details per key concept*	*Included 4–5 details per key concept*	*Included 2–3 details per key concept*	*Included 1 or fewer details per key concept*	
Applications (questions, links to personal experience)	*Generated at least one application or question for each key concept*	*Generated at least one application or question for half of the key concepts*	*Generated at least one application or question for ¼ of the key concepts*	*Generated at least one application or question for fewer than ¼ of the key concepts*	
				Total points earned:	

Skill assessed: *Managing performance anxiety*

Element	Criteria				Value
	4	3	2	1	
Making classroom presentations with ease	*Using a 1–5 scale, I rate performance as a 5 (minimum anxiety)*	*Using a 1–5 scale, I rate performance as a 4 (mild anxiety)*	*Using a 1–5 scale, I rate performance as a 2–3 (moderate anxiety)*	*Using a 1–5 scale, I rate performance as a 1 (severe anxiety)*	
Completing tests without anxiety	*Using a 1–5 scale, I rate performance as a 5 (minimum anxiety)*	*Using a 1–5 scale, I rate performance as a 4 (mild anxiety)*	*Using a 1–5 scale, I rate performance as a 2–3 (moderate anxiety)*	*Using a 1–5 scale, I rate performance as a 1 (severe anxiety)*	
Doing homework without worrying about perfection	*Using a 1–5 scale, I rate performance as a 5 (minimum anxiety)*	*Using a 1–5 scale, I rate performance as a 4 (mild anxiety)*	*Using a 1–5 scale, I rate performance as a 2–3 (moderate anxiety)*	*Using a 1–5 scale, I rate performance as a 1 (severe anxiety)*	
				Total points earned:	

Skill assessed: *Keeping science notebook organized*

Element	Criteria				Value
	4	3	2	1	
Contains relevant sections	*Includes all sections assigned by teacher*	*Missing 1 section*	*Missing 2 sections*	*Missing more than 2 sections*	
Includes relevant material	*No missing materials*	*Missing no more than 1 paper per section*	*Missing no more than 2 papers per section*	*Missing 3 or more papers per section*	

Material placed in appropriate section	No loose or misplaced papers	1–2 loose or misplaced papers	3–5 loose or misplaced papers	More than 5 misplaced papers	
Handwriting and papers are neat (not wrinkled)	No wrinkled papers; handwriting rated as 5 (very neat) on 1–5 scale	1–2 wrinkled papers; handwriting rated as 4 on 1–5 scale	3–4 wrinkled papers; handwriting rated as 3 on 1–5 scale	More than 4 wrinkled papers; handwriting rated as 1–2 on 1–5 scale	
				Total points earned:	

Exercise 13

Problem-Solving Worksheet

What is the problem?
Unequal participation; not all students participating equally.

What are some possible things I could do to solve the problem?
1. *Talk with teacher and ask him to intervene.*
2. *Raise the problem with the group and suggest the group break down the project into individual steps and have group members sign up for different steps.*
3. *Use "I"-messages (e.g., "I'm getting stressed out because the group seems pretty dysfunctional and it doesn't seem fair that some people are doing more work than others") and ask the group to talk about possible solutions.*

What will I try first?
Use "I"-messages and ask the group to brainstorm solutions.

If this doesn't work, what can I do?
Offer my own solution and ask the group to react.

How did it go? Did my solution work?

What might I do differently the next time?

Exercise 14A

With the assistance of a coach, student will create an end-of-day checklist and will use it with verbal prompts as necessary from coach.

Exercise 14B

With the assistance of a coach, student will estimate how long assignments will take and will make a plan for assignment completion by dividing the assignment into reasonable chunks.

Exercise 14C

Student will review test answers before handing them in and show that she has done so by placing a checkmark next to each test answer after it has been reviewed. Teacher will remind student to double-check work if test is handed in without checkmarks.

Exercise 15A

Tier 1: Teacher instructs students on how to study for tests and asks students to make a study plan in advance of tests.

Tier 2: Small-group coaching with direct instruction in test-taking strategies and making study plans.

Tier 3: Individual coaching, with time spent assessing study strategies that work best for the student and coaching and supervision around using those strategies.

Exercise 15B

Tier 1: Teacher gives students 5 minutes at the end of class to make sure they've written down homework assignments and have all the necessary materials in backpack; class divided into pairs, with each member of the pair checking on the other.

Tier 2: Small-group coaching at end of day in which students are supervised in checking assignment books and making sure they have all the necessary materials they need to complete homework.

Tier 3: Individual coaching, including creating a checklist the student can use to make sure he or she remembers everything needed to complete assignments.

APPENDICES

Reproducible Materials

The material in the appendices is referenced throughout the book, sometimes more than once and in multiple chapters. Rather than simply presenting the material in the order referenced, we felt it would be more accessible to readers if we grouped the appendices by category or function. Each section is described next, including lists of handouts and forms and page numbers.

BACKGROUND MATERIAL

Material in this section includes forms and rating scales that can be used to gather information about students before the coaching process begins.

This two-page survey is designed to gather information about students to be coached. It asks students to identify preferred leisure time activities, talents and personal strengths, knowledge or skills they'd like to become expert in, as well as preferred learning styles.

This interview-format questionnaire is designed to elicit information about students' executive skills strengths and weaknesses by asking about common school-related and leisure time activities.

Coaches can take this self-assessment to identify their own executive skills strengths and weaknesses. It can help coaches identify potential trouble spots they may encounter in the coaching process and equip them with greater insight and knowledge, which they can share with the students they are coaching.

This is a quick self-assessment students can complete to identify their own executive skills strengths and weaknesses.

COACHING FORMS

The forms in this section are to be used by coaches in basic coaching for academic success, as outlined in Chapter 3. They are presented as templates and examples. Coaches may want to modify them to fit the specific needs of the students they are coaching.

Coaches can use this form as the basis for their interview with students in the first stage in the coaching process to help students identify a long-term goal they want to work toward as well as interim goals to help them achieve their long-term goal. For younger students, coaches may want to shorten or even bypass this discussion.

Coaches sometimes find it helpful to focus on marking period goals rather than longer term goals. This form is designed for this purpose.

This form is a component of the daily coaching session. Its purpose is to help students keep track of everything they have to do, make plans for doing their work, and evaluate how well they followed their plans. It also includes space for them to track longer term work as well as other incidental things they have to remember to do.

This form allows the coach and student to plan for how coaching will be "faded" as a strategy. Together, the coach and student determine the steps in the fading process, including both frequency and mode of contact.

An alternative to the Daily Coaching Form, this form focuses more specifically on making daily homework plans. It is particularly well suited to a group-coaching format.

This is a modification of the Daily Coaching Form to be used with elementary school students. Here, students identify and select a daily goal to work on and then, along with their coach, evaluate how well they met their goal for the day.

TEACHING ROUTINES

This section includes a number of teaching routines that coaches can incorporate into daily coaching sessions to help students develop specific academic skills.

PROGRESS MONITORING FORMS

A critical element of coaching, in addition to goal setting, is determining how well the goals have been met. This section of appendices contains blank forms that supplement Chapter 4's presentation of a variety of progress monitoring techniques and examples.

COACH COORDINATOR FORMS

These forms are designed to facilitate the establishment of a coaching program in which a coach coordinator recruits and trains coaches (either peer or adult) to work with students.

CLASSWIDE PEER COACHING FORMS

The forms in this section are designed for use with the classwide peer coaching strategy described in detail in Chapter 6. Students and coaches use these self-monitoring forms to assess daily how well the student has performed the specific tasks associated with each skill being taught. There is also a blank score sheet included so that teachers/coaches can target skills other than those described in the chapter. Finally, there is a record-keeping sheet for the classroom teacher's use to track the progress of the class as a whole.

FORMS FOR PEER COACHING FOR SOCIAL SKILLS DEVELOPMENT

The forms in this section are designed for peer coaching for social skills development, as described in Chapter 7. They include instructions for coaches and students, permission letters for the parents of coaches and students, daily goal-setting forms, and other record-keeping forms.

Appendix 31. Peer Coaching Steps for the Peer Coach

This form identifies the daily steps for the peer coach. It can be laminated and left in the student's desk as a reminder.

Appendix 32. Student's Daily Goal Steps

This form identifies the daily steps for the focus student. It can be laminated and left in the student's desk as a reminder.

Appendix 33. Daily Goal Form

The peer coach and focus student complete this form together daily. Once completed, it should be kept in the peer coaching binder.

Appendix 34. Reward Menu

This menu can be completed with the peer coaching pair during the training session to determine their choices for weekly rewards.

Appendix 35. Weekly Goal Table

This table can be used to keep track of the number of points students earn each day and week.

This letter can be sent home at the end of each week to update parents on how their child did that week working on his or her goals.

This letter can be sent home at the end of each week to update parents on how their child did that week working with the focus student on his or her goals.

This form can be used during the training session to determine potential appropriate goals. It should be kept in the peer coaching binder so the students can refer back to it if necessary.

This form can be completed by the supervisor to ensure the students are following the necessary peer coaching steps.

Getting to Know You

Name: _____   Date: _____

1. How do you spend your spare time? Check (✓) all that apply and draw a circle around your favorite three activities.

☐ with family   ☐ TV/DVDs ☐ reading   ☐ theater/dance   ☐ part-time job
☐ with friends   ☐ alone   ☐ sports   ☐ Internet, IM   ☐ video/computer games
☐ outdoors   ☐ sleeping ☐ writing   ☐ listening to music   ☐ volunteering
☐ arts, crafts, building things   ☐ playing an instrument ☐ extracurricular activities at school
☐ dirt biking/four-wheeling   ☐ OTHER: _____

2. What talents do you have? Check all that apply and provide an example if you can.

☐ Athletic: _____   ☐ Artistic: _____
☐ Musical: _____   ☐ Writing: _____
☐ Communication: _____   ☐ Leadership: _____
☐ Performing arts: _____ ☐ Technology: _____
☐ Mechanical skills: _____ ☐ Math/sciences: _____
☐ Cooking, sewing: _____ ☐ Interpersonal skills: _____
☐ OTHER: _____

3. What personal qualities do you have that you consider to be strengths? Check up to five.

☐ leadership   ☐ patience   ☐ creativity   ☐ sense of humor ☐ independence
☐ caring, empathy ☐ hard worker   ☐ loyalty   ☐ imagination   ☐ dependability
☐ determination   ☐ optimism   ☐ self-control   ☐ coping skills   ☐ problem solving
☐ persistence   ☐ ambition   ☐ honesty   ☐ organization   ☐ courage
☐ competitiveness ☐ extraversion (outgoing)   ☐ working well with others
☐ OTHER: _____

4. What areas of skill or knowledge would you like to become an expert in? List *any* topic that interests you, even if it is something you don't usually learn about in school (e.g., skateboarding, video games, sports statistics, cheerleading, horseback riding).

(cont.)

5. How do you learn best? Check all that apply.

    a. Group size:

    ☐ alone   ☐ small group (2–4 people)

    ☐ medium group (5–7 people)   ☐ whole class

    b. Learning style:

    ☐ visual   ☐ hands on

    ☐ listening   ☐ memorizing

    ☐ discussion   ☐ activity/experiential learning

    ☐ apprenticeship   ☐ taking notes

    ☐ reading   ☐ thinking about what I've read or heard

    ☐ OTHER: _____

    c. What is your preferred study environment?

    ☐ library   ☐ study hall at school

    ☐ bedroom   ☐ other room in my house

    ☐ with friends   ☐ public place (e.g., coffee shop)

    ☐ resource room   ☐ OTHER: _____

6. What are your preferred classroom activities? Check all that apply.

    ☐ lecture   ☐ discussions   ☐ projects

    ☐ debates   ☐ group games   ☐ presentations

    ☐ reading   ☐ creative writing   ☐ worksheets

    ☐ labs/experiments   ☐ cooperative learning   ☐ brainstorming

    ☐ outdoor activities   ☐ field trips   ☐ learn, then teach others

    ☐ role playing   ☐ simulations   ☐ taking tests

    ☐ self-directed learning   ☐ individual research   ☐ doing homework

    ☐ movies/DVDs   ☐ working on the computer ☐ teacher-led instruction

    ☐ doodling   ☐ daydreaming   ☐ talking with friends

    ☐ OTHER: _____

Executive Skills Semistructured Interview—Student Version

Name: _____ Date: _____

I'm going to ask you some questions about situations related to your success as a student. All of these are situations in which you have to use planning and organizational skills in order to be successful. Some will be directly related to school, whereas other questions will touch on extracurricular activities, any job situations you've been in, and how you spend your leisure time.

HOMEWORK. I'm going to ask you some questions about homework and the kinds of problems kids sometimes have with homework. Please tell me if you think these are problems for you. I may ask you to give me examples of how you see it as a problem.

Item	Not a Problem	Notes
Getting started on homework. (TI) *Related questions:* What makes it hard? When is the best time to do homework? Are some subjects harder to start than others?		
Sticking with it long enough to get it done. (SA) *Related questions:* Is this worse with some subjects than others? What do you say to yourself that leads you to either give up or stick with it? Does the length of the assignment make a difference in your ability to complete it?		
Remembering assignments. (WM) *Related questions:* Do you have trouble remembering to write down assignments, bring home necessary materials, or hand in assignments? Do you lose things necessary to complete the task?		
Becoming distracted while doing homework. (SA) *Related questions:* What kinds of things distract you? Have you found places to study that minimize distractions? How do you handle the distractions when they come up?		
Having other things you'd rather do. (P, GDP) *Related questions:* Are there things you have trouble tearing yourself away from to do homework? Do you resent having homework or too much homework? Do you think there are other things in your life that are more important than homework?		

(cont.)

LONG-TERM PROJECTS. Now let's talk about long-term assignments. Which of the following, if any, are hard for you?

Item	Not a Problem	Notes
Choosing a topic (M)		
Breaking the assignment into smaller parts (P)		
Developing a timeline (P)		
Sticking with a timeline (TM)		
Estimating how long it will take to finish (TM)		
Following directions (e.g., Do you forget to do part of the assignment and lose points as a result?) (WM, M)		
Proofreading or checking your work to make sure you followed the rules and haven't made careless mistakes (M)		
Finishing the project by the deadline (GDP)		

STUDYING FOR TESTS. Here are some problems students sometimes have when studying for tests. Which ones, if any, are a problem for you?

Item	Not a Problem	Notes
Making yourself sit down and study (TI)		
Knowing what to study (M)		
Knowing how to study (M)		
Putting off studying/not studying at all (TM)		

(cont.)

STUDYING FOR TESTS. *(cont.)*

Item	Not a Problem	Notes
Taking breaks that are either too frequent or too long (SA)		
Giving up before you've studied enough (GDP)		
Memorizing the material (WM)		
Understanding the material (M)		

HOME CHORES/RESPONSIBILITIES. What kinds of chores, if any, do you have to do on a regular or irregular basis?

Chore	Regular (When do you do it?)	Occasional
1.		
2.		
3.		
4.		
5.		

What aspects of completing chores, if any, do you have trouble with?

Item	Not a Problem	Notes
Remembering to do them (WM)		
Doing them when you're supposed to (TI)		
Running out of steam before you're done (SA)		
Doing a sloppy job and getting in trouble for it (M)		

(cont.)

ORGANIZATIONAL SKILLS. Now I'm going to ask some questions about how organized you are. Tell me if you have problems with any of the following.

Item	Not a Problem	Notes
Keeping your bedroom neat (O)		
Keeping your notebooks organized (O)		
Keeping your backpack organized (O)		
Keeping your desk clean (O)		
Keeping your locker clean (O)		
Leaving your belongings all over the house (O)		
Leaving belongings other places (e.g., school, friend's houses, at work) (O)		
Losing or misplacing things (O)		

MANAGING EMOTIONS. Sometimes emotions can get in the way of doing well in school or getting along with others. Tell me if you have problems with any of the following.

Item	Not a Problem	Notes
Losing your temper (EC)		
Getting nervous in some situations (e.g., when taking tests, speaking up in class, with peers or adults you don't know well (EC)		
Getting easily frustrated (e.g., when you don't understand homework or when parents get on your nerves (EC)		
Saying or doing something without thinking that you later regret (RI)		
Giving up quickly when a task is hard or boring (RI)		
Difficulty adjusting to changes in plans or disruptions to routines (F)		
Having trouble with open-ended assignments (such as writing assignments where there's no one right answer) (F)		

(cont.)

WORK/LEISURE TIME. Let's talk about how you spend your time when you're not in school. What kinds of extracurricular activities, if any, are you involved in? Do you have a job? How do you spend your leisure time?

Activity	Amount of time (approximate per day or week)
1.	
2.	
3.	
4.	
5.	
6.	
7.	

Here are some problems that students sometimes have with how they spend their spare time. Which ones, if any, are problems for you?

Item	Not a Problem	Notes
Spending too many hours at a job (TM)		
"Wasting" time (e.g., hanging out, playing computer/ video games, talking on the phone, time on Facebook, watching too much TV) (TM)		
Hanging out with kids who get in trouble (RI)		
Not getting enough sleep (RI)		
Spending money as soon as you get it (RI)		

(cont.)

LONG-TERM GOALS. Do you know what you want to do after high school?

Possible goals
1.
2.
3.
4.

Have you formulated a plan for reaching your goal(s)? If so, what is it?

What are some of the potential obstacles that might prevent you from reaching your goal(s)?

Potential obstacle	Ways to overcome the obstacle
1.	
2.	
3.	
4.	
5.	

If you have not yet identified a goal or developed a plan for reaching the goal, when do you think you will you do this?

Note. TI, Task initiation; WM, Working memory; O, Organization; GDP, Goal-directed persistence; RI, Response inhibition; SA, Sustained attention; P, Planning; F, Flexibility; EC, Emotional control.

Executive Skills Questionnaire—Adult Version

Name: _____   Date: _____

Read each item below and then rate that item based on the extent to which you agree or disagree with how well it describes you. Use the rating scale below to choose the appropriate score. Then add the three scores in each section. Use the key on the last page to determine your executive skills strengths (2–3 highest scores) and weaknesses (2–3 lowest scores).

Strongly disagree	1	Tend to agree	5
Disagree	2	Agree	6
Tend to disagree	3	Strongly agree	7
Neutral	4		

Item   Score

1. I don't jump to conclusions.   _____
2. I think before I speak.   _____
3. I don't take action without having all the facts.   _____
                                                              TOTAL SCORE: _____

4. I have a good memory for facts, dates, and details.   _____
5. I am very good at remembering the things I have committed to do.   _____
6. I seldom need reminders to complete tasks.   _____
                                                              TOTAL SCORE: _____

7. My emotions seldom get in the way when performing on the job.   _____
8. Little things do not affect me emotionally or distract me from the task at hand.   _____
9. I can defer my personal feelings until after a task has been completed.   _____
                                                              TOTAL SCORE: _____

10. No matter what the task, I believe in getting started as soon as possible.   _____
11. Procrastination is usually not a problem for me.   _____
12. I seldom leave tasks to the last minute.   _____
                                                              TOTAL SCORE: _____

13. I find it easy to stay focused on my work.   _____
14. Once I start an assignment, I work diligently until it's completed.   _____
15. Even when interrupted, I find it easy to get back and complete the job at hand.   _____
                                                              TOTAL SCORE: _____

(cont.)

Item	Score
16. When I plan out my day, I identify priorities and stick to them.	_____
17. When I have a lot to do, I can easily focus on the most important things.	_____
18. I typically break big tasks down into subtasks and timelines.	_____
	TOTAL SCORE: _____
19. I am an organized person.	_____
20. It is natural for me to keep my work area neat and organized.	_____
21. I am good at maintaining systems for organizing my work.	_____
	TOTAL SCORE: _____
22. At the end of the day, I've usually finished what I set out to do.	_____
23. I am good at estimating how long it takes to do something.	_____
24. I am usually on time for appointments and activities.	_____
	TOTAL SCORE: _____
25. I take unexpected events in stride.	_____
26. I easily adjust to changes in plans and priorities.	_____
27. I consider myself to be flexible and adaptive to change.	_____
	TOTAL SCORE: _____
28. I routinely evaluate my performance and devise methods for personal improvement.	_____
29. I am able to step back from a situation in order to make objective decisions.	_____
30. I "read" situations well and can adjust my behavior based on the reactions of others.	_____
	TOTAL SCORE: _____
31. I think of myself as being driven to meet my goals.	_____
32. I easily give up immediate pleasures to work on long-term goals.	_____
33. I believe in setting and achieving high levels of performance.	_____
	TOTAL SCORE: _____
34. I enjoy working in a highly demanding, fast-paced environment.	_____
35. A certain amount of pressure helps me to perform at my best.	_____
36. Jobs that include a fair degree of unpredictability appeal to me.	_____
	TOTAL SCORE: _____

(cont.)

KEY			
Items	Executive Skill	Items	Executive Skill
1–3	Response inhibition	4–6	Working memory
7–9	Emotional control	10–12	Task initiation
13–15	Sustained attention	16–18	Planning/prioritization
19–21	Organization	22–24	Time management
25–27	Flexibility	28–30	Metacognition
31–33	Goal-directed persistence	34–36	Stress tolerance

Strongest Skills

_____

_____

_____

_____

Weakest Skills

_____

_____

_____

_____

Executive Skills Questionnaire for Students

Name: _____   Date: _____

Big problem	1
Moderate problem	2
Mild problem	3
Slight problem	4
No problem	5

Item   Score

1. I act on impulse.   _____
2. I get in trouble for talking too much in class.   _____
3. I say things without thinking.   _____
                                                               TOTAL SCORE: _____

4. I say, "I'll do it later" and then forget about it.   _____
5. I forget homework assignments or forget to bring home needed materials.   _____
6. I lose or misplace belongings such as coats, notebooks, sports equipment, etc.   _____
                                                               TOTAL SCORE: _____

7. I get annoyed when homework is too hard or confusing or takes too long to finish.   _____
8. I have a short fuse; am easily frustrated.   _____
9. I get upset easily when things don't go as planned.   _____
                                                               TOTAL SCORE: _____

10. I have difficulty paying attention and am easily distracted.   _____
11. I run out of steam before finishing my homework.   _____
12. I have problems sticking with chores until they are done.   _____
                                                               TOTAL SCORE: _____

13. I put off homework or chores until the last minute.   _____
14. It's hard for me to put aside fun activities in order to start homework.   _____
15. I need many reminders to start chores.   _____
                                                               TOTAL SCORE: _____

16. I have trouble planning for big assignments (knowing what to do first, second, etc.). _____
17. It's hard for me to set priorities when I have a lot of things to do.   _____
18. I become overwhelmed by long-term projects or big assignments.   _____
                                                               TOTAL SCORE: _____

(cont.)

_____

Item   Score

19. My backpack and notebooks are disorganized.   _____

20. My desk or work space at home is a mess.   _____

21. I have trouble keeping my bedroom tidy.   _____

                 TOTAL SCORE: _____

22. I have a hard time estimating how long it will take to do something (such as homework).   _____

23. I often don't finish homework at night and rush to get it done in school before class.   _____

24. I'm slow getting ready for things (e.g., school or appointments).   _____

                 TOTAL SCORE: _____

25. If the first solution to a problem doesn't work, I have trouble thinking of a different one.   _____

26. It's hard for me to deal with changes in plans or routines.   _____

27. I have problems with open-ended homework assignments (e.g., don't know what to write about when given a creative writing assignment).   _____

                 TOTAL SCORE: _____

High School Students Only

28. I don't have effective study strategies.   _____

29. I don't check my work for mistakes even when the stakes are high.   _____

30. I don't evaluate my performance and change tactics in order to increase success.   _____

                 TOTAL SCORE: _____

31. I can't seem to save up money for a desired object.   _____

32. I don't see the value in earning good grades to achieve a long-term goal.   _____

33. If I should be studying and something fun comes up, it's hard for me to make myself study.   _____

                 TOTAL SCORE: _____

KEY			
Items	**Executive Skill**	**Items**	**Executive Skill**
1–3	Response inhibition	4–6	Working memory
7–9	Emotional control	10–12	Sustained attention
13–15	Task initiation	16–18	Planning/prioritization
19–21	Organization	22–24	Time management
25–27	Flexibility	28–30	Metacognition
31–33	Goal-directed persistence		

Your Executive Skills Strengths   **Your Executive Skills Weaknesses**

_____   _____

_____   _____

_____   _____

Long-Term Goal-Setting Form

Creating the Link between Today's Plans and Tomorrow's Goals

LONG-TERM GOAL: LIFE AFTER HIGH SCHOOL. What do you see yourself doing after you finish high school? Do you plan to go to college? What kind of college? Do you plan to get a job? What kind of job? Create a picture of what you see your life like after high school. If this question is to difficult to contemplate, then think about this: What is *one thing* you would like to get out of school?

Identify a single goal to focus on now—highlight it in the list above. Now identify the things you need to do in order to meet your goal.

(cont.)

What are some of the potential obstacles that might prevent you from reaching your goal? How can those obstacles be overcome or avoided?

Potential obstacle	Ways to overcome the obstacle
1.	
2.	
3.	
4.	
5.	

INTERIM GOALS. Think about where to start in order to achieve your long-term goal. Check off which of the following you might like to work on.

Possible interim goals	I want to work on this
Improve class attendance	
Improve homework completion	
Increase homework handed in on time	
Improve grades on homework assignments	
Improve test or quiz grades	
Improve class participation	
Decrease discipline referrals	

(cont.)

Take one or more of the above goals (or others you may have considered), and carry out the following steps:(1) Estimate your current performance; (2) create a goal; (3) identify in which classes or settings you want the goal to apply; (4) describe the strategies you will use to achieve your goal; (5) decide on a criterion for success; and (6) decide how many weeks you will meet the criterion before you begin to fade coaching or select a new goal. Your coach can provide examples and help you do this. *Note:* You may want to delay completing the last column until the coaching process is up and running for a couple of weeks.

Current performance	Interim goal	In what classes?	Strategies to achieve goal	Success criterion	Length of time at criterion before beginning new goal or fading coaching

Are there supports or assistance you need from others to help you achieve your goal? This might include working with a coach; having someone, such as a parent, friend, or teacher, give you reminders; staying after school for extra help; or signing up for a study skills class.

1.	
2.	
3.	
4.	
5.	

(cont.)

Now that you've defined your goal and have a plan, do you think the goal and plan are realistic?

_____ Yes

_____ No

If No, how can the plan be modified to make it more realistic?

Marking Period Goal-Setting Form

Name: _____ Date: _____

SUBJECT: _____

Current grade (if applicable):   Desired grade:

What do you need to do to earn your desired grade in this subject?

1.   3.

2.   4.

SUBJECT: _____

Current grade (if applicable):   Desired grade:

What do you need to do to earn your desired grade in this subject?

1.   3.

2.   4.

(cont.)

SUBJECT: _____

Current grade (if applicable):   Desired grade:

What do you need to do to earn your desired grade in this subject?

1.   3.

2.   4.

SUBJECT: _____

Current grade (if applicable):   Desired grade:

What do you need to do to earn your desired grade in this subject?

1.   3.

2.   4.

SUMMARY: These are the things I need to do to meet my marking period goals:

1.

2.

3.

4.

APPENDIX 7

Daily Coaching Form

Name: _____   Date: _____

LONG-TERM GOAL(S): _____

THE BIG PICTURE:

Upcoming tests/quizzes:

Subject:	Date:

Long-term assignments:

Assignment:	Date due:	Task:	Date:

Other responsibilities:

_____

_____

TODAY'S PLANS: (include homework assignments as well as any work to be done on long-term projects or studying for tests)

LOOKING BACK:

What are you going to do?	When will you do it?	Did you do it?	How did you do?*
1.	1.	Yes No	1 2 3 4 5
2.	2.	Yes No	1 2 3 4 5
3.	3.	Yes No	1 2 3 4 5
4.	4.	Yes No	1 2 3 4 5
5.	5.	Yes No	1 2 3 4 5
6.	6.	Yes No	1 2 3 4 5

*Use this scale to evaluate: 1—Not well at all; 2—So-so; 3—Average; 4—Very well; 5—Excellent

THINGS I NEED TO REMEMBER (check off item when taken care of)

1. _____
2. _____
3. _____
4. _____
5. _____

OTHER NOTES:

_____
_____
_____
_____

Plan for Fading Coaching

Coaching step	Frequency of sessions		Type of contact
1	____ Daily ____ Twice weekly ____ Biweekly	____ Every other day ____ Once a week ____ Monthly	____ Face to face ____ Telephone ____ Electronic (specify):
2	____ Daily ____ Twice weekly ____ Biweekly	____ Every other day ____ Once a week ____ Monthly	____ Face to face ____ Telephone ____ Electronic (specify):
3	____ Daily ____ Twice weekly ____ Biweekly	____ Every other day ____ Once a week ____ Monthly	____ Face to face ____ Telephone ____ Electronic (specify):
4	____ Daily ____ Twice weekly ____ Biweekly	____ Every other day ____ Once a week ____ Monthly	____ Face to face ____ Telephone ____ Electronic (specify):
5	____ Daily ____ Twice weekly ____ Biweekly	____ Every other day ____ Once a week ____ Monthly	____ Face to face ____ Telephone ____ Electronic (specify):
6	____ Daily ____ Twice weekly ____ Biweekly	____ Every other day ____ Once a week ____ Monthly	____ Face to face ____ Telephone ____ Electronic (specify):

Daily Homework Planning Form

Name: _____   Date: _____

Subject/assignment	Do I have all the materials?	Do I need help?	Who will help me?	How long will it take?	When will I start?	How long did it take?
	Yes ☐ No ☐	Yes ☐ No ☐			Start time: Stop time:	
	Yes ☐ No ☐	Yes ☐ No ☐			Start time: Stop time:	
	Yes ☐ No ☐	Yes ☐ No ☐			Start time: Stop time:	
	Yes ☐ No ☐	Yes ☐ No ☐			Start time: Stop time:	
	Yes ☐ No ☐	Yes ☐ No ☐			Start time: Stop time:	
	Yes ☐ No ☐	Yes ☐ No ☐			Start time: Stop time:	

Did I follow my plan?   Yes ☐   No ☐   If no, what got in the way?

Coaching for Kids Form

Name: _____   Date: _____

My goals are:

1.

2.

3.

Today I am working on: _____

_____

_____

_____

_____

MY RATING

How did I do? (Circle one)	Great!	Pretty good	OK	Not so good	Pretty bad
	5	4	3	2	1

COACH RATING

	Great!	Pretty good	OK	Not so good	Pretty bad
	5	4	3	2	1

How to Write an Essay

Executive skills addressed: task initiation, sustained attention, planning, organization, time management, metacognition.

Students with a variety of executive skills weaknesses struggle with writing papers because this is one of the most complicated tasks we expect students to do. Use the following steps to help them through the process.

1. **Brainstorm topics.** If the student has to come up with a topic to write about, the process should begin with brainstorming. The rules of brainstorming are that any idea is accepted and written down in the first stage—the wilder and crazier the better because wild and crazy ideas often lead to good, usable ideas. No criticism is allowed at this point. If the student has trouble thinking of ideas on his or her own, the teacher or aide can throw out some ideas to "grease the wheels." We recommend that the adult working with the student write down the ideas rather than expecting the student to because youngsters with weak writing skills often struggle with the act of writing itself. When a reasonable number of ideas have been generated, have the student read the list and circle the most promising ones. The student may know right away what he or she wants to write about. If not, talk about what he or she likes and dislikes about each idea to make it easier to zero in on a good choice.

2. **Brainstorm content.** Once a topic has been selected, the brainstorming process begins again. Ask the student to "Tell me everything you know or would like to know about this topic." Again, write down any idea or question: the crazier the better at this point.

3. **Organize the content.** Now look at all the ideas or questions that have been written down. With the student, decide whether the material can be grouped together in any way. If the assignment is to do a report on aardvarks, for instance, the information might cluster into categories such as what they look like, where they live, what they eat, who their enemies are, how they protect themselves. Create topic headings and then write the details under each topic heading. Sometimes it's helpful to use Post-its for this process. During the brainstorming phase, each individual idea or question is written on a separate Post-it. The Post-its can then be organized on a table under topic headings to form an outline of the paper. The paper can then be written (or dictated) from this outline.

4. **Write the opening paragraph.** This is often the most difficult part of the paper to write. The opening paragraph, at its most basic level, describes very succinctly what the paper will be about. For instance, an opening paragraph on a report about aardvarks might read:

   This paper is about a strange animal called an aardvark. By the time you finish reading it, you will know what they look like, where they live, what they eat, who their enemies are, and how they protect themselves.

   The one other thing that the opening paragraph should try to do is "grab the reader"—give the reader an interesting piece of information to tease his or her curiosity. At the end of the prior opening paragraph, for instance, two more sentences might be added:

   The reader will also learn the meaning of the word "aardvark" and what language it comes from. And if that hasn't grabbed your interest, I will also tell you why the aardvark has a sticky tongue—although you may not want to know this!

(cont.)

Children with writing problems will have trouble writing the opening paragraph by themselves and may need help. Help can be provided by asking general questions, such as "What do you want people to know after they read your paper?" or "Why do you think people might be interested in reading this?" If they need more help than that, they may need a model to work from—for example, an opening paragraph on a topic similar to the one the student is working on or the paragraph on aardvarks provided here. If the student needs more guided help writing this paragraph, provide it. Then see if he or she can continue without the need for as much support.

5. **Write the rest of the paper.** To give the student a little more guidance, suggest that the rest of the paper be divided into sections with a heading for each section. Help the student make a list of the headings and then see if he or she can continue with the writing task alone. If not, continue to provide support until the paper is written. Each paragraph should begin with a main or topic sentence that makes one main point. Following the topic sentence should be three to five sentences that expand or explain the main point. It's helpful to use connecting words to link sentences or paragraphs. Examples of simple linking words are *and, because, also, instead, but, so.* Examples of more complex linking words are *although, moreover, on the other hand, therefore, as a result, finally, in conclusion.*

In the early stages of learning to write, children with writing problems need a great deal of help. This skill should get better with time, especially if each writing session concludes by giving the student some positive feedback about something done well. Note in particular any improvement since the last writing assignment (e.g., "I really like the way you were able to come up with the headings on your own this time, with no help from me.").

For students with more significant writing impairments: More modeling, guidance, and support will need to be provided for students with writing disabilities. Furthermore, the process may need to be broken down a good deal more. For those with significant impairments or those who are highly resistant to the writing process, we recommend the following sequence:

- **Step 1:** Spend a few minutes (e.g., 5 minutes) each day practicing any kind of writing. Here, the goal is to get words down on paper. For many students, just having them write any words they can think of is the place to start. If children have difficulty generating words on their own, give them organizing or retrieval strategies, such as looking around the room and writing down the name of anything you see or having them write rhyming words by giving them the first word (e.g., *cat, man*). Count the number of words written and keep a graph, challenging them to write a few more words each day.
- **Step 2:** Give them a picture and have them write down words to describe the picture or have them describe the picture and you write down the words. Use pictures that reflect their interests.
- **Step 3:** Give them a picture and have them write a sentence or two describing the picture.
- **Step 4:** Have them draw a picture and write sentences describing the picture or telling a story to go along with the picture.
- **Step 5:** Finally, give them a story starter and have them write for 5 minutes based on the story starter. They may want to choose a story starter or to think up one on their own.

This approach can be very effective when combined with curriculum-based measurement—that is, keeping the time frame constant, counting the number of words written, and graphing the results. The graph should be constructed with the child and might incorporate small stickers (obtainable at office supply stores like Staples) to construct the graph. Watching the graph progress indicator go up can be very motivating for young children, in particular those with writing production problems.

(cont.)

Additional Resources

- Harvey, V. S., & Chickie-Wolfe, L. A. (2007). *Fostering independent learning: Practical strategies to promote student success*. New York: Guilford Press.—This book has a chapter devoted to writing that includes a number of useful checklists and handouts. One of these lists presents a wide variety of "genre ideas" to remind teachers that there are myriad forms of writing and that going beyond the traditional essay may help stimulate writing in reluctant writers.

- Harris, K. R., Graham, S., Mason, L. H., & Friedlander, B. (2008). *Powerful writing strategies for all students*. Baltimore: Brookes.—This book describes the process of self-regulated strategy development and applies it to the writing process. Packed with helpful lesson plans and handouts, it details explicit strategies for specific writing genres as well as general writing strategies with an overarching goal of developing self-regulated learners. Thus, not only does the book teach writing, but it also helps students learn self-regulation strategies (i.e., executive skills!) such as goal setting, self-monitoring, self-reinforcement, and self-instruction.

(cont.)

WRITING TEMPLATE FOR A FIVE-PARAGRAPH ESSAY

Introductory Paragraph

Sentence 1 summarizes what your essay is about:

Sentence 2 focuses on the main point you want to make:

Sentence 3 adds more detail or explains why the topic is important:

Body Paragraphs

Paragraph 1, topic sentence:

Supporting detail 1:

Supporting detail 2:

Supporting detail 3:

(cont.)

Paragraph 2, topic sentence:

Supporting detail 1:

Supporting detail 2:

Supporting detail 3:

Paragraph 3, topic sentence:

Supporting detail 1:

Supporting detail 2:

Supporting detail 3:

(cont.)

Concluding Paragraph

Restate the most important point from the paper you want to make (what the reader should go away understanding).

How to Plan and Complete Long-Term Projects

Executive skills addressed: task initiation, sustained attention, planning, time management, metacognition.

Even more than writing assignments, long-term projects involve many of the more advanced executive skills. For this reason, students in general benefit from teacher support, not only when this kind of assignment is first introduced but to some degree or other throughout their schooling (at least until well into high school).

The steps involved in teaching students to complete long-term projects are as follows:

1. With the student, look at the description of the assignment to make sure the student understands what is expected. If the student is allowed a choice of topic, topic selection is the first task. Many children have trouble thinking up topics, and you may need to brainstorm ideas—and include a variety of suggestions—starting with topics that are related to the student's areas of interests.

2. Using the Long-Term Project Planning Sheet, write down the possible topics. Once three to five topics have been generated, ask the student what he or she does or does not like about each choice.

3. Help the student make a final selection, taking into consideration not only the topic of greatest interest but also (a) a topic that is neither too broad nor too narrow; (b) the level of difficulty involved in tracking down references and resources for the topic; and (c) whether there is an interesting "twist" to the topic that will make it either fun to work on or appealing for the teacher.

4. Using the Long-Term Project Planning Sheet, decide what materials or resources will be needed, where the student will get them, and when (this last variable may be determined after completing Step 5). Possible resources include Internet websites, library books, travel brochures, and similar items that may need to be ordered, people who might be interviewed, and relevant places to visit (e.g., museums, historical sites). You may need to "walk" the student through the process of tracking down sources (e.g., going to the library or accessing the Internet to show how to conduct a search). Also consider any construction or art materials needed if the student's plan includes a visual presentation.

5. Using the Long-Term Project Planning Sheet, list all the steps required to carry out the project and then develop a timeline so the student knows when each step will be done. It may be helpful at this point to transfer this information onto a monthly calendar that can be placed in the student's binder to make it easier to keep track of what needs to be done when.

6. Assist the student in following the timeline. Before he or she begins each step, you may want to discuss what exactly is involved in completing the step—this may mean making a list of things to be done for each step. Planning for the next step could be done as each step is completed, so that the student has some idea what's coming next and to make it easier to get the next step started.

(cont.)

LONG-TERM PROJECT-PLANNING SHEET

Step 1: Select Topic

What are possible topics?	What I like about this choice:	What I don't like:
1.		
2.		
3.		
4.		
5.		

Final Topic Choice:

Step 2: Identify Necessary Materials

What materials or resources do you need?	Where will you get them?	When will you get them?
1.		
2.		
3.		
4.		
5.		

(cont.)

Step 3: Identify Project Tasks and Due Dates

What do you need to do? (List each step in order.)	When will you do it?	Check off when done
Step 1:		
Step 2:		
Step 3:		
Step 4:		
Step 5:		
Step 6:		
Step 7:		
Step 8:		
Step 9:		
Step 10:		

Reminder List. Include here any additional tasks or details you need to keep in mind as you work on the project. Cross out or check each one off as it is taken care of.

1. _____
2. _____
3. _____
4. _____
5. _____
6. _____
7. _____
8. _____
9. _____
10. _____

How to Study for Tests

1. Keep a monthly calendar with the student to record any upcoming tests.

2. From 5 days to 1 week before the test, devise a study plan with the student.

3. Using the Menu of Study Strategies, have the student decide which strategies he or she wants to use to study for the test. Make sure the student understands what is involved in each strategy, providing further explanation if necessary (e.g., if the student chooses "Study flash cards," ask him or her to show what the flash cards will look like, giving additional suggestions for flash card design).

4. Have the student make a plan for studying that starts 4 days before the test. Vast psychological research shows that in learning new material, *distributed practice is more effective than massed practice.* In other words, if a student plans to spend 2 hours studying for a test, it is better to break down the study time into smaller segments over a longer period (e.g., 30 minutes a night for four nights) than study for a 2-hour block the night before the test. Research also shows that learning is consolidated through sleep, so getting a good night's sleep before an exam is more beneficial than "cramming" the night before.

5. If the student has problems with sustained attention, it may be easier to use several strategies, each for a short amount of time, than using one strategy for the full study period. You can suggest that the student set a kitchen timer for the length of time for each strategy, and when the bell rings, the student can move on to the next strategy (unless he or she prefers the strategy being used and wants to continue it).

6. After the student takes the test, have him or her complete the posttest evaluation. This builds self-evaluation so that improvements can be made and implemented for the next test.

(cont.)

MENU OF STUDY STRATEGIES

Check off the ones you will use.

___ 1. Reread text	___ 2. Reread/organize notes	___ 3. Read/recite main points
___ 4. Outline text	___ 5. Highlight text	___ 6. Highlight notes
___ 7. Use study guide	___ 8. Make concept maps	___ 9. Make lists/organize
___ 10. Take practice test	___ 11. Quiz myself	___ 12. Have someone else quiz me
___ 13. Study flash cards	___ 14. Memorize/rehearse	___ 15. Create a "cheat sheet"
___ 16. Study with friend	___ 17. Study with study group	___ 18. Study session with teacher
___ 19. Study with a parent	___ 20. Ask for help	___ 21. Other: _____

STUDY PLAN

Date	Day	Which strategies will I use? (write #)	How much time for each strategy?
	4 days before test	1. 2. 3.	1. 2. 3.
	3 days before test	1. 2. 3.	1. 2. 3.
	2 days before test	1. 2. 3.	1. 2. 3.
	1 day before test	1. 2. 3.	1. 2. 3.

POSTTEST EVALUATION: How did your plan for studying work out? Answer the following questions:

1. What strategies worked best?
2. What strategies were not so helpful?
3. Did you spend enough time studying? Yes No
4. If no, what more should you have done?
5. What will you do differently the next time?

How to Organize Notebooks/Homework

1. With input from the student, decide on what needs to be included in the organizational system: A place to keep unfinished homework? A separate place to keep completed homework? A place to keep papers that need to be filed? Notebooks or binders to keep notes, completed assignments, handouts, and worksheets? A sample list is included in the checklist that follows.

2. Once you've listed all these elements, decide how best to handle them, one at a time. For example, you and the student might decide on a colored folder system, with a different color for completed assignments, unfinished work, and other papers. Or you might decide to have a separate small three-ring binder for each subject or one large binder to handle all subjects.

3. Make a list of the materials the student needs—these might include a three-hole punch, lined and unlined paper, subject dividers, and small Post-it packages the student can use to flag important papers.

4. Ask the student to procure the necessary materials if they are not available at school. It may be necessary to e-mail the student's parents to ensure that the materials are obtained.

5. Set up the notebooks and folders, labeling everything clearly.

6. Help the student maintain the system over time. This generally means a daily check-in, which might include having the student take out the folders for completed assignments, unfinished work, and material to be filed. Have the student make a decision about each piece of material and where it should go.

(cont.)

SETTING UP A NOTEBOOK/HOMEWORK MANAGEMENT SYSTEM

System element	What will you use?	Got it (✓)
Place for unfinished homework		
Place for completed assignments		
Place to keep materials for later filing		
Notebooks or binder(s) for each subject		
Other things you might need: 1. 2. 3. 4.		

MAINTAINING A NOTEBOOK/HOMEWORK MANAGEMENT SYSTEM

Task	Monday	Tuesday	Wednesday	Thursday	Weekend
Clean out "to be filed" folder.					
Go through notebooks and books for other loose papers and file them.					
Place all assignments (both finished and unfinished) in appropriate places.					

How to Take Notes

- Solicit from student the reasons why note taking is important. If the student has difficulty answering the question, point out that note taking not only enables students to record important information needed to understand the lecture topic and provides material to use when studying for tests, but it also is a way to help them pay attention and focus on the class.
- Ask the student how he or she takes notes now and to assess the usefulness of the method. Explain that learning is most likely to occur when three things happen: (1) The student is able to absorb the relevant information in a way that is organized appropriately for the material being presented; (2) the student is able to extract the key concepts or main ideas as a way to help him or her understand and retain the factual information presented in lecture; and (3) the student is able to apply what he or she is learning to prior learning or relate it to personal experiences in order to have a meaningful context within which the new material can be placed. The more a student can make the information *emotionally* relevant, the more he or she will likely understand and remember.
- If the student's current note-taking style does not incorporate these three elements, explain that you will be teaching a couple of different note-taking strategies for the student to try and then to decide which one works best.

NOTE-TAKING STRATEGY 1: CORNELL METHOD

This strategy uses a three-column system, and begins with sequential note taking (writing down what the teacher is saying in the sequence provided) in the center column (see the following sample). As the lecture progresses, the student writes down key concepts and "big ideas" in the left-hand column. Sometimes a teacher is direct in identifying those key concepts; other times students have to listen carefully and draw conclusions on their own. In the right-hand column, the student is instructed to jot down personal reflections—a word or two that relates the material to a personal experience, an emotional reaction to what is being said, or a question that the material brings to mind. The first and third columns can be filled in during the lecture as well as later, when the student reviews the notes from the day's class.

The strategy should be modeled using relevant material from the class in which the note taking will be used. The student may need particular helping identifying key concepts or relating the material to personal experiences, and can be guided through this process by asking probing questions (e.g., "Can you think of anything in your life that you could relate this to?" "What's your opinion about this—do you agree or disagree?").

If teachers provide PowerPoint notes, the student can use a highlighter to emphasize key concepts and write down personal reactions/questions in the margins. This, too, may need to be modeled.

NOTE-TAKING STRATEGY 2: CONCEPT MAPPING

This visual strategy uses graphic organizers to link key concepts to details. Concept maps begin with a central topic (e.g., the title of the day's lecture), to which main branches are added to represent the main subdivisions of the lecture. Each branch can be extended with details illustrating or clarifying the subdivision. (See the following example, based on the theme of Chapter 4 of this book.)

The concept map is a more difficult approach to note taking for students to learn, but the graphic display makes it easier for them to learn the content to study for tests. The best way to teach this skill is to model it. When working with individual students, it may be easier to teach concept mapping using a chapter from the student's text (e.g., social studies or science) before applying the method to lectures. Giving students partially completed concept maps and having them fill in the missing pieces is a way to shape the skill (or fade the support).

(cont.)

SAMPLE CORNELL METHOD FORM

Name: _____   Date: _____   Class: _____

Lecture topic: _____

Key terms and concepts	Running notes	Reflections, questions, links to personal experience

(cont.)

EXAMPLE OF CONCEPT MAP

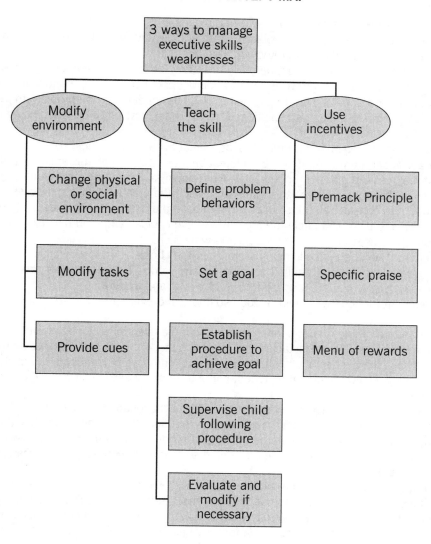

Learning to Solve Problems

Executive skills addressed: metacognition, flexibility, planning

1. Talk with the student to identify the problem. This generally involves three steps: (a) empathizing with the student or letting him or her know you understand how he or she feels ("I can see that makes you really mad" or "That must be really upsetting for you"); (b) getting a *general* sense of what the problem is ("Let me get this straight—you're upset because the friend you were hoping to play with at recess doesn't want to play with you); and (c) defining the problem more narrowly so that you can begin to brainstorm solutions ("You're not sure what to do when you go out to recess").
2. Brainstorm solutions. Together with the student, think of as many possible solutions as you can. You may want to set a time limit (e.g., 2 minutes) because this sometimes speeds up the process or makes it feel less like an open-ended task. Write down all the possible solutions. Do not criticize the solutions at this point because this tends to squelch the creative thinking process.
3. Ask the student to consider all the solutions and choose the one he or she likes best. You may want to start by having the student circle the top three to five choices and then narrow them down by talking about the pluses and minuses associated with each.
4. Ask the student if he or she needs help carrying out the choice.
5. Talk about what will happen if the first solution doesn't work. This may involve choosing a different solution or analyzing where the first solution went wrong and fixing it.
6. Praise the student for coming up with a good solution (and again after the solution is implemented.

This is a standard problem-solving approach that can be used for all kinds of problems, including interpersonal problems as well as obstacles that prevent a student from getting what he or she wants or needs. Sometimes the best solution will involve figuring out ways to overcome the obstacles, while at other times it may involve helping the student come to terms with the fact that what he or she wants is unobtainable.

Sometimes the problem-solving process may lead to a "negotiation," where you and the student both agree on what will be done to reach a satisfactory solution. In this case, you should explain to the student that whatever solution you come up with, you both have to be able to live with it. You may want to talk about how labor contracts are negotiated so that both workers and bosses get something they want out of the bargain.

After you've used the process (and the worksheet) with the student for a number of different kinds of problems, the student may be able to use the worksheet independently. Because your goal is to foster independent problem solving, you may want to ask the student to fill out the following Problem-Solving Worksheet alone before coming to you for your help (if needed). Eventually, the student will internalize the whole process and be able to solve problems "on the fly."

(cont.)

PROBLEM-SOLVING WORKSHEET

What is the problem?

What are some possible things I could do to solve the problem?

What will I try first?

If this doesn't work, what can I do?

How did it go? Did my solution work?

What might I do differently the next time?

Goal Attainment Scale Form

Level of attainment	Behavior
−2 (much less than expected)	
−1 (somewhat less than expected)	
0 (expected outcome level)	
+1 (somewhat more than expected)	
+2 (much more than expected)	
Monitoring schedule	Monitor: _____ daily _____ weekly _____ other (specify): _____

Rubric Form

Skill assessed: _____

Element	Criteria				Value
	4	3	2	1	
				Total points earned:	

RTI Progress Monitoring Form

Student's Name: _____

Tier level	Intervention	Start date	Review date	Criterion for success	Measurement procedure	Outcome	Next step

Coach Job Description

Prerequisite Knowledge/Skills/Training/Experience

- The ability to communicate clearly and diplomatically with diverse populations, including parents, students, teachers, and other professionals; communication skills include paraphrasing, reflective listening, asking open-ended questions, and scaffolding as well as the ability to provide clear instructions and effective praise.
- Specialized knowledge of executive skills deficits and how they impact school performance in students at different developmental levels.
- Effective planning/organizational skills, including the ability to manage and keep track of time, maintain records to document how the coaching time is spent, and collect and depict in graphic form objective data to evaluate the efficacy of the coaching in achieving agreed-upon goals.
- Skill in problem solving so that when obstacles arise, coaches can help students as well as those in the students' support network (e.g., parents, teachers, case managers) identify the barriers and brainstorm ways to overcome those barriers to get the students back on track.
- A working understanding of schools, both their culture and organization, including special education and Section 504 services, as well as typical teacher expectations regarding how homework is assigned, monitored, and completed and how grading systems typically work at different age levels.

Job Responsibilities

The job of a coach is to work with students to help them develop more effective executive skills, such as time and task management, planning/prioritization, and organization, as well as to set and achieve long-term goals. Specific coaching functions include:

- Daily contact with students either face to face or via phone or e-mail to help them make a daily homework plan, keep track of due dates for long-term assignments and tests, and break down long-term assignments into subtasks with timelines.
- Regular contact with teachers or school-based case managers to track student performance (including information about missing assignments, upcoming assignments and tests, grades on test/ quizzes, and so on and other due dates or classroom obligations).
- Contact with parents to inform them about how the coaching process is going and when problems arise, including providing concrete objective data about the efficacy of coaching in achieving agreed-upon goals.
- Troubleshooting with parents, students, or teachers to correct any recurring problems.

Permission Letter

Dear Parents:

_____ Middle/High School has developed a program we call "coaching" to provide academic support to at-risk students, helping them to stay on top of their course work and pass their classes. Your son/daughter has expressed an interest in participating in the coaching program, and we are seeking your permission for this to happen.

If you agree, we will match your son/daughter with a compatible member of our staff, who will act as a coach. The job of a coach is to meet with the student every day for 10–15 minutes to help with the time and task management demands required for academic success. Coaching will not take place during academic classes, but will occur during your child's free time (such as lunch, study halls, or just before or after school).

Coaches typically use the time to help the student (1) review all homework assignments, including daily homework, upcoming tests, and long-term projects or papers; (2) break down long-term assignments into subtasks and develop timelines; (3) create a study plan for tests; (4) make a homework plan for the day; and (5) monitor how well the plan is followed and track assignment completion. Coaches typically check in with teachers at least weekly to track any missing assignments and to double-check long-term assignments. Coaching includes an instructional component so that the student can gradually take on more and more of the coaching tasks with less input from the coach. As your child experiences success, coaching will be faded from a daily check-in to less frequent check-ins on a gradual basis.

Coaching has been shown to be an effective intervention for struggling students—or for students who are doing well but want to do better. We hope you will agree to have your child participate. If so, please sign and return the permission slip at the bottom of this letter. If you have questions about the program, I can be reached at:

_____ (Tel). or _____ (e-mail)

Sincerely,

_____ Middle/High School Coach Coordinator

- -

_____ Yes, I give permission for _____ to work with a coach.

_____ I am interested but would like to talk with the Coach Coordinator to discuss it. I can be reached at: (Tel.) _____.

_____ No thanks.

_____
(Parent signature)

_____

Coach Coordinator Master List

Student	Coach	Meeting time	Meeting location	Current goal	Schedule change	Goal change

Coach Coordinator Weekly Monitoring Form

Week of: _____

Student	No. of sessions	Reason for missed session(s)	Daily goals score*	Comments about process

*Daily goals score is based on the percentage of daily goals met by the student for the week, using the following key:

<10%—1   10–25%—2   25–50%—3   51–75%—4   75–100%—5

Coach Feedback Form—Student Version

Tell us how much you agree or disagree with the following statements, using the following scale:

5—Strongly agree

4—Somewhat agree

3—Not sure

2—Somewhat disagree

1—Strongly disagree

Compared with before I started coaching, I . . .

1. Completed more of my homework assignments.	5	4	3	2	1
2. Handed in more of my homework assignments on time.	5	4	3	2	1
3. Spent more time studying for tests.	5	4	3	2	1
4. Got better grades on tests/quizzes.	5	4	3	2	1
5. Got better grades on homework assignments.	5	4	3	2	1
6. Managed long-term assignments better (e.g., not leaving them until last minute).	5	4	3	2	1
7. Got fewer detentions or other discipline referrals.	5	4	3	2	1
8. Was less likely to get in trouble in class or other school settings.	5	4	3	2	1

Tell us how helpful the different coaching components were, using the following scale:

4—Very helpful

3—Somewhat helpful

2—Not sure

1—Not helpful

1. Daily (or regular) contact with my coach.	4	3	2	1
2. Setting daily goals.	4	3	2	1
3. Talking about whether I met my goals (reviewing the daily plans).	4	3	2	1
4. Making daily work plans.	4	3	2	1
5. Having my coach remind me of things I might have forgotten.	4	3	2	1
6. Getting help from my coach to solve academic or social problems.	4	3	2	1
7. Getting tips from coach on specific strategies (e.g., how to study for tests, write papers, manage time).	4	3	2	1
8. Having my coach check with my teachers to make sure I was on track.	4	3	2	1
9. Having my coach listen to me vent about school problems.	4	3	2	1

(cont.)

What worked best about coaching?

How could coaching be improved?

Other comments:

Coach Feedback Form—Coach Version

Tell us how much you agree or disagree with the following statements, using the following scale:

    5—Strongly agree

    4—Somewhat agree

    3—Not sure

    2—Somewhat disagree

    1—Strongly disagree

Coaching helped this student . . .

1. Complete homework assignments.	5 4 3 2 1
2. Hand in homework assignments on time.	5 4 3 2 1
3. Spend time studying for tests.	5 4 3 2 1
4. Get better grades on tests/quizzes.	5 4 3 2 1
5. Get better grades on homework assignments.	5 4 3 2 1
6. Manage long-term assignments (e.g., not leaving them until last minute).	5 4 3 2 1
7. Avoid detentions or other discipline referrals.	5 4 3 2 1
8. Avoid getting in trouble in class or other school settings.	5 4 3 2 1

Tell us how helpful you feel the different coaching components were for this student, using the following scale:

    4—Very helpful

    3—Somewhat helpful

    2—Not sure

    1—Not helpful

1. Daily (or regular) contact with the coach.	4 3 2 1
2. Setting daily goals.	4 3 2 1
3. Talking about whether the student met his/her goals (review the daily plans).	4 3 2 1
4. Making daily work plans.	4 3 2 1
5. Having the coach remind the student of things that might have been forgotten.	4 3 2 1
6. Helping the student solve academic or social problems.	4 3 2 1
7. Providing tips on specific strategies (e.g., how to study for tests, write papers, manage time).	4 3 2 1
8. Checking with teachers to make sure the student was on track.	4 3 2 1
9. Listening to the student vent about school problems.	4 3 2 1

(cont.)

What worked best about coaching?

How could coaching be improved?

Other comments:

Score Sheet for Math Facts Goal

Student:				Job	Coach:			
Rating					**Rating**			
Self		Coach			Self		Coach	
1 2 3		1 2 3		Has materials	1 2 3		1 2 3	
1 2 3		1 2 3		Stays on job	1 2 3		1 2 3	
1 2 3		1 2 3		Completes job (on time/with correction)	1 2 3		1 2 3	
1 2 3		1 2 3		Meets goal	1 2 3		1 2 3	

Has materials:
- 3 = Has pencil, math facts sheet, work folder
- 2 = Missing one of above
- 1 = Missing two or more of above

Stays on job:
- 3 = Completes tasks without reminder
- 2 = Needs one reminder from coach
- 1 = Needs reminder from teacher after coach

Completes job and meets goal:
- 3 = Improves on previous day's performance
- 2 = Gets same score as yesterday
- 1 = Gets lower score than yesterday

Score Sheet for Independent Work Time

Student:				Coach:		
Rating		Job		**Rating**		
Self	Coach			Self	Coach	
1 2 3	1 2 3	Listens to direction		1 2 3	1 2 3	
1 2 3	1 2 3	Stays in seat		1 2 3	1 2 3	
1 2 3	1 2 3	Stays on job		1 2 3	1 2 3	
1 2 3	1 2 3	Completes job or asks for help		1 2 3	1 2 3	

Listens to directions:
- 3 = Starts work immediately
- 2 = Needs directions from coach
- 1 = Needs directions from teacher

Stays in seat:
- 3 = Stays in seat—no reminder
- 2 = Leaves seat once—returns with coach cue
- 1 = Leaves seat more than once

Stays on job
- 3 = Attends to job—no reminder
- 2 = Needs one reminder from coach
- 1 = Needs reminder from teacher after coach

Completes job:
- 3 = Finishes all work
- 2 = Finishes most of work
- 1 = Finishes only a little work

Score Sheet for Morning Meeting Behaviors

Student:				Coach:			
Rating				**Rating**			
Self	Coach	Job		Self	Coach		
1 2 3	1 2 3	Listens to speaker		1 2 3	1 2 3		
1 2 3	1 2 3	Raises hand to speak		1 2 3	1 2 3		
1 2 3	1 2 3	Sits in space		1 2 3	1 2 3		
1 2 3	1 2 3	Follows directions		1 2 3	1 2 3		

3 = No reminders

2 = One reminder from coach

1 = Two or more reminders from coach or one from teacher

Score Sheet for End-of-Day Routine

Student:				Coach:		
Rating		Job		**Rating**		
Self	Coach			Self	Coach	
1 2 3	1 2 3	Desk cleared off/wiped		1 2 3	1 2 3	
1 2 3	1 2 3	Tools (e.g., pencils) in containers		1 2 3	1 2 3	
1 2 3	1 2 3	Folders in correct area		1 2 3	1 2 3	
1 2 3	1 2 3	Notices and homework materials in backpack		1 2 3	1 2 3	

Desk cleared off/wiped:
   3 = No materials or substances on desk
   2 = One object on desk or top not clean
   1 = Objects out and top not clean

Tools in containers:
   3 = All personal items stored
   2 = One item left out
   1 = Two or more items left out

Folders in correct area:
   3 = Folders (e.g., writing, math) in correct area
   2 = One folder out
   1 = Two or more folders out or missing

Notices and homework materials in backpack:
   3 = All materials in backpack
   2 = One notice or homework sheet missing
   1 = More than one notice or worksheet not in backpack or missing

Blank Score Sheet

SCORE SHEET FOR: _____

Student:		Job	Coach:	
Rating			**Rating**	
Self	Coach		Self	Coach
1 2 3	1 2 3	A.	1 2 3	1 2 3
1 2 3	1 2 3	B.	1 2 3	1 2 3
1 2 3	1 2 3	C.	1 2 3	1 2 3
1 2 3	1 2 3	D.	1 2 3	1 2 3

Description of job elements:

A. _____

   3. _____

   2. _____

   1. _____

B. _____

   3. _____

   2. _____

   1. _____

C. _____

   3. _____

   2. _____

   1. _____

D. _____

   3. _____

   2. _____

   1. _____

Class Roster for Teams and Coaches

Team Orange	M	T	W	T	F	Total	Team Purple	M	T	W	T	F	Total

Peer Coaching Steps for the Peer Coach

1. Pick the daily goal together with _____ and write it on the Daily Goal Form at the beginning of the day.

2. Remind _____ what his/her goal is at the beginning of the period.

3. Look and see what _____ is doing during that period.

4. At the end of the period, circle your rating in the "_____'s rating" section of the Daily Goal Form.

5. Record the number of points _____ earned for that day on the Daily Goal Form and the Weekly Goal Table.

6. Place the Daily Goal Form in the peer coaching binder.

Student's Daily Goal Steps

1. You and _____ will select a goal together at the beginning of the day and write it on the Daily Goal Form.

2. _____ will remind you what your goal is at the beginning of the period.

3. You will try to achieve your goal and _____ will observe how you are doing during this period.

4. At the end of the period, circle your rating in the "_____'s rating" section of the Daily Goal Form.

5. You and _____ will record the number of points you earned during the day on the Daily Goal Form and the Weekly Goal Table.

6. You and _____ will place the Daily Goal Form in the peer coaching binder.

Daily Goal Form

Name: _____   Date: _____

My goal is:

_____

_____

_____

How did I do?

My rating: (circle one)

Unsatisfactory	Needs improvement	Satisfactory	Honors
1	2	3	4

_____'s rating: (circle one)

Unsatisfactory	Needs improvement	Satisfactory	Honors
1	2	3	4

Points for the day: _____

Reward Menu

Reward 1: _____

Reward 2: _____

Reward 3: _____

Point Range for Rewards

Reward 3: Average of 3.0–3.9 points

Reward 2: Average of 4.0–4.9 points

Reward 1: 5 points

Weekly Goal Table

		Scores					
	Monday	Tuesday	Wednesday	Thursday	Friday	Average score	Reward earned
Week 1							
Week 2							
Week 3							
Week 4							
Week 5							
Week 6							
Week 7							
Week 8							
Week 9							
Week 10							

Letter to Family for Focus Student

Date: _____

Dear _____ ,

This letter is to let you know how _____ did in earning his/her goals for this week.

This week he/she earned a total of _____ points and DID/DID NOT earn a weekly reward.

The reward was _____ .

Other comments:

Sincerely,

Letter to Family for Peer Coach

Date: _____

Dear _____,

This letter is to let you know how _____ did working

with _____ this week.

This week they earned a total of _____ points and they DID/DID NOT earn a
weekly reward.

The reward was _____.

Other comments:

Sincerely,

Sample Goal Form

Goal 1: _____

_____

_____

_____

Goal 2: _____

_____

_____

_____

Goal 3: _____

_____

_____

_____

Goal 4: _____

_____

_____

_____

Goal 5: _____

_____

_____

_____

Treatment Integrity Questions

Can the students state the peer coaching steps to you during your weekly meeting?

Pick a goal/write together at the beginning of every day?	Yes	No
Peer coach reminds student of goal?	Yes	No
Student works on goal and peer coach looks/checks?	Yes	No
Circle their ratings?	Yes	No
Record their points on Daily Goal Form and Weekly Goal Table?	Yes	No

Comments?

_____

_____

_____

_____

_____

Did the students remember to fill out their forms every day?   Yes   No

Did the students forget any steps throughout the week?   Yes   No

If they forgot, which ones did they forget?

_____

_____

_____

_____

Any other problems/challenges this week?

_____

_____

_____

_____

_____

_____

_____

_____

References

Anderson, D. H., Munk, J. H., Young, K. R., Conley, L., & Caldarella, P. (2008). Teaching organizational skills to promote academic achievement in behaviorally challenged students. *Teaching Exceptional Children, 40,* 6–13.

Antshel, K. M., & Remer, R. (2003). Social skills training in children with attention deficit hyperactivity disorder: A randomized-controlled clinical trial. *Journal of Clinical Child and Adolescent Psychology, 32,* 153–165.

Babyak, A. E., Luze, G. J., & Kamps, D. M. (2000). The good student game: Behavior management in diverse classrooms. *Intervention in School and Clinic, 35*(4), 216–223.

Barkley, R. A. (1997). *ADHD and the nature of self-control.* New York: Guilford Press.

Bevill-Davis, A., Clees, T. J., & Gast, D. L. (2004). Correspondence training: A review of the literature. *Journal of Early and Intensive Behavioral Intervention, 1,* 17–26.

Biederman, J., Monuteaux, M. C., Doyle, A. E., Seidman, L. J., Wilens, T. E., Ferrero, F., et al. (2004). Impact of executive function deficits and attention-deficit/hyperactivity disorder (ADHD) on academic outcomes in children. *Journal of Consulting and Clinical Psychology, 72,* 757–766.

Bransford, J., Brown, A., & Cocking, R. (2000). *How people learn: Brain, mind, experience, and school.* Washington, DC: National Academy Press.

Brewer, R. D., Reid, M. S., & Rhine, B. G. (2003). Peer coaching: Students teaching to learn. *Intervention in School and Clinic, 39,* 113–126.

Broussard, C., & Northup, J. (1997). The use of functional analysis to develop peer interventions for disruptive classroom behavior. *School Psychology Quarterly, 12,* 65–76.

Brown, T. E. (1996). *Brown Attention-Deficit Disorder Scales for Adolescents and Adults.* San Antonio, TX: Psychological Corporation.

Buron, K. D., & Curtis, M. B. (2003). *The incredible 5-point scale.* Shawnee Mission, KS: Autism Asperger Publishing Company.

Clark, C., Prior, M., & Kinsella, G. (2002). The relationship between executive function abilities, adaptive behavior, and academic achievement in children with externalizing behavior problems. *Journal of Child Psychology and Psychiatry, 43,* 785–796.

Coffee, G., & Ray-Subramanian, C. E. (2009). Goal attainment scaling: A progress-monitoring tool for behavioral interventions. *School Psychology Forum: Research in Practice, 3*(1), 1–12.

Corkum, P., Corbin, N., & Pike, M. (2010). Evaluation of a school-based social skills program for children with attention-deficit/hyperactivity disorder. *Child and Family Behavior Therapy, 32,* 139–151.

Dawson, M. M., & Guare, R. (1998). *Coaching the ADHD student.* Toronto: Multi-Health Systems.

233

Dawson, P., & Guare, R. (2004). *Executive skills in children and adolescents: A practical guide to assessment and interventions.* New York: Guilford Press.

Dawson, P., & Guare, R. (2009). *Smart but scattered: The revolutionary "Executive Skills" approach to helping kids reach their potential.* New York: Guilford Press.

Dawson, P., & Guare, R. (2010). *Executive skills in children and adolescents: A practical guide to assessment and intervention* (2nd ed.). New York: Guilford Press.

de Boo, G. M., & Prins, P. J. M. (2007). Social incompetence in children with ADHD: Possible moderators and mediators in social-skills training. *Clinical Psychology Review, 27,* 78–97.

DeLuca, C. R., & Leventer, R. J. (2008). Developmental trajectories of executive functions across the lifespan. In V. A. Anderson, P. Jacobs, & P. Anderson (Eds.), *Executive functions and the frontal lobes: A lifespan perspective* (pp. 23–55). New York: Taylor & Francis.

Diamantopoulou, S., Rydell, A., Thorell, L. B., & Bohlin, G. (2007). Impact of executive functioning and symptoms of attention deficit hyperactivity disorder on children's peer relations and school performance. *Developmental Neuropsychology, 32,* 521–542.

DuPaul, G. J., Ervin, R. A., Hook, C. L., & McGoey, K. E. (1998). Peer tutoring for children with attention deficit hyperactivity disorder: Effects on classroom behavior and academic performance. *Journal of Applied Behavior Analysis, 31,* 579–592.

DuPaul, G. J., & Henningson, P. N. (1993). Peer tutoring effects on the classroom performance of children with attention deficit hyperactivity disorder. *School Psychology Review, 22,* 134–143.

DuPaul, G. J., & Stoner, G. (2003). *ADHD in the schools: Assessment and intervention strategies* (2nd ed.). New York: Guilford Press.

Elliott, S. N., & Gresham, F. M. (1993). Social skills interventions for children. *Behavior Modification, 17,* 287–313.

Fantuzzo, J. W., & Polite, K. (1990). School-based behavioral self-management: A review and analysis. *School Psychology Quarterly, 5,* 180–198.

Fantuzzo, J. W., Rohrbeck, C. A., & Azar, S. T. (1987). A component analysis of behavioral self-management interventions with elementary school students. *Child and Family Behavior Therapy, 9,* 33–43.

Field, S., Martin, J., Miller, R., Ward, M., & Wehmeyer, M. (1998). *A practical guide to teaching self-determination.* Reston, VA: Council for Exceptional Children.

Fisher, D., & Frey, N. (2010). *Guided instruction: How to develop confident and successful learners.* Alexandria, VA: ASCD.

Frankel, F., Myatt, R., Cantwell, D. P., & Feinberg, D. T. (1997). Parent-assisted transfer of children's social skills training: Effects on children with and without attention-deficit hyperactivity disorder. *Journal of the American Academy of Child and Adolescent Psychiatry, 36,* 1056–1064.

Gewirtz, S., Stanton-Chapman, T., & Reeve, R. (2009). Can inhibition at preschool age predict ADHD symptoms and social difficulties in third grade? *Early Child Development and Care, 179,* 353–368.

Gioia, G. A., Isquith, P. K., Guy, S. C., & Kenworthy, L. (2000). *Behavior Rating Inventory of Executive Function.* Odessa, FL: Psychological Assessment Resources.

Greenwood, C. R., Arreaga-Mayer, C., Utley, C. A., Gavin, K. M., & Terry, B. J. (2001). ClassWide Peer Tutoring Learning Management System: Applications with elementary-level English language learners. *Remedial and Special Education, 22,* 34–47.

Greenwood, C. R., & Delquadri, J. (1995). Classwide peer tutoring and the prevention of school failure. *Preventing School Failure, 39*(4), 21–25.

Greenwood, C. R., Delquadri, J., & Carta, J. J. (1997). *Together we can!: Classwide peer tutoring to improve basic academic skills.* Longmont, CO: Sopris West.

Greenwood, C. R., Maheady, L., & Delquadri, J. (2002). Class-wide peer tutoring. In G. Stoner, M. R. Shinn, & H. M. Walker (Eds.), *Interventions for academic and behavior problems* (2nd ed., pp. 611–649). Washington, DC: National Association of School Psychologists.

Gresham, F. M. (2002). Teaching social skills to high-risk children and youth: Preventive and remedial strategies. In M. R. Shinn, H. M. Walker, & G. Stoner (Eds.), *Interventions for academic and behavior problems II: Preventive and remedial approaches* (pp. 403–432). Washington, DC: National Association of School Psychologists.

Gresham, F. M., & Elliott, S. N. (2008). *Social Skills Improvement System Rating Scales.* Minneapolis, MN: NCS Pearson.

Hallowell, E. M., & Ratey, J. J. (1994). *Driven to distraction*. New York: Pantheon.

Hart, T., & Jacobs, H. E. (1993). Rehabilitation and management of behavioral disturbances following frontal lobe injury. *Journal of Head Trauma Rehabilitation, 8*, 1–12.

Hinshaw, S. P. (1992). Intervention for social competence and social skill. *Child and Adolescent Psychiatric Clinics of North America, 1*, 539–551.

Hofmeister, A., & Lubke, M. (1990). *Research into practice: Implementing effective teaching strategies*. Boston: Allyn & Bacon.

Hogan, K., & Pressley, M. (Eds.). (1997). *Scaffolding student learning: Instructional approaches and issues*. Cambridge, MA: Brookline Books.

Hoza, B., Mrug, S., Pelham, W. E., Greiner, A. R., & Gnagy, E. M. (2003). A friendship intervention for children with attention-deficit/hyperactivity disorder: Preliminary findings. *Journal of Attention Disorders, 6*, 87–98.

Hunley, S., & McNamara, K. (2010). *Tier 3 of the RTI model*. Bethsda, MD: National Association of School Psychologists.

Kaufman, C. (2010). *Executive function in the classroom: Practical strategies for improving performance and enhancing skills for all students*. Baltimore: Brookes.

Kiresuk, T. J., & Sherman, R. E. (1968). Goal attainment scaling: A general method for evaluating community mental health programs. *Community Mental Health Journal, 4*, 443–453.

Landau, S., Milich, R., & Diener, M. B. (1998). Peer relations of children with attention-deficit hyperactivity disorder. *Reading and Writing Quarterly, 14*, 83–105.

Landau, S., & Moore, L. A. (1991). Social skills deficits in children with attention-deficit hyperactivity disorder. *School Psychology Review, 20*, 235–251.

Larkin, M. J. (2001). Providing support for student independence through scaffolded instruction. *Teaching Exceptional Children, 34*(1), 30–34.

Lezak, M. D. (1983). *Neuropsychological assessment* (2nd ed.). New York: Oxford University Press.

Locke, E. A., & Latham, G. P. (2002). Building a practically useful theory of goal setting and task modification. *American Psychologist, 57*, 705–717.

Loney, L., & Milich, R. (1982). Hyperactivity, inattention, and aggression in clinical practice. In M. Wolraich & D. K. Routh (Eds.), *Advances in developmental and behavioral pediatrics* (Vol. 3, pp. 113–147). Greenwich, CT: JAI Press.

Maheady, L., Mallette, B., & Harper, G. F. (2006). Four classwide peer tutoring models: Similarities, differences and implications for research and practice. *Reading and Writing Quarterly, 22*, 65–89.

Martin, C., Dawson, P., & Guare, R. (2007). *Smarts: Are we hardwired for success?* New York: American Management Association.

Martin, C., Guare, R., & Dawson, P. (2010). *Work your strengths: A scientific process to identify your skills and match them to the best career for you*. New York: American Management Association.

Mathur, S. R., & Rutherford, R. B. (1991). Peer-mediated interventions promoting social skills of children and youth with behavioral disorders. *Education and Treatment of Children, 14*, 227–242.

McQuade, J. D., & Hoza, B. (2008). Peer problems in attention deficit hyperactivity disorder: Current status and future directions. *Developmental Disabilities Research Reviews, 14*, 320–324.

Merrell, K. W. (2002). *School social behavior scales* (2nd ed.). Eugene, OR: Assessment-Intervention Resources.

Merriman, D. E. (2010). *The effects of group coaching on the homework completion of secondary students with homework problems*. Unpublished doctoral dissertation, City University of New York.

Merriman, D. E., & Codding, R. S. (2008). The effects of coaching on mathematics homework completion and accuracy of high school students with attention-deficit/hyperactivity disorder. *Journal of Behavioral Education, 17*, 339–355.

Miller, M., & Hinshaw, S. P. (2010). Does childhood executive function predict adolescent functional outcomes in girls with ADHD? *Journal of Abnormal Child Psychology, 38*, 315–326.

Miranda, A., & Presentacion, M. J. (2000). Efficacy of cognitive-behavioral therapy in the treatment of children with ADHD, with and without aggressiveness. *Psychology in the Schools, 37*, 169–182.

Mitchem, K. J., Young, R. K., West, R. P., & Benyo, J. (2001). CWPASM: A classwide, peer-assisted, self-management program for general education classrooms. *Education and Treatment of Children, 24*(2), 111–140.

Paniagua, F. A. (1992). Verbal–nonverbal correspondence training with ADHD children. *Behavior Modification, 16*, 226–252.

Parker, D. R., & Boutelle, K. (2009). Executive function coaching for college students with learning disabilities and ADHD: A new approach for fostering self-determination. *Learning Disabilities Research and Practice, 23*(4), 204–215.

Pfiffner, L. J., & McBurnett, K. (1997). Social skills training with parent generalization: Treatment effects for children with attention deficit disorder. *Journal of Consulting and Clinical Psychology, 65,* 749–757.

Plumer, P. J. (2007). Using peers as intervention agents to improve the social behaviors of elementary-aged children with attention deficit hyperactivity disorder: Effects of a peer coaching package. *Dissertation Abstracts International: Section A. Humanities and Social Sciences, 68*(7), 2813.

Plumer, P. J., & Stoner, G. (2005). The relative effects of classwide peer tutoring and peer coaching on the positive social behaviors of children with ADHD. *Journal of Attention Disorders, 9,* 290–300.

Pogrow, S. (1996, June). Reforming the wannabe reformers: Why education reforms almost always end up making things worse. *Phi Delta Kappan,* pp. 656–663.

Quinn, P. O., Ratey, N. A., & Maitland, T. L. (2000). *Coaching college students with AD/HD: Issues and answers.* Silver Spring, MD: Advantage Books.

Raffaelli, M., Crocket, L. J., & Shen, Y.-L. (2005). Developmental stability and change in self-regulation from childhood to adolescence. *Journal of Genetic Psychology, 166,* 54–75.

Rafferty, L. A. (2010). Step-by-step: Teaching students to self-monitor. *Teaching Exceptional Children, 43*(2), 50–58.

Reyna, V., & Farley, F. (2006). Risk and rationality in adolescent decision-making: Implications for theory, practice, and public policy. *Psychological Science in the Public Interest, 7,* 1–44.

Risley, T. R., & Hart, B. (1968). Developing correspondence between the nonverbal and verbal behavior of preschool children. *Journal of Applied Behavioral Analysis, 1,* 267–281.

Rutherford, L. E., DuPaul, G. J., & Jittendra, A. K. (2008). Examining the relationship between treatment outcomes for academic achievement and social skills in school-age children with attention-deficit hyperactivity disorder. *Psychology in the Schools, 45,* 145–157.

Schumaker, J. B., Nolan, S., & Deshler, D. D. (1985). *Learning strategies curriculum: The error monitoring strategy.* Lawrence: University of Kansas, Institute on Learning Disabilities.

Schunk, D. H. (2003). Self-efficacy for reading and writing: Influence of modeling, goal setting, and self-evaluation. *Reading and Writing Quarterly, 19,* 159–172.

Steinberg, L. (2007). Risk taking in adolescence: New perspectives from brain and behavioral science. *Current Directions in Psychological Science, 16,* 55–59.

Steinberg, L., Graham, S., O'Brien, L., Woolard, J., Cauffman, E., & Banich, M. (2009). Age differences in future orientation and delay discounting. *Child Development, 80*(1), 28–44.

Swartz, S. L., Prevatt, F., & Proctor, B. E. (2005). A coaching intervention for college students with attention deficit/hyperactivity disorder. *Psychology in the Schools, 42,* 647–656.

Twachtman-Cullen, D., & Twachtman-Bassett, J. (2011). *The IEP from A to Z: How to create meaningful and measurable goals and objectives.* San Francisco: Jossey-Bass.

Utley, C. A., Mortweet, S. L., & Greenwood, C. R. (1997). Peer mediated instruction and interventions. *Focus on Exceptional Children, 29*(5), 1–23.

Vilardo, B. A., & DuPaul, G. J. (2010, March). *Cross-age peer coaching: Enhancing the peer interactions of first graders exhibiting symptoms of ADHD.* Poster session presented at the annual convention of the National Association of School Psychologists, Chicago.

Vygotsky, L. (1978). *Mind in society.* Cambridge, MA: Harvard University Press.

Walker, H. M., & Severson, H. H. (1992). *Systematic screening for behavior disorders (SSBD): User's guide and administration manual* (2nd ed.). Longmont, CO: Sopris West.

Whalen, C. K., & Henker, B. (1991). The social impact of stimulant treatment for hyperactive children. *Journal of Learning Disabilities, 24,* 231–241.

Wiener, J., & Mak, M. (2009). Peer victimization in children with attention-deficit/hyperactivity disorder. *Psychology in the Schools, 46,* 116–131.

Wolters, C. A. (2003). Regulation of motivation: Evaluating an underemphasized aspect of self-regulated learning. *Educational Psychologist, 38,* 189–205.

Young, K. R., West, R. P., Smith, D. J., & Morgan, D. P. (1991). *Teaching self-management strategies to adolescents.* Longmont, CO: Sopris West.

Zimmerman, B. J. (2001). Theories of self-regulated learning and academic achievement: An overview and analysis. In B. J. Zimmerman & D. H. Schunk (Eds.), *Self-regulated learning and academic achievement* (pp. 1–37). Hillsdale, NJ: Erlbaum.

Index

Page numbers followed by an *f* indicate a figure, *t* indicate a table

237